THE RAPE OF THE AMERICAN WORKER

The Rape of the American Worker

John J. Parker

EXPOSITION PRESS   HICKSVILLE, NEW YORK

FIRST EDITION

© 1976 by John J. Parker
Copyright © under the Universal Copyright and
Berne Conventions

All rights reserved, including the right of reproduction in whole or in part, in any form or by any means, electronic or mechanical, including photocopying, recording, or by any information storage and retrieval system, without permission in writing from the Publisher. Inquiries should be addressed to Exposition Press, Inc., 900 South Oyster Bay Road, Hicksville, N.Y. 11801.

ISBN 0-682-48560-8

LIBRARY OF CONGRESS CATALOG CARD NUMBER: 76-20051

Printed in the United States of America

COPYRIGHT ACKNOWLEDGMENTS

Grateful acknowledgment is made for permission to use material from the following sources:

A Monetary History of the United States, 1867-1960, by Milton Friedman. Copyright © by the National Bureau of Economic Research, Inc. Used by permission.

Barron's. Reprinted by courtesy of Barron's National Business and Financial Weekly.

Better Investing (The publication of the National Association of Investment Clubs, Royal Oak, Michigan). Reprinted by permission.

Challenge. Copyright © 1974 by International Arts and Sciences Press, Inc. Reprinted by permission of International Arts and Sciences Press, Inc.

Economics, by Paul Samuelson. Ninth edition copyright © McGraw-Hill Book Company. Used with permission of McGraw-Hill Book Company.

Energy Regulation by the Federal Power Commission, by Stephen G. Breyer and Paul W. MacAvoy. Copyright © 1974 by the Brookings Institution, Washington, D.C. Used by permission.

Energy: The New Era, by S. David Freeman. Copyright © by Walker & Company, New York. Used by permission.

Facts and Figures on Government Finance. 1975 edition. Tax Foundation, Inc. Used by permission.

Fortune. Reprinted by permission.

Tax Loopholes: The Legend and the Reality, by Roger Freeman. (Washington: The American Enterprise Institute for Public Policy Research, 1973.)

The Detroit News. Used by permission.

The Economist. London.

The Outline of History, by H. G. Wells. Used by permission of the Estate of H. G. Wells.

The Real America. Copyright © 1974 by Ben J. Wattenberg. Reprinted by permission of Doubleday & Co., Inc.

The Wall Street Journal. Reprinted with permission of the Wall Street Journal, © Dow Jones & Company, Inc., 1972, 1973, 1974, 1975, 1975, 1976. All Rights Reserved.

Two Cheers for the Affluent Society, by Wilfred Beckerman. (New York: St. Martin's Press, Inc., Macmillan & Co., Ltd.) Used by permission.

Acknowledgment is also made to the following individuals: Joseph Adelson, Professor of Psychology, University of Michigan; Peter Berger; Frank Ikard, President, American Petroleum Institute; and Geoffrey Moore, President, National Bureau of Economic Research, Inc.

*To my wife Joyce
and our children:
Constance Parker
Joan Sutton
Carolyn Starr
Arthur T. Prew*

"There is no lie worse than truth misunderstood by the listener."

—William James

CONTENTS

	INTRODUCTION	xiii
I	Myths and Realities of Corporate Profits	3
II	Facts and Fancies on Prices	33
III	Illusions and Fallacies of Price Control	57
IV	Profits: The Road to Workers' Capitalism	73
V	Philosophical and Moral Aspects of Profits	93
VI	The Propaganda and the Rhetoric	107
VII	The Harvest of the Whirlwind	119
VIII	Economic Growth: Its Necessity, Desirability and Feasibility	137
IX	The Distribution of Income and a Social Philosophy Thereof	163
X	Tax Loopholes: Rhetoric Versus Reality	193
XI	The "Slumpflation" of 1974-75	207
XII	Inflationary Aspects of Government Spending	223
XIII	Wage Rates, Inflation and Unemployment	245
XIV	Economic Growth at Full Employment Without Inflation	275
XV	Community of Interests and the Coming Workers' Capitalism	297
XVI	Energy: Geopolitics and Politics	313
XVII	Slippery Rhetoric on Oil	341
XVIII	Perspectives on Energy	361
XIX	Conclusions: The Real Issues	373

INTRODUCTION

Our economic rapists are the rip-off artists of pseudo-liberalism and the wisenheimers of the left.

By means of diabolically contrived lies, distortions, and sophistries, the leftist intelligentsia in literature, education, the media, unionism, politics and even religion are depriving the American worker and the consumer of the benefits of relatively steady economic growth at reasonably full employment with minimal inflation. Further, they are impeding the growth of the pension fund base that can lead to a workers' capitalism.

It is the objective of this put-it-in-perspective book to expose their arrant economic claptrap that has engendered deliberately and/or naively false and erroneous propaganda about the true nature and role of profits, prices, the capitalist system, our democracy and our social system. Among our workers, students and our unfortunate destitute, they have spawned and fostered an unwarranted amount of mischief, mistrust and discontent. They are the Pied Pipers who have insidiously and invidiously engendered the "Crisis in Expectations" and the "Revolution in Entitlements."

It all boils down to a simple proposition that someone is being screwed and someone is doing the screwing. We all know who is being screwed—the American worker and the American consumer. But the authentic screwers, the Marxists and their servile lackeys of pseudo-liberalism, by their sophistries, lies, distortions and false propaganda, have successfully shifted the blame from themselves to American business and the middle and upper income classes. These sham intellectuals, in their specious outpourings and diatribes against profits and corporate pricing, have fabricated an adversary relationship between employer and employee that in reality should not exist.

By brazenly ignoring the true facts on profits and the limits of income distribution, the sham intellectuals have unleashed a rising tide of false hopes leading to a crisis of unfulfillable expectations culminating in a revolution of entitlements. If the anti-bourgeois prevaricators would honestly and objectively analyze corporate returns, they would find that the composite income statements in recent years would show a profit margin of 4 to 6 cents per each dollar of sales. In 1973, one of the best profit making years on record, total profits after taxes were $43 billion. If confiscated and distributed to each family in U.S. that would amount to a meager $800 per family. Also if the highbrows (those educated beyond their intelligence) of the "new class" were to analyze the U.S. Internal Revenue Service Statistics of Income for Individuals, they would learn to their amazement that in 1972 the earnings of the income class group earning $50,000 or more comprised only 7.2% of adjusted gross income or $53 billion.

If the polemicists of the left were unfettered by Marxist dogma and scrutinized the foregoing data objectively, they would find that not only are there limits to income distribution but also that the tax base is limited to finance bureaucratic throwing of money at problems—some of which in

Introduction

truth do exist but some are merely creations of career reformers, bureaucrats and demagogues.

Since there are limits as to the amount that they can extract from the so-called "rich bitches" and "capitalist bastards" and the "fat cat" corporations, the free-wheeling spenders pick the pockets of the working and middle classes. The intelligentsia have engendered a climate of hostility between employer and employee, conning workers into demands for wage increases exceeding productivity growth upon the false premises that these can be financed by corporations out of profits instead of by the consumer and the worker himself by the resultant inflation.

The anti-profit and anti-bourgeois propaganda is to a large degree responsible for creating the condition where there appears to be a fundamental contradiction between full employment and price stability. They have generated what Professor Daniel Bell has aptly called "a psychology of entitlements." The ensuing psychological momentum in expectations and entitlements is to a large degree responsible for stagflation and what the London *Economist* calls slumpflation.

If this nation is to maintain steady economic growth with relatively stable prices at reasonably full employment, a means must be found to counter the misleading propaganda against profits, thereby defusing the explosion in expectations and entitlements.

In his most recent edition of his monumental *Economics*[1] Paul Samuelson asks, "Can a nation simultaneously

---

[1] Paul Samuelson, *Economics*, Ninth Edition (New York: McGraw-Hill Book Company, 1973).

enjoy the blessings of full employment and price stability? Or is there a fundamental dilemma of choice between high employment and reasonable price stability? Must full employment lead to creeping inflation?" Further he states, "In the current state of knowledge about the modern mixed economy, no jury of competent economists can reach a broad agreement on how to recommend a feasible and optimal incomes policy" (page 825). He poses the stagflation dilemma in the following words as he zeroes in on cost-push inflation, "In modern cost-push inflation, prices and wages begin to creep upward even before employment is full and industrial capacity fully utilized. To clamp down on monetary and fiscal policy to fight such inflation will only result in unemployment and stagnation. But not to act is to accept creeping inflation that may accelerate into a canter or gallop. An 'incomes policy' is needed to supplement fiscal and monetary policy. . . . But it remains an unsolved problem of modern economics to get experts to agree to an incomes policy" (page 837).

It is the writer's conviction that a feasible modified incomes policy can become a reality. But it can be asked, "What are your credentials? Are you an economist?" No, the author is not a professional economist. His formal education was confined to high school. He undertook a rigorous self-study in accounting, economics and finance, involving going through over 500 books. In addition, he was exposed to the rigors of the business world. He gave up on journalism and for shop experience worked as a machine operator at Ford and General Motors, producing gears for axles and transmissions. He took a special course in gear mathematics and advanced to a position as gear mathematician at two different concerns for attaining as broad as possible an experience in different types of gear tools. In 1946, the author and his partner founded a company to manufacture precision gauges and tools. From the inception in 1946 through 1974, when he retired and sold his share in the business at a lucrative figure, the writer was accorded 31 patents as inventor and co-inventor of gauges and tools for machines. The items are internationally patented and renowned as the most productive in their field.

As to the question facetiously and mischievously asked of ivory tower economists, "Have you ever signed a paycheck?" The answer is a proud "Yes!" When the company was started with three employees, the writer set up the accounting system—acknowledged by accountants as one of most efficient that they have seen and still in existence. The writer also wrote the sales brochures, directed sales and aided in supervising the engineering and production departments. In his sales contacts, domestic and overseas, the writer has been exposed to the explosion in machine technology, of which we just see the tip of the iceberg. His experience has been about 10% with buyers and 90% with production engineers and plant managers.

The foregoing comments are presented not in the spirit of boasting, but essentially as showing exposure to revealing and informative micro-economic factors in the context of a macro-economic environment in the study of markets and forecasts—domestic and worldwide.

As an employee, the writer has seen the great improvement in working conditions that resulted from emergence of unions. As an employer he instituted a profit-sharing pension plan, in the management of which he outperformed some of the most prestigious investment counselors. As a matter of record, the writer and the fund were fully liquid in March, 1973.

All in all the writer thinks he has a feel for what makes corporations and the economy tick.

Before the presentation of a modified incomes policy, analyses will be made of the myths and realities of profits, myths and realities of prices and corporate pricing, the true nature and role of profits and prices, and among other topics the roles of capital formation and technology. Suggestions will also be made toward the attainment and maintenance of guaranteed full employment, by the establishment of a National Technical Center as fully outlined in Chapter Fourteen. All unemployed scientists, engineers, technicians and skilled workers would be employed on research and development projects until recalled by their former employers.

In this book, we will also point out that the seeds have been planted for the development of a phenomenon of profound and startling implications that could change the economic environment for a long time. We are speaking of the potential emergence and fruition of a workers' and middle class capitalism via funds set aside in pension plans. Thus the true facts on profits and the possibilities of a workers' capitalism are creating the conditions for a "new class conflict." The antagonists of this new struggle will be the workers and the middle classes on one side and what Irving J. Kristol calls the "new class"—the intelligentsia, the elitist leftists, the regulatory and service bureaucracies —on the other. This conflict will pit middle class workers and the middle class producers against the elite "new class" non-producers.

Introduction

This phenomenon of the workers' and middle class capitalism will pose a problem for the union leader, who up to now has fostered an adversary relationship between the worker and the corporation. This, combined with true facts on profits and income distribution, will force him to decide to maintain his illicit association with the pseudo-liberals of the left or make a 180-degree about-face.

Thus, it behooves the middle class workers and middle classes to launch a counteroffensive against the malicious rhetoric of the intelligentsia, the "new class" elitists, about profits and the free enterprise system because their deceitful propaganda is delaying the potential of the workers' capitalism.

Also, in this book, we will propound a theory that profits through their cost control discipline have socially redeeming values conducive to social progress.

Workers of America, YOU have nothing to lose but the chains of Marxist dogmas.

THE RAPE OF THE AMERICAN WORKER

I

MYTHS AND REALITIES OF CORPORATE PROFITS

Myths and misconceptions about profits are undermining the economic base of our society and the growth that is desirable and necessary to provide employment for a growing population. Deliberate falsehoods and distortions are concocted by the pseudo-intellectuals and purveyed by them and their naive dupes. They appeal to the economically illiterate and pander to their prejudice, envy and resentment to perpetuate the myth of the adversary relationship and the class conflict. They have spawned a "new class" of anti-establishment propagandists—consisting of a good part of the educational complex, the media, the regulatory and service bureaucracies and trade unionism. This motley crowd of sham intellectuals and their willful lackeys have conjured up the rhetoric of high profits, surging profits and obscene profits among their epithets.

They could not substantiate their deceitful blather with statistics so they resort to the technique of Lenin and Goebbels—that the persistent repetition of the lie, the half-truth, the distortion, the slanted report, will result in their acceptance as truths. Just how well they have succeeded is illustrated by the conventional opinion about profits. The public, according to a survey by Opinion Research Corporation of Princeton, believes that profits run to some 28% of sales. As a matter of fact average after-tax profits, fluctuate from 4 to 6 cents per dollar of sales, and play an indispensable role in capital formation that creates future jobs.

Now let us consider the economic consequences of this myth that profits run to 28 cents per dollar of sales. The producers are considered greedy and should be regulated if not punished. "Soak the rich" and "soak the corporation" attitudes are engendered and fostered to the eventual detriment of both laborers and companies.

Furthermore, the public holds a distorted view of potentials in the wage negotiation process. Two-thirds of the adults who were sampled in a poll believe that a 10% hourly wage increase can be paid by American companies without raising prices. As a matter of fact, wages can be increased on average only 3%—equal to the growth of productivity—without increasing prices.

This myth of the 28% profit margin also has a deleterious effect on productivity. When Gallup pollsters asked a cross-section of American adults last year, "Could you accomplish more each day if you tried?" one-half said, "Yes." They did not accomplish more because 80% of hourly wage workers believed, "Companies benefit from increased productivity at the expense of workers." This attitude also arises from union encouragement in the adversary relationship to get "more" and do less.

What is the arrant rhetoric that misrepresents profit statistics? Let us now consider how the so-called champions of labor appraise these developments. Are they fair, honest and objective or do they exploit economic ignorance to further ensconce their positions in their little empires?

So first let us get a sampling from the labor leaders. George Meany, president of the AFL-CIO, was reported as stating in his annual Labor Day message of 1974: "Corporate profits, despite inflation, are up 28% in the second quarter of 1974. And this is on top of profit increases of 26% in 1973; 25% in 1972 and 17% in 1971. This is not sacrifice, this is greed."

Leonard Woodcock, president of the UAW, cast his economic eye on profit developments in an article which he wrote for the *Detroit Free Press*, in which he quoted manufacturing corporations' profits as having shot up 36 percent from their recession low. Why, he asks, since the facts show an upsurge, do administration spokesmen insist that profits are low?

He goes on to say that, without restraints, corporate profit growth will so far exceed national income growth that the living standard of the American family will suffer.

I. W. Abel, president of the United Steel Workers, was quoted by *Iron Age* in its issue of March 30, 1972, as follows:

> In the second half of the last year, corporate after-tax profits were up 18% from the same period in 1970.
>
> This is a rate nearly three times faster than the 6.5% rise of the total wage and salary payments to all employees. . . .

It is hard to understand how an economist of the stature of Gardner Ackley could stoop so low as to be a willful participant in the dissemination of irresponsible misinformation regarding the true perspective on profits. The then chairman of the Council of Economic Advisers under President Johnson was taken to task in an editorial "An Ominous Swipe at Profits" in *Fortune* of June, 1966. *Fortune* said:

> In one especially disturbing passage, Ackley said, ". . . it is time to ask whether a further rise in the share of profits in the national income is either in the interest of the health of the nation's economy or in the interest of business itself." . . . after tax business profits, he noted, increased 85% from early 1961 to 1965 . . .

In his presentations, Ackley was guilty of two dubious practices, unbecoming a man of his sensitive position. First, he did not give a true perspective on profits by failing to state that in 1960 and 1961 profits were at a depressed level, and second, he failed to cite data on profit ratios. A much more objective and truer picture was given in the following passage of the same *Fortune* editorial:

> It is certainly not surprising that profit ratios are a lot higher now than they were in recession-pinched 1961. For one thing, capacity is being much more fully utilized than it was then. It is not surprising, either, that "the share of profits in the national income," as Ackley put it, has increased since 1961—meaning, in effect, that profits have risen faster than wages. That is the

normal pattern in periods of economic expansion, just as the reverse is normal in periods of recession. Profits are much more volatile than wages. Over a period of years, wage rates go up, up, up, while profit ratios go up, down, up, down. Corporate profits dropped from $46 billion in 1956 to $41 billion in 1958, but over the same span, average hourly earnings in manufacturing industries crept up from $1.95 to $2.11, and total personal income increased from $333 billion to $361 billion.

In the unwarranted attack on profits let us have a look at the rhetoric contrived by the politicians. In the *New York Times* Senator Hubert H. Humphrey, Democrat of Minnesota, was quoted as criticizing "record high profits" that showed "a 19% increase" in the last year. Henry S. Reuss, Democratic senator from Wisconsin, chimes in with this observation in a signed article in the *New York Times* of July 7, 1974: ". . . corporate profits rose during the end of 1973 and the beginning of 1974 at an annual rate of over 46%."

In our analysis of profits, we shall demonstrate vividly that this is political opportunism of the rankest sort. The politicians, like their union brethren, in effect take profit aggregates out of their historical context, through wishful deceit or economic naivete, to create misconceptions about profits and profit trends.

However, in considering profits, it is important to distinguish between the aggregates and the profit margin. In order to show that profits were not excessive, actually hardly reasonable, we present a table from *Facts and Figures on Government Finance* published by the Tax Foundation, Inc., New York, 1975. (See Table I-1.)

Profits in their true perspective can be seen in the table. A false picture is obtained by looking only at the absolute amounts in the columns of profits before Federal income taxes and profits after Federal income taxes. The most relevant figures are obtained in the column on after-tax profits as a percentage of sales. It is here that charges of excessive or obscene profits are proven or shown to be false. Note should be taken of the fact that dividends are paid out of that profit margin. Thus, it can be seen that any notions of the ability of manufacturers to pay for wage increases exceeding productivity gains are erroneous. Furthermore, it follows logically that to arouse such expectations is a hoax, which contributes to inflation, excessive government expenditures in search of problems, some genuine but a good number just fabrications of the elitists, and inhibits economic growth. The self-styled benefactors of the worker are the ones who give him a shafting.

Charges are often made by union leaders and the intelligentsia that inflation is caused by higher profits and that business benefits most from inflation. In consideration of these charges, Table I-2 on weekly earnings and profit margins was constructed for all manufacturers. The data are shown in current dollars and in constant dollars to reflect the effects of inflation on each series.

The tables debunk the myths of excessive, obscene, and unconscionable profits and reveal the falsehood in Woodcock's assertion that profits rise "at the expense of the living standards of the great majority of America's families." In real terms, profit margins have plunged to record lows while weekly earnings were up substantially.

Before continuing this discourse on the relationship of profits and wages relative to the working man's welfare, a severe reprimand should be dished out to businessmen for

SALES, PROFITS, AND STOCKHOLDERS EQUITY [...]
Calendar Years 1950-1973[b] (Dollar Figures in Billions)

Year	Sales (net)	Profits Before Federal Income Taxes	Profits After Federal Income Taxes	Stockholders' Equity[c]	After-tax Profits as a Percentage of Sales	After-tax Profits as a Percentage of Equity
1950	$ 181.9	$23.2	$12.9	$ 83.3	7.1	15.4
1951	245.0	27.4	11.9	98.3	4.8	12.1
1952	250.2	22.9	10.7	103.7	4.3	10.3
1953	265.9	24.4	11.3	108.2	4.3	10.5
1954	248.5	20.9	11.2	113.1	4.5	9.9
1955	278.4	28.6	15.1	120.1	5.4	12.6
1956	307.3	29.8	16.2	131.6	5.3	12.3
1957	320.0	28.2	15.4	141.1	4.8	10.9
1958	305.3	22.7	12.7	147.4	4.2	8.6
1959	338.0	29.7	16.3	157.1	4.8	10.4
1960	345.7	27.5	15.2	165.4	4.4	9.2
1961	356.4	27.5	15.3	172.6	4.3	8.9
1962	389.9	31.9	17.7	181.4	4.5	9.8
1963	412.7	34.9	19.5	189.7	4.7	10.3
1964	443.1	39.6	23.2	199.8	5.2	11.6
1965	492.2	46.5	27.5	211.7	5.6	13.0
1966	554.2	51.8	30.9	230.3	5.6	13.4
1967	575.4	47.8	29.0	247.6	5.0	11.7
1968	631.9	55.4	32.1	265.9	5.1	12.1
1969	694.6	58.1	33.2	289.9	4.8	11.5
1970	708.8	48.1	28.6	306.8	4.0	9.3
1971	751.4	53.2	31.3	320.9	4.2	9.8
1972	849.5	63.2	36.5	343.4	4.3	10.6
1973	1,017.1	81.4	48.1	374.2	4.7	12.9

[a] For years before 1969, excludes newspapers.
[b] Because of changes in accounting and other procedures, data are not strictly comparable from one period to another.
[c] Annual average based on four end-of-quarter equity figures.
Source: Federal Trade Commission, and Securities Exchange Commission.

Table I-2
MANUFACTURING INDUSTRIES

	Average Gross Weekly Earnings (Billion Dollars)		Profit Margin on Sales	
	Current Dollars	1967 Dollars	Current Dollars	1967 Dollars
1955	$ 75.7	$ 94.4	5.4%	7.1%
1960	89.7	101.2	4.4	4.9
1965	107.5	113.8	5.6	5.9
1968	122.5	117.6	5.1	4.9
1969	129.5	118.0	4.8	4.4
1970	133.7	115.0	4.0	3.5
1971	194.2	117.1	4.2	3.5
1972	154.7	123.5	4.3	3.5
1973	165.7	124.5	4.7	3.6
	Percentage Increases, 1955-1973			
	118.9%	31.9%	−13.0%	−49.3%
	Percentage Increases, 1970-1973			
	23.9%	8.3%	17.5%	2.9%

Sources: Earnings—U.S. Bureau of Labor Statistics.
Profit Margins—Federal Trade Commission.
Profit margins in constant dollars computed by using implicit proce deflater for non-residential structures and durable goods of Department of Commerce—Bureau of Economic Analysis.

their inept and really stupid handling of profit figures for the media. They and their public relations experts should be castigated for contributing to the dissemination of distorted profit data by failing to show profit margin statistics.

Corporate oligarchies vote themselves generous salaries and bonuses and there is no excuse for not adhering to their primary function—the management of the business for its long-term benefit to the long-term welfare of its employees

Myths and Realities of Corporate Profits

and stockholders. They must devote their efforts to removing the myth of the adversary relationship or that myth will destroy our society. Businessmen are as much at fault as union leaders in presenting a distorted picture of profits. Mr. Meany and Mr. Woodcock were merely following the prevailing but dubious practice of most businesses in announcing the percentage increase in dollar profits without mentioning profit margins.

Union leaders, competing with aspirants in the wings, and political demagogues portray "Big Business" and the "Working Man" as supposedly representing two different enemy camps. This myth was tackled admirably and demolished in an article by John O'Riley in the *Wall Street Journal* of April 17, 1972. Excerpts follow:

> The record suggests that the welfare of business and the welfare of the people on the payroll are almost one and the same thing.
>
> As good a definition as any of a big business is just a big payroll—and a generator of other payrolls.
>
> Take, for example, the biggest business of them all—the General Motors Corporation. Here are some highlights from its recently released annual report for 1971, showing all the money General Motors took in—and where the money went. Dollar figures represent billions.
>
> | | |
> |---|---:|
> | GM Received | $28,328 |
> | **THE REVENUE WENT** | |
> | To Suppliers | 13,512 |
> | To Employes | 9,448 |
> | For Taxes | 2,560 |
> | For Depreciation, Obsolescence | 873 |
> | To GM Stockholders | 985 |
> | For Expanding, Modernizing, etc. | 950 |

The tax collectors alone got more than two and a half times as much of GM money as went to stockholders. And the employes received just a whisker under ten times as much as the stockholders—who got only a thin 3.5% slice of the pie. On a dollars-and-cents basis, the people on the payroll thus have ten times as much at stake in the corporation's welfare as those who receive the stock dividends.

O'Riley points out that from 1965 to 1972 wages and salaries increased 60%, double the 30% increase in dividend income. However, O'Riley perceptively asserts that pension plan assets have grown from $58 billion in 1961 to $138 billion in 1970, or nearly 140% in just one decade. O'Riley concludes with this remark:

Yes, many a punch will land in the "business eye" in this as in all election years. But somewhere along the line, employe-voters may begin to wonder more just whose eye is really being punched.

In his conclusion, O'Riley is stressing the fact that the viability of the corporation means more to the employe than it does to the stockholder. For the worker it bears noting that, as O'Riley put it, "On a dollar-and-cents basis, the people on the payroll thus have ten times as much at stake in the corporation's welfare as those who receive stock dividends." In this quote, O'Riley was referring to General Motors, but this conclusion is just as valid for all manufacturers, in fact all business enterprises.

Because it is so representative of unfounded, wild charges against profits, we will again revert to Woodcock's assertion that profits rise "at the expense of the living standards of the great majority of America's families." By a logical extension, we can conclude from his remarks that the stock-

Myths and Realities of Corporate Profits

holder gains at the expense of the worker and his family. To get some perspective in this area, we have compiled Table I-3 on shares in the national income.

Table I-3
National Income by Distributive Shares
(As Percentages of National Income)

	Compensation of Employes	After-Tax Profits	Dividends
1929	59.0%	9.9%	6.7%
1939	66.3	7.7	5.2
1949	64.8	8.5	3.3
1959	69.8	7.1	3.2
1969	73.9	5.8	3.2
1973	73.8	6.8	2.8
1974	74.9	7.4	2.9

Percentage changes from 1929 to 1973
+25.1%   −25.3%   −62.3%

The table graphically demonstrates the shocking deterioration in profit and dividend trends. This should not be accepted complacently by Woodcock and his leftward-oriented cohorts in academia, the media, unionism and the bureaucracies. Before they wring their hands in sadistic glee, they should realize that today's profits and dividends are tomorrow's investments and the jobs of the day after tomorrow and tomorrow's energy. The union worker should also realize that he has a vital stake in the profitability and viability of corporations because his pension fund allotments are invested in businesses. It behooves him to take cognizance of the fact that he may be in position to own and control the huge corporations via his pension fund money. We briefly mentioned this in the introduction and will expound on this theme more extensively later.

The tables cited in the foregoing paragraphs debunk conclusively the myth of huge profits as depicted by pseudo-liberals and their fellow travelers. It is a picture of inadequate profits that are necessary for steady growth in capital formation, which will be discussed more fully in a later chapter.

"Soaking big business" through exorbitant wage demands in excess of productivity increases and heavy taxes is not only contributing to inflation but really undermining capital formation, wherein lie future jobs, paychecks and pensions.

It is sad to conclude that the worker is not being shafted by the profits of corporations but by the "obscene profits" of political opportunism in government and unionism.

Now it will be fitting to delve into the motives of the detractors of profits, the profit system, capitalism and our society. Who are the detractors? What is their basic economic philosophy? Why do they concoct the lie, the half-truth, the distortion, the slanted interpretation? Most have or aspire for a vested interest so they must have a target. So they pick on what they consider their most appealing target—profit. They conjure up the picture of the bloated plutocrat—the greedy fat cat. In their appeals to the economically ignorant they succeed in creating and perpetuating an adversary relationship that in fact should not exist. The union leadership has a vested interest in a position of power and prestige. They seem to think that economic statesmanship would be suicidal. They appear to feel that if they are not militant enough in their demands some ambitious firebrand will challenge them in the next union election. They ignore the facts that adequate profits are of

Myths and Realities of Corporate Profits

common and mutual concern to management as well as labor. After all, today's profits are tomorrow's jobs, tomorrow's paychecks, tomorrow's pension and tomorrow's viable economic base that will provide better jobs, paychecks, and pensions for their children and grandchildren.

Attention, now, will be focused on the political demagogue. He apparently sees more votes among the economic illiterates than those who are informed in such matters, so he crassly panders to inequalities and envies, which he exploits to preserve his vested interest. Objectivity and fairness are sadly lacking.

The charge has been made that union leaders and certain politicians take advantage of the fact that the great majority of the populace is not too well versed on finance and economics. Why this dismal state of affairs about a science that has been erroneously misnamed the "dismal science"? After all, it deals with human economic welfare, which affects the present and the future. It is an exciting and intriguing science that reaches into numerous ramifications of life that have a bearing on the psychological, emotional and moral aspects of life. Our educational system and the media are mainly responsible, with an assist by business managers. A course on the economic facts of life should be one requirement for graduation from high school. In our universities, economics should be required of all students. These high school and college texts should at a minimum present facts and data on prices, profits, wages, taxes in their true perspective. A discourse should be included on the merits and demerits of all economic systems.

Our business managers have been remiss in their presentation of profit figures. Their public relations or publicity departments have done a lousy job in this respect, as well as in the area of propounding and defending the virtues of the free enterprise system. In the latter aspect, John A. Davenport in the *Wall Street Journal* of July 27, 1973, made the following cogent observations in an article from which we present the following excerpts:

FREE ENTERPRISE'S FORGOTTEN VIRTUES

The standard defense of capitalism is that it is the most *efficient* system of production yet devised, and in a world wracked by poverty and food shortages efficiency is surely not something to be sneered at. Yet with the U.S. gross product now running over the trillion dollar mark, efficiency of and by itself has lost some of its old appeal. The young, in particular, are not apt to be impressed by massive statistics on steel output or million digit figures on kilowatt hours generated and consumed (the more so since the country has been suffering from brownouts and fuel shortages). The young are looking for *significance* in their lives in this bewildering world of gadgets and mass communication. Man does not live by bread alone.

The true case for enterprise rests on higher grounds. It is that in providing bread it also yields two things which men in all ages have craved—namely Freedom and Order. In a Socialist economy where government owns the means of production, the bureaucrat must decide what goods are to be produced and where and how men should work. Sad experience has shown that this is the road to tyranny whether under Communist or Fascist banners. The same is true of any system of planned economy all too often favored by our wooly-headed liberals and technocrats. The planners may think they know what people want or should have. The people themselves are denied choice in the matter.

By contrast, the enterprise economy, working within the framework of strong but limited government, does provide freedom of choice and voluntary collaboration. Its basic postulate is that the consumer rather than the producer or bureaucrat is king and should be given a vote in the economic arena no less than at the ballot box. The means to this end is the much maligned price, wage and profit system which is a signalling device for translating consumer demands into productive output. If consumers want more meat, as has been the case recently, the price of meat not only will rise but *should* rise, and farmers in their own interest and in quest of profit will produce more hogs and beef cattle. So too with all other commodities and manufactured products from automobiles to hairpins. In such a system even the biggest corporation must respond to the public will or go under.

The market is also a means for organizing and coordinating the most precious thing a man has to offer society, namely his own skill and ability. In the Soviet Union and other Socialist societies men are driven to work at such times and places as commissars choose, when they are not actually subjected to slave labor camps. In Western societies men are still free to sell their work where it will fetch the highest return (unless prevented by union restrictions and government minimum wage laws). As Walter Lippmann put it in his book *The Good Society:* "The market is not something invented by businessmen and speculators for their profit, or by classical economists for their intellectual pleasure. The market is the only possible means by which labor that has been analyzed into its separate specialties, can be synthesized into useful work. Failure to understand that truth is a sure sign of failure to understand the technical principle of production in the modern world."

Above all, public misunderstanding of the market system is manifest in the constant attack on profits which though a tiny part of the national income are the vital *enzyme* in the economy's metabolism. In a complex economy such as ours someone must undertake the risks of bringing labor, materials and capital together before a single bushel of wheat or a single automobile can be produced. That function falls to the businessman. If he is right in judging the market, his reward will be profit. If he is wrong he will suffer loss. On the short-run ours is not a profit economy but a *profit-and-loss* system. (Ask Penn-Central!) On the longer run a continuous flow of profits is essential to capital formation on which rising living standards and all welfare schemes depend. To talk of profitless prosperity is really a contradiction in terms.

Businessmen have a chance—perhaps a last chance—to help mobilize public opinion toward a different outcome where government and business will each attend to their respective roles. They can no longer claim that capitalism is some kind of God-given dispensation. They can with reason and good conscience argue that the market economy and limited constitutional government stand or fall together and that both are deeply rooted in the Nature of Man.

This is no doubt a difficult and high-sounding mission. It is also one that can be based on hard common sense. The hour is late. The need pressing. The funds for such an educational campaign are available. What in the world are businessmen waiting for?

In current vogue among many educators and passed on to their students is the idea that there is something antisocial about working for profit. This has aroused the ire of a certain Mr. George W. Betz of Villanova, Pennsylvania, who made these caustic and perceptive comments in a letter to the editor appearing in the *Wall Street Journal* of February 26, 1974. Excerpts follow:

... The initiative, imagination and application of businessmen for 150 years is never mentioned. Even the most superficial knowledge of our economic history would disclose the enormous losses absorbed by the businessman in the course of our history—losses largely taken by reason of ventures that failed. Risk taking is the very essence of economic growth. If there had been none to take the risks we would still be a nation of farmers.

Is it really supposed that the railroad system of this country, so effectively ruined by regulation, could have been built without Vanderbilt, Harriman or Gould? Or that the electric grid could have been organized by a committee of journalists, politicians or professors?

To hell with appeasement. Teach the young what and who built this country and, incidentally, got rich at it. Teach them the truth. Teach them that the most critical shortages with which we now must contend are in regulated industries—regulated because of an educational system that instilled an abiding mistrust of corporate profits. Teach them, for a change, what happens to corporate profits. Best of all, offer a course in the economic development of, say, India. Or maybe Russia. Teach them that one-half of them would likely be dead if it weren't for the drugs discovered and merchandised by these corporate pigs.

If our high school teachers don't know how our national income is distributed, how can they instill the proper information to their students? When the Opinion Research Corporation asked a cross-section of the nation's high school teachers whether they thought employes or owners get the larger portion of national income, 52% said they thought owners got the larger portion. This is not surprising since they get most of their information from union-biased news reporters and the biased propaganda sheets of the educational complex.

In the opening paragraphs of this chapter, we alluded to the Opinion Research Corporation poll in which people exhibited the fantastically erroneous belief that corporations made 28 cents on each sales dollar. As the second draft of this chapter was being written, a new poll by Opinion Research disclosed that the public understanding of corporate profits was not improving but getting worse. This development elicited this editorial response in the *Detroit News* of June 28, 1975:

PUBLIC EXAGGERATES CORPORATE PROFITS

The public estimated the average manufacturer's after-tax profit at 33 percent, more than six times the actual amount; the auto companies' profit at 39 percent, more than 20 times the actual amount, and the oil companies' profit at 61 percent, more than eight times the actual amount.

Two other disappointing facts about the survey results ought to be noted.

One is that the public understanding of corporate profits is getting worse, not better. In a similar survey in 1973, the public estimate of the average manufacturer's after-tax profit was 28 percent or 5 percentage points lower than the current finding.

The other is that for the first time in 30 years a majority of the public believes the government should put a limit on corporate profits.

Those results appear to confirm the fear that the foes of the free enterprise system are doing a better job of tearing it down than the corporations and other capitalists are in defending it.

Beyond that, however, what's the explanation for the erroneous public attitudes?

Perhaps corporations aren't explaining their profit margins very well to the public. Perhaps economics courses in schools and colleges are not emphasizing the essential role of profits to private enterprise. And perhaps reporting has overemphasized profit increases rather than the actual level of profits.

Perhaps the mistaken views about profits also stem from the desire on the part of some politicians to "soak the rich," including the corporations, without realizing that taxes on business either are passed on to the public in the form of higher prices or absorbed by the stockholders in the form of lower returns on their investments.

Whatever the reason for the public's mistaken views about profits, American business and industry leaders and the public as well ought to be concerned about attitudes which contribute to public confusion, lead to bad legislation and threaten the future of the private enterprise system.

"What's the explanation for the erroneous public attitudes?" the *Detroit News* asks and answers, "Perhaps corporations aren't explaining their profit margins very well to the public." That "perhaps" puts it too mildly and too kindly. In our opinion corporate managements and their publicity departments have been remiss and negligent in their faulty handling of profit reports in their press releases and advertisements. With an eye toward the Translux Tape, they overstress per share results and in most cases completely ignore profit margins. Thus, unwittingly or stupidly, they provide the grist that anti-business radicals and liberals exploit to sow misconceptions about profits and distrust of the free market system.

The results of the new opinion poll prompted the following remarks in the *Wall Street Journal* in an editorial on June 20, 1975:

NICE GOING

No one should underestimate the power of a little demagoguery to sow distrust of business and free markets during periods of excessive inflation.

Any halfway competent economist knows that inflation results from government creating an excess of money, usually to cover its own debts. But it is very easy for Congressmen to transfer the blame to business, since businessmen, after all, are the ones who are changing the price tags.

The problem, we are told by illustrious Senators, is that, all of a sudden, businessmen are trying to reap "obscene profits." And sure enough, an Opinion Research poll shows that those sampled are currently overestimating after-tax business profit margins by some six times.

All we can say to such Congressmen is "nice going." If you wanted to confuse the electorate and thus complicate the politics of coping with inflation you certainly have succeeded.

However, the treatment of profits reports by the *Wall Street Journal* in its news sections is not above reproach. One would expect that the *Wall Street Journal* would be an effective counter-force to the faulty dissemination and interpretation of profit figures. But has it been? The *Journal's* handling of profit reporting has aroused the indignation of *Better Investing*, the official publication of the

National Association of Investment Clubs. Following is in its entirety an editorial that appeared in the issue of December, 1973:

NOTABLE & QUOTABLE?
NO; MORE LIKE IGNOBLE,
WALL STREET JOURNAL

* * *

Accuracy! Accuracy! Accuracy!
Paucity of It Would Make
Old Joe Pulitzer Roll Over

* * *

Is it Reportage or Pottage?
QUESTION: If THE WALL STREET JOURNAL doesn't know how to report business news then who does?

We aren't sure the WSJ knows that business is a game of margins. At least they don't seem to understand the importance of margins.

Take, for instance, the reporting of GENERAL MOTORS' third-quarter sales and profits. The front page item stressed the 41% jump in sales and record profits that were "more than double" the previous year.

Then, in a longer story on the inside pages, WSJ is quick to point out (in the third paragraph) that third-quarter profits edged out the 1965 previous record, $0.92 to $0.91. Ah, but wait, and wait and wait. Six paragraphs further at the very end of the article, we learn one of the most important facts. "GM's third-quarter profit margin on sales was a slim 3.5% compared to the 7% of 1965."

This low margin occurred despite the fact the corporation is operating at a high volume when margins should be at their best. It is occurring in a corporation that traditionally had margins of over 10%.

The WSJ reporting doesn't show that GENERAL MOTORS had to double its sales to get a penny more in profits per share.

It doesn't stress the dangerously low margin. By stressing profits, it tends to make the public less sympathetic with the struggles of the corporation to meet the pollution and safety challenges, retool for smaller cars and new engines and just pay for the research and development necessary in a highly competitive industry.

We think it might be more productive for WSJ to point out that government pressures to meet standards that many people feel are ridiculous are a major cause of this low margin, that such standards are endangering the economic health of GENERAL MOTORS.

Let's take another look at the WSJ, this time at a dumb editorial. In an editorial called "Those Oil Industry Profits," the WSJ stresses how the oil industry is "choking with embarrassment" and "shamefaced" over third-quarter profits, then reels off some of the figures. But don't be embarrassed, says the WSJ. (We don't know whether this is sarcastic or just cute commentary.) Not until the second last paragraph are we enlightened. "The reason profits have soared is that the industry has been operating flat out . . . there is no excess capacity in the system and efficiencies are at a peak. The reason there is no excess capacity is that it was not built when it should have been, because the government was both limiting the importation of oil and holding down earnings with price controls."

Frankly we've read some of the releases from the oil industry, and they didn't sound embarrassed.

Like the WSJ says in the LAST paragraph, the industry will need income growth increases estimated at 16% compared to historical averages of 8% to meet "the stupendous capital requirements it faces."

That was probably the lead for your editorial, WSJ, not your kicker. Those readers who stopped after the first few paragraphs of your items on GENERAL MOTORS or your editorial on the oil industry, missed some fairly important facts in your paper. And if they don't get them from you, where will they come from?

Because they are such a tremendous force in shaping public opinion, TV commentators have a grave responsibility in reporting profit data and in presenting them in their true perspective so as not to leave a false impression. The writer was quite perturbed when he heard a TV commentator in 1972 report that the earnings of Chrysler surged 42%. There was no mentioning of the fact that the earnings were from a depressed level to which they had fallen. Profit margin data, likewise, were not given. The profit margin rise was 55½%, ostensibly a prodigious rise until one digs deeper to discover that profit margins improved from 2.7 cents to 4.2 cents on the dollar. What galled the writer was the tenor of presentation when the commentator very slowly and deliberately intoned *"surged forty-two percent."* There was no doubt that he tried to impress millions of his naive listeners with the enormity of the profit rise. Is it any wonder that public opinion is led to believe that corporations have a huge reservoir of untapped wealth from which they should be able to grant generous wage increases and fringe benefits without raising prices?

Since the advent of the American Newspaper Guild, there has been a perceptible change in newspaper reporting and editorial writing. Before the days of the Guild, the advertising department and the publisher and editor-in-chief favored slanting news in favor of big business. Now it appears that the Guild members are tending to slant the news in favor of unions, consumerists, environmentalists and left-of-center politicians. So it would not be surprising that news reports of profits are not accorded treatment in true perspective.

It is of paramount importance that a drastic change should be made in reporting profits in order to present to the public a true and an unbiased picture of profits. The profit margin should be given not only in the lead paragraph but also in the first sentence. This practice should be put into effect immediately by all public relations officers, publicity agents and corporate officers and by all news wire services. Corporate officers and their public relations staffs should take their eye off the stock market, forget financial analyst meetings and spend more time managing their businesses and improving communications with their employes. This is one important way in which they will impress their employes that they have a big stake in healthy profits and encourage them to improve productivity for their mutual benefit. Productivity gains should be distributed in ratios favoring employes with the balance allocated to the corporations and price reductions.

The anti-profits propaganda conducted by union leaders, educators and the media is having far greater economic consequences than they have ever contemplated. It is suspected that, in some instances, the myth of huge and unwarranted profits was created with the mischievous purpose of creating an adversary relationship; in other instances, for throwing a monkey wrench into the machinery of the capitalist system. Consequences of this propaganda have been changes in labor attitudes. "Me-tooism" has resulted in a chain of events that has been a contributory factor in the inflationary spiral. This has led to a more serious development—the eruption of "more" fever. The *Detroit Free Press* printed a cartoon depicting *their* editorial policy: the weary and much put-upon figure of Unemployment is shown sitting on a park bench and reading a newspaper article headlined CORPORATE PROFITS SOAR.

In conjunction with the cartoon, please note the following terminology in the allusion to profits:

Mr. Meany—"Greed"
Mr. Woodcock—"Skyrocketed" "Upsurge"
Sen. Humphrey—"Record high profits"

Having been subjected to this type of biased news reporting and cartoons, is it any wonder that the worker freezes at his post at the machine and fails to produce what he is capable of doing? Also it is not surprising that our high school and college students are easy prey to the Marxist school of historical revisionists. In their constant reiteration of lies, distortions and myths, our educators, union leaders, avant-garde writers and movie producers have succeeded in creating an anti-bourgeois culture. As examples take the movies *The Graduate* and *Love Story*, and such publications as *Rolling Stone* and *Playboy*, which cast aspersions on industry. Irving Kristol theorizes that "these critics, intellectuals and men of letters above all, never did like modern liberal society because it was 'vulgar'—i.e., it permitted ordinary men and women, in the marketplace, to determine the shape of this civilization, a prerogative that intellectuals and men of letters have claimed for themselves. (This is why so many intellectuals and men of letters naturally tend to favor some form of benevolent despotism, in our time called a 'planned society.')" According to the pseudo-intellectuals—the intelligentsia—bureaucrats, enlightened by the wisdom of the intelligentsia, will usher in the economic, social and political utopia. In their myopic economic vision, further hindered by the blinkers of ideology, they fail to make an honest and comparative study of the merits

Myths and Realities of Corporate Profits

and demerits of capitalism on the one hand and socialism on the other. Because of their prejudices, they fail or don't want to perceive that what in human nature renders capitalism imperfect renders socialism unworkable. They gloss over the failure of socialist bureaucratic planners to solve problems of such a basic industry as agriculture as evidenced by the creaking inefficiencies of agricultural production in Russia, China and India. They now propose that we entrust the management of our industrial complex to bureaucrats. It is not within the powers of their putative all-wise intelligence to see through the economic fog they have let loose that over-regulation has crippled many of our industries. In this respect, George Orwell said, "You have to belong to the intelligentsia to believe things like that: No ordinary man can be such a fool."

The attack on profits and the profit motive is the main basis of the intellectual prostitutes of the left in creating the anti-bourgeois culture. These creators and purveyors of economic claptrap about exorbitant profits that putatively exploit the worker have succeeded in brainwashing our youth that working for profit is anti-social. Businessmen will have to abandon their defensive stance about our industrial complex and take an aggressive attitude about extolling the virtues of the free enterprise system and the profit motive and the benefits that accrue to the benefit of the worker and society. They should be aware of the fact that they have a formidable undertaking in tackling the elitist pseudo-intellectuals in our educational complex as evidenced in the following analysis appearing in the *Wall Street Journal* of August 11, 1970:

CONFESSIONS OF A CONSERVATIVE SOCIOLOGIST
by Edwin Harwood

We always assumed that free public higher education would raise the sons and daughters of the less privileged into better jobs. Did we ever consider, as the economist Joseph Schumpeter pointed out over 30 years ago, that the expansion of mass higher education could lead easily to a deterioration in teaching, with the result that students would be psychologically prepared for elite occupations in the Establishment without getting the necessary training to enter those occupations? Colleges were not, Schumpeter emphasized, just a matter of money, if nature set limits to the number of good scholars and teachers she chose to furnish for the task.

Consequently, today there is a good chance that the young man who once would have been content to follow his dad into the plant or apprentice himself in his uncle's craft, will now—thanks to the deterioration of college education accompanying its rapid spread—become psychologically unemployable.

He finds he cannot become a doctor, a lawyer, a corporation executive or a professor, but he will not take some lowly salaried white-collar job that would subject him to the indignities of taking other people's orders and following a bureaucracy's routines. After having touched the great traditions of Western thought, that would be a "cop out." But neither can he go back to his dad's plant and work as an operative, a plumber or a maintenance man. He is in limbo.

College, with its well-tended lawns and gardens, plushly furnished student gathering rooms and library alcoves, sauna, squash and tennis facilities, theater and concerts has introduced him to an affluent life-style—I would say, to the upper middle class life-style. (Can you think of any country club more richly equipped than the ordinary state college campus?) To graduate from that will mean for many students to graduate down to something infinitely less desirable. It means, as one Rice senior explained his contempt for a nine-to-five job to me, giving up the leisured and rich campus life for the discipline that most lower middle class and working class Americans are subject to, of being an order-taker and an early-riser.

It is not the strange paradox many think that the University of California at Santa Barbara—one of the loveliest, best situated and most lavishly equipped schools in the California system—should have become the scene of some of the worst rioting, that included the precincts of the business community serving it. Nor is it odd that well-dressed, suntanned kids could be found moving between dorms and classroom buildings covered with Eldridge Cleaver's enraged visage. That campus has the affluent American life-style and more, a West Coast Waikiki with the difference that while some study is expected of the guests there are no hotel bills to be paid.

Yet students can see that others work in the adjoining business district, and that these others have to get up much earlier in the morning than they to serve their needs: To take their orders for books, clothing, food and whatever else the student needs.

Guilt at the "oppression" of a business routine afflicting others, that the student is being adjusted to reject, weakens his self-confidence. If *he* doesn't want to face the harsh routines of adult life, how can he expect the blacks to accept theirs, or any group in society that must toil from 8 to 5 in return for a two or three week vacation at the end of the year? Because he is guilty, he cannot stand up to black militants. And he is also angry because he knows that the good life on campus will not go on forever.

Students see that their professors can take off at any time of the day to run errands, and that instead of the one-and-a-half or two-day weekend, they can arrange a teaching schedule that will give them three or even four days. If an old friend comes to town and wants a tour or a conference beckons, classes can be canceled or re-scheduled. Naturally many students would like to have the very same freedoms for themselves. Academic salaries being what they are today, the economic privations that used to insure that only dedicated scholars would want these freedoms are no longer available to stem the flood of seekers after academic positions. It is this factor, not the draft as is so often claimed, that explains why so many undergraduates want to continue in graduate school.

The New Leisured Class

Radicals, who once told us that the leisured classes of society were parasitical for taking goods while refusing to work, are now defending the abuses of the new leisured class, of students and ex-students and anyone else in rebellion against society. In *The Making of a Counter Culture,* Theodore Roszak defends the college dropout's rejection of a job. Why, he asks, should hippies be expected to work, even when they continue to demand the services others must produce, if America has "an economy of cybernated abundance that does not need their labor, that is rapidly severing the tie between work and wages, that suffers from hard-core poverty due to maldistribution, not scarcity." Given these "facts" about the American economy, Roszak believes the college dropout's refusal to get a "good respectable forty-hour-week job" is just simple good sense.

In another book addressed to young people "dedicated to the possibility of radical change," a sociologist, also teaching in the California system, tells us that since full automation is just one decade off, "If you wanted to lie on the beach and do nothing, you could obtain the necessities of life, produced in abundance by machines . . . nobody would be forced by economic necessity to work for somebody else or take a job he did not like." Only if the person wants luxury goods will he have to work to earn the money for them. (Frank Lindenfeld, "Work, Automation, and Alienation" in *Radical Perspectives on Social Problems.* MacMillan.)

Just how those automated bicycles, shoes, radios and telephones—none of them luxury goods in the article's view—are to be packaged, marketed and brought down to the beach is unclear. This sociologist raises the important question only to dismiss it: "Would people work if they didn't have to? That this question can be raised seriously is a reflection of the pecuniary twist of our values."

Who can blame the Middle American for getting sore at us when his youngster comes home from college and confronts the folks with *that.*

This chapter on huge profit myth would not be complete without reference to the so-called "oligopolistic and monopolistic profits." The intelligentsia and the political windbags have raised the myth that consumers have been ripped off by huge profits resulting from monopolistic and oligopolistic price gouging. The truth is that redistributing monopoly profits would shift less than 1% of income, according to a study by economist Arnold Harberger of the University of Chicago. Just imagine all that political rhetoric and economic buncombe over a mere 1%. Perhaps, greed for political profit must pay off handsomely.

In more than one way we have submitted irrefutable statistical proof that profits are not excessive, and that they have not been made at the expense of the worker. In fact, measured in real terms, profits and dividends have been shown to lag woefully behind other economic series, posing a threat to economic growth, employment and price stability and energy supplies. These important factors will be considered in future chapters. Briefly, here we will summarize some of the deleterious consequences ensuing from the irresponsible and unfounded rhetoric against profits: It has

—Led to the "crisis of rising expectations."
—Spawned the "psychological momentum in expectations and entitlements."
—Laid groundwork for "governmental throwing of money at problems."
—Supplied erroneous bases for wage increases exceeding productivity gains.
—Contributed to inflation in a major degree by supplying false rationale for government spending, demand-pull inflation and unwarranted wage increase cost-push inflation.
—Impeded economic growth.

—Inhibited employment gains.
—Fostered an unnecessary adversary relationship between employer and employe.
—Undermined the work ethic.
—Sowed discontent and distrust among our young people.
—Provided some of the misleading rationale to criminal activity.
—Threw stumbling blocks to reasonable long-term solutions for the energy crunch.
—Delayed the potential emergence of a workers' capitalism.

All of these factors will be accorded a more extensive treatment in future chapters.

In the following chapter, consideration will be given to another set of myths about corporate pricing and prices.

II

FACTS AND FANCIES ON PRICES

The arrant sophistries that have spawned an inflation of myths about profits have spilled over into the area of prices, especially corporate pricing. As profits are the result of price and cost factors we cannot compartmentalize our thinking about prices only. This is natural as the prices of one industry are the costs of another. Further, in our complex, interdependent economic system, the myriad factors of prices, profits, wages, inflation and economic growth intertwine inextricably.

Consideration first will be given to the myths and fallacies about the alleged excessive prices of monopolistic and oligopolistic corporations. It has been the contention of liberal and leftward-leaning economists, such as Gardiner Means and John Kenneth Galbraith, that big corporations are so powerful that they can administer prices independent of the market. Hence, they propound their theories of "administered" prices, "rigid" prices and producer sovereignty. The data of Gardiner Means and Adolph Berle were accepted at face value. Apparently, they were looking for evidence to support their preconceived notions in a so-called monopolistic market structure. They made no genuine, sincere efforts to differentiate between the nature of the beasts that result in highly flexible prices of agricultural products on the one hand and the less flexible prices of manufactured goods. It is absurd to equate a market of millions of producers with a market of relatively few producers. Steel mills, auto plants and durable goods manufacturing entail huge sums in equipment and in relatively large research and administrative staffs, resulting in huge fixed overhead costs. The natural results are market pricing for agricultural products and "mark-up" pricing for manufactured goods. Instead of evaluating objectively, the purveyors of antibourgeois propaganda imply that there exist some ulterior machinations that engender less flexible prices of manufactured goods. They ascribe what they consider rigid prices to produce suzerainty. As for big business market sovereignty, it is fitting to ask what happened to Ford's Edsel, GM's Corvair, Chrysler's De Soto, Lockheed's Electra, Du Pont's Corfam and GE's and RCA's computers? Somehow, the pseudo-intellects are so victimized by their Marxist dogma that they cannot rationalize developments that don't conform to their ideology. They are strangely silent.

It has been indicated that it would be unusual for prices

of manufactured goods to be as flexible as farm products. Here the theory of price rigidity will be debunked. In their eagerness to fit data to preconceived notions, the anti-big-business propagandists took listed prices at their face value without inquiring into their validity. They saw listed prices as being rigid and farm prices as fluctuating, leading them to the conclusion that the price administrators were rigging the market, gouging the consumer and unduly piling up corporate profits. As proof they cited data showing farm prices plunging in the depression of the 1930s while prices of manufactured goods supposedly remained rigid. This is a fallacy, a typical distortion of the elitist intelligentsia. Historical perspective shows that prices of manufactured goods fluctuate less than those of farm products in *both* directions. They rise less in the upward phase of the business cycle and also fall less in the declining phase of business.

The self-styled detractors of profits, the establishment and corporate pricing are guilty of failing to inquire if list prices are the actual transaction prices. If they would slough off their anti-bourgeois bias they would discover that discounts, rebates and delivery terms play a significant role in prices. In business upswings, they disappear; in business declines, they reappear.

Transaction prices were considered by George J. Stigler and James K. Kindall in their scholarly study, *The Behavior of Industrial Prices* (National Bureau of Economic Research, N.Y., 1970—Columbia University Press). They found ". . . no evidence here to suggest that price rigidity or 'administration' is a significant phenomenon." Referring to the theory of Gardiner Means that prices of concentrated industries do not respond to reductions in demand, Stigler and Kindahl state that "We raise grave doubts of the validity of this belief." They did not use list prices as used by the Bureau of Labor Statistics from data supplied by sellers. Instead, they used transaction prices supplied by buyers. In their summary they found prices of concentrated industries "moving in the same direction as business 56% of the time; remaining constant 17% of the time; and moving perversely 27% of the time."

Long-term historical perspective shows the trend of industrial prices declining slowly. This is a resounding rebuttal to the specious theories of the self-serving detractors of our efficient economic system, which merits more freedom and less government intervention. The intelligentsia aspire to supplant this machine with a system that has shown an amazing ineptitude in as basic an industry as agriculture; a system that cannot compete in manufactured goods as well; a system that has failed signally as a dynamic productive force; a system where life is better for the stagnator than the innovator; and a system where economic regulation cannot countenance criticism, thus ending in political regimentation. Rather than brickbats American industry should be accorded bouquets. It should be admired and congratulated for the maintenance or reduction of industrial prices in the face of rising real wages and slowly declining profit margins.

In their great crescendo of spurious polemics, the leftists and phony liberals of academia, the media, unionism and populist demagoguery, have concocted myths of greedy monopolies extorting excessive prices and amassing unconscionable and obscene profits. In the vein of Lenin and

Facts and Fancies on Prices

Goebbels, communists and fascists alike, their persistent reiterations of falsehoods and distortions about profits and prices have created an unwarranted atmosphere of hostility against business and our society. This society, composed of human beings endowed with the imperfections and proclivities of human nature, is naturally imperfect but up to this time the most effective in providing food, clothing, shelter and the amenities of life. After all, that in human nature that makes capitalism imperfect renders socialism unworkable. These merchants of mendacity do not bother to provide statistical proof, unbiased and in true historical perspective. If they did, they would find that their hollow, bombastic rhetoric would not face up to the fact that redistributing monopoly profits would shift only about 1% of income.

A truer picture of the price structure was provided by Stigler and Kindahl in their differentiation between list prices and transaction prices—a scholarly, objective search for truth in the tradition of Plato. However, price is but one element of competition. Pricing uniformity, an outcome of mark-up pricing, is but a cover for other vectors of competition such as quality and productivity among others. Quality competition would be most largely confined to consumer goods and productivity competition to producer goods.

First, we will consider the quality aspect. Quality is in effect a price differential. A product with a slightly higher price but much higher quality will provide more utility than the lower-priced product. Price uniformity masks the fierce quality competition that rages among producers to maintain or increase their share of the market. This is especially true of declining phases of the business cycle. This results from the exploitation of science and technology to the benefit of the consumer. Here the innovators of capitalism outperform the stagnators of socialism.

The story of refrigeration provides a commendable example of both price reduction and quality improvement. For countless eons food was cooled in streams, wells and cellars until the advent of the icebox in 1860, followed by the electric refrigerator in 1915. Around 1930 industry came out with evaporator coils and freon as a refrigerant. Sepaate freezer chambers were added in 1939. Since then, the appliance industry tapped science and technology to develop autodefrost, ice makers, magnetic door seals, thinner walls, better insulation and safety grounding. For over 50 years, the consumer has been getting more for much less. According to *Appliance Manufacturing*, in 1921 about 5,000 refrigerators were sold for about $600 apiece; in 1931, some 850,000 averaged for $275; in 1941 over 4,000,000 sold at an average price of $154. Counterparts can be seen in the washing machine, the mangle, electric stoves and radar ranges. The drudgery of home keeping has been reduced immeasurably.

All these gains have accrued to the benefit of the consumer while industry has been operating at a profit margin of about 4 to 6 cents of the sales dollar. If the left-wing and liberal elitists think that this is exorbitant, why don't they create a competitive product? It's a million to one bet that they couldn't do it because, being indoctrinated with Marxism and populism, they can only produce invectives and sophistries to brainwash students, unionists and voters.

Facts and Fancies on Prices

Here also it would be fitting to cite the auto industry. Senator Phillip Hart sees price uniformity but fails to observe the intense quality competition. This quality competition exists not only between the four American manufacturers, but is as intense between the different divisions of one company. As an example, in the case of General Motors, the divisions of Chevrolet, Buick, Oldsmobile and Pontiac vie against each other as they do against their counterparts of Ford and Chrysler. This quality competition has caused the innovators to bring forth among others the self-starter, the mechanical or electrical windshield wiper, the windshield washer, automatic transmission, power steering, power brakes, electronic ignition, and air conditioning. All this has occurred in the face of meager profits of 3 to 6 cents on the sales dollar while wage rates have inexorably gone up and up. The auto industry sells to the buyer a product incorporating about 10,000 parts for less than $2 a pound. This is a terrific bargain. This stacks up well against European competition. The London *Economist* of April 5, 1975, writes, "The American car remains a good buy, often half the cost per cubic centimetre of engine capacity of its European equivalent."

One of the best measures of gauging benefits accruing to the consumer-worker is the calculation showing how many hours of work are required to purchase the different items. According to *Fortune*, April, 1975 (p. 94), "Today's factory worker has to work only half as long as his counterpart did in 1939 to earn the wherewithal to buy the goods and services that make up the consumer price index . . . Prices are more than three and a half times as high as they were then, but the average wage in manufacturent is up seven-fold, from 63¢ an hour to $4.40." This means that real compensation has increased 100% or doubled.

The aforementioned issue of *Fortune* presents a significant chart showing the hours of work needed to pay for goods and services. It is most revealing to observe that where 50% as much in work hours were needed in 1974 in comparison with 1939, four items are listed below the 50% line. These four are gasoline, requiring 47% as many hours; new autos, about 38%; electricity, 21%; and refrigerators, about 12%. *Fortune* states, "It's a fortunate thing these real costs have fallen. The average worker . . . now works 15% of his time to pay his Federal income taxes and social security compared with 1% in 1939." The rise in taxes has roughly offset the workers' fringe benefits. It is ironic that the four best-performing industries should be the so-called concentrated industries—the oligopolists. The lines in the chart for new autos and refrigerators show a persistent and continuous downtrend with no deviations. Electricity showed a parallel pattern until 1974, revealing a rise from 20 to 22% in required working hours; largely due to OPEC, gasoline's indicator rose from 37 to 47%.

This kind of performance merits praise and admiration rather than bombast, fulminations and invectives of the Marxist and liberal pseudo-intellectuals and their willful or naive followers in politics, education, the press, TV and unionism.

In their lies, distortions and half-truths about profits and prices, what have they perpetrated? Among our student body, in high school as well as college, they have indoctrinated a sizable segment with contempt and mistrust for the work ethic, the profit system and society as a whole. Among the unionists, they demean productivity and encourage "more for less." To the voters, they hypocritically appeal with calls for price rollbacks, soaking the rich and more government regulation to solve problems that were caused by government interference or regulation in the first place.

It appears credible that the leftist purveyors of economic and sociological pap may have contributed to the rising crime rate. They have transformed a picture of inadequate or meager profits into one of excessive, exorbitant, unconscionable, obscene and "rip-off" profits. In this unwarrantedly pernicious atmosphere, some see justification for soaking the rich and others for robbing the rich.

In contrast to the mischief that leftist theoreticians have produced, let us consider what corporate managers have produced. Operating under a profit margin of a picayune 4 to 6 cents on the sales dollar and further motivated by a sense of fulfillment, they have formed a team of managers, scientists, technologists and workers to enable the average American to avail himself of the following:

—To consume over eight times as much electricity in 1974 as he did in 1940
—To make seven times as many telephone calls
—To travel two and a half times as many miles
—To eat twice as much beef

Assembling the facts concerning electricity, we find that an average worker worked only 12% as long in 1974 to buy as much electricity as he did in 1939, and as a result in 1974 he consumed more than eight times as much electricity for his comfort and enjoyment. He and his wife used more electrical appliances than ever before for preparing meals, washing clothes and dishes and enjoying their TV, radio, stereo console, tape recorder, movie and slide projectors, and so forth. These reveal amenities above the basics of food, clothing and shelter.

In the case of the auto, we see a picture of a worker putting in only 38% as many hours and traveling two and a half times as many miles. This has been a tremendous egalitarian factor. At one time long distance travel was practically the exclusive domain of the ultra-rich. Now the scenic wonders of Niagara, Yosemite, the Tetons, the Grand Canyon, and so on, are accessible to practically all Americans.

Compared with socialist societies, capitalism presents this stark contrast:

> A relatively free market system in which innovators and managers motivated by profits which are hardly reasonable and adequate, providing the majority of consumers with amenities and luxuries far above the basics of food, clothing and shelter. To the above must be added the freedom of religion, free speech and mobility.
> A socialistic society operating under the dogmas of Marx and Lenin, revealing a startling ineptitude in providing the basics of life, with the attendant restrictions on mobility and on political and religious expression.

It has been demonstrated that pricing uniformity is but a cover for the quality competition that rages underneath in the case of consumer goods. In the case of producer goods, we have the element of productivity competition that is in effect quality competition applicable to durable goods. In considering this factor we will delve into the intricacies of production engineering. Let's assume that our hypothetical chief production engineer has to process a new automatic transmission. It is his function with the aid of numerous process engineers to determine how each individual item is to be produced and assembled into components that are finally assembled into a transmission. This will entail spending anywhere from $50,000,000 to $200,000,000 worth of equipment. The purchases will include machines costing around $10,000, to more sophisticated machines costing as much as $200,000 and automated transfer machines costing millions of dollars. The process engineer will have to specify the chucks (attachments on machines holding parts while they are being machined), cutting tools, feed rate of cutting tool to part, speed rate at which machine spindle and part rotate, production rate, and so forth. Some concerns buy on price only. The machine suppliers and in turn their suppliers compete savagely to get those sales. Needless to say, the producers offering the most productive machines and components get the business. Herein lies one of the secrets enabling American manufacturers to deliver autos and appliances at stable or falling prices while simultaneously increasing wage rates and reducing working hours.

General Motors reached its position because of its lead in quality competition. IBM attained its status because of its superiority in productivity competition. It would be tragic to penalize their successes by demands for dismemberment and divestiture to satisfy the idiotic rhetoric of the educational, journalistic, union and political grandstanders and charlatans. Their false assertions relative to profits and prices should not go unchallenged. A massive counteroffensive should be organized by our business leaders, responsible educators, journalists, political leaders and, if feasible, union leaders. This educational undertaking should stress that corporate profits and price trends are not economic ogres and that Senator Hart's "reorganization bill" would effectively destroy the efficiency of American industry because it would reward success with another piece of surgery—that is, any company that performed too well would be dismantled by a government commission for its success. Senator Hart's bill would not give us viable, highly competitive, cost- and price-reducing industries but major industries reduced to a safe level of mediocrity. The true picture on profits and prices should be given to every employe with his paycheck. Perhaps a better way would be to distribute this message to all students and their teachers and above all to union leaders and to everyone working in the media and to authors of "contemporary" novels and plays and television documentaries.

Headlines and the pseudo-profundities of the leftists leave the suggestion that the so-called concentrated industries are price gougers. John O'Riley rebuts these charges effectively in his column in the *Wall Street Journal* of May 7, 1973. His tabulation and some of his comments follow:

> The table below traces the rise in (1) living costs and (2) wages from 1947 through March of this year. "All L-C Items" is the official (1967=100) Labor Department consumer price index. Following it are price indices on some individual categories that make up the big index. And "Weekly Earnings" is the Labor Department's average for all nonsupervisory employes in the private economy.

Facts and Fancies on Prices

LIVING COSTS AND WEEKLY EARNINGS

	1947	1973	Rise
All L-C Items	66.9	129.8	94%
Food	70.6	134.5	91%
Meat, Poultry, Fish	76.3	152.7	100%
Dairy Products	73.2	121.5	66%
Fruits, Vegs.	67.2	136.8	104%
Durable Goods	80.3	120.2	50%
Apparel and Upkeep	78.2	124.8	60%
All Services	51.1	136.6	167%
Medical Care	48.1	135.8	182%
Weekly Earnings	$45.58	$140.23	208%

With incomes vastly outstripping the cost of things, what this adds up to is the greatest growth in average-man living standards in the history of mankind.

Lo and behold, what do we find? The alleged price gouger turns out to be the best performer. The tabulation shows that durable goods increased in price least of all. From 1947 to 1973, manufacturers of durable goods paid out 208% more in weekly earnings while increasing prices only 50%. It should be noted that of all the major categories listed, the rise in prices was the least for durable goods. Contrary to the Marxist propagandists, this is not exploitation of labor but the exploitation of science and technology for the benefit of the masses.

As indicated above, the historical perspectives on prices prove that the free market is working, refuting the charges of Means and Senator Hart. Business is forced by competition to pass on to the consumer the benefits of technology. Reverting to our studies in Chapter I, we have indicated that profits have declined sharply as a percentage of National Income. This would not have occurred if competition were not an effective force. These facts of economic life are ignored by theoretical economists. Another factor that is overlooked is one of cost competition. The appellations "process engineer" or "production engineers" are misnomers. They should be called "cost reduction engineers." They are the real unsung heroes who have benefited the worker and consumer alike.

We have been exposed in our contacts with engineers to note a development of which the theoretical economists and politicians are unaware. It is the competition of engineers and plant managers for recognition and possible promotion. Herein lies the real secret of the competitive market and the free market. The freedom to express individuality and originality is given full reign. And who benefits the most? The price data in this chapter and the profit data of the previous chapter show that the worker and purchaser are the prime beneficiaries.

The writer has admired the zeal with which process engineers and plant managers face up to challenges and end up with a sense of fulfillment. This proves the thesis of a substantial body of psychiatric literature that holds that people are happiest when challenged.

Another fact of corporate life that is overlooked is its self-policing. Corporations buy from and sell to each other, and the product design engineer and the process engineer and the purchasing agent are constantly looking at alternatives. The sellers know this and are not as free as Means and Hart erroneously conclude. Means' bogey of the interlocking directorships is a theoretical abtraction of no meaningful consequences. In essence, corporate pricing is mark-up pricing consisting of cost plus the profit margin. Thus it is the cost competition that is the main driving force that has been so beneficial to labor and consumer. This is the beauty of the cost discipline of the profit motive. We will treat the merits of its social redeemability in Chapter V on the philosophical aspects of profits.

From all of the above considerations, it should be obvious that profits are more dependent on cost trends than pricing power.

This is not to say that the conduct of industry is exemplary and above reproach at all times. But those companies or industries that have exploited a situation to what they thought was their advantage have discovered to their regret that in the end they invited competition and/or expansions that resulted in overcapacity that in the end lowered profit margins.

Long-range perspective on profits and prices prove that competition rages fiercely and yet the theoreticians hate to slough off their blinkers, as attested by the following news report in the *Wall Street Journal* on April 15, 1975:

> INDUSTRIES WITH LITTLE COMPETITION CITED
> FOR ABOUT HALF OF RECESSION'S INFLATION
>
> WASHINGTON—About half the inflation experienced in the current recession can be traced to industries where there's little competition, the government's wage-price monitoring agency was told.
>
> Economic consultant Gardiner C. Means said that while last year's fourfold jump in foreign oil prices has accounted for "something like a half" of the 12.5% rise in wholesale prices of the past 12 months, "most of the rest" can be attributed to price increases in concentrated industries. He defined such industries as those in which four companies do at least 25% of the business.
>
> Mr. Means, participating at a one-day conference by the Council on Wage and Price Stability, which is examining the

effects on inflation of pricing in concentrated industries, contended that unless prices in concentrated sectors of the economy are constrained, the U.S. is likely to have "continued strong single-digit inflation." He said such an inflation pace will occur "whether we have a continued stagnation, a deepening depression or a recovery restricted by inflation."

Basic Economic Theory

Mr. Means observed that basic economic theory calls for prices to fall during business slumps and rise during economic expansion. But he presented data showing that prices in concentrated industries often don't react that way to changes in business conditions. He urged that guidelines be established to curb what he considers abuses of market power in concentrated industries.

Mr. Means' assertions drew opposition from other participants. Phillip Cagan, an economist at the National Bureau of Economic Research, New York, said he believes concentrated industries respond very slowly to economic changes. He contended that these industries only now are catching up with price boosts taken by other industries several months ago. He said this process of catch-up "is spread out over a number of years."

J. Fred Weston, professor at the University of California at Los Angeles, argued that prices in large companies and in concentrated industries respond to market forces that aren't in ways "fundamentally different" from what take place in industries that aren't regarded as concentrated.

Expansion Period

He contended that during the 1958-65 period of economic expansion, the most concentrated industries actually decreased prices on the average.

Another participant, University of Chicago economist Sam Peltaman, said that pricing practices in concentrated industries have presented a "relatively minor problem with inflation."

"We're talking about a tempest in a teapot because over any cycle there's no difference in (pricing) behavior," he declared.

Mr. Means clings to a theory that he concocted in the 1930s and that has been widely circulated by so-called

Facts and Fancies on Prices 49

liberal economists. Apparentely this theory, unsubstantiated by logical analysis and statistics, is accepted because it conforms to their preconceived notions of the evils of big business. The objective and thorough investigations of Stigler and Kindahl have been ignored. Mr. Means' conclusions are at variance with the findings of Stigler and Kindahl and a chart that appeared in the previously cited issue of *Fortune*.

The charts clearly show that "concentrated industries" *always* outperformed the "unconcentrated industries" in price restraint, either declining while others were increasing or increasing less than the others. This is a graphic illustration of market competition at work. It should be added that this admirable price performance occurred in the face of rising wages.

In this respect, Mr. Woodcock's commentary relative to the automotive industry is of interest, as reported in the following interview as reported in *Barron's* of May 12, 1975:

> Q. Aside from the national mood, hasn't there been a tremendous rise in automobile prices over the past two or three years?
> A. I got into all sorts of trouble on *Meet the Press* on a question like that. This time I'm armed. Let me read you some figures that relate the average expenditure for a domestic car to median family income. Back in 1950, it took 8.1 months of income to buy a car. In 1955, 6.8 months. In 1960, 6.2 months. In 1965, 5.4 months. In 1970, it dropped to 4.7, in 1971 to 4.6, in 1972 to 4.5 and in 1973 to 4.3. In 1974, it rose again to 4.4, but that's almost half what it was in 1950.

The above charts and Woodcock's assertions certainly do make Mr. Means look ridiculous. He just doesn't seem able to shake off his obsession with theoretical "posted" prices as distinguished from the real world's "transaction" prices. Price performance over the entire business cycle and in long-term historical perspective is also ignored by Means.

"Book" or "posted" prices have been a fact of our industrial life, even though "transaction" prices have been the significant factor in the final consummation of transactions. However, posted prices assume a significance they never were accorded before because of the fear of the imposition of price controls. This explains the significance of the "rebates."

At any time that an industry has resorted to excessive price increases, the excesses have corrected themselves in time. A case in point is the comeuppance that the chemical industry brought down upon itself in the 1950s. Instead of taking a long-term view, the industry took advantage of the shortages created by the Korean war and boosted prices in excess of cost increases. Profits rose fantastically, invited competition that culminated in excess capacity, which in turn caused lower prices and meager profit margins for 20 years. No price controls were needed to correct the abuses. The market did a very effective job.

All the evidence we have cited so far discredits Means' espousal of guidelines to curb what he considers abuses of market power in concentrated industries. Means and economists oriented toward statism fail to perceive the damages wrought in the regulated industries. It cannot be overstressed that when industry makes a mistake it pays the consequences, most often to the benefit of the consumer, but when the bureaucrat makes a mistake, he blithely goes his way but the consumer pays indefinitely. As an example, witness the mess in natural gas, in oil, transportation and postal services.

Facts and Fancies on Prices

In the final analysis, business as a whole has furnished a commendable record, as indicated by our numerous references to profit and price developments. What deviations occur are of no major consequence and we would rather accept the warts of capitalism than the cancer of socialism. It would be apropos here to show how the American worker fares in comparison with the Russian worker. A revealing comparison chart appeared in the *New York Times* of February 21, 1971.

The chart compared on-the-job times that an average industrial worker needed to earn enough to purchase various items. Thus, a New Yorker had to work 32 hours to have enough money to buy a refrigerator; his Moscow counterpart had to work 343 hours. A color TV called for 147 working hours in New York, and in Moscow 1,111! The New Yorker toiled 46 minutes to buy 10 cotton diapers, while the Muscovite labored 983 minutes for the same. Among the items listed, Ivan had an advantage only in haircuts: he worked 39 minutes for his; the New Yorker needed 7 minutes more.

Very appropriately, the following appeared in the London *Economist* of January 31, 1976:

Here's how much more than a Parisian or New Yorker the poor Muscovite has to pay for his fun:

THE PRICE OF LUXURY

Hours (months for car) of average paid work necessary to buy:

	Moscow	Paris	New York
Zhiguli/Fiat 124	43	11	4
Petrol (10 litres)	1.4	2	.5
Sugar (kg)	1.4	.4	.1
Vodka (litre)	10	6	1.6

Source: Revue de l'Est

Here is a striking portrayal of efficiency versus bungling ineptitude—a stark contrast of the effectiveness of a relatively free market system and the inefficiency of socialist planning and regimentation. In the next chapter on price controls, we will delve more fully into the economics of socialist planning. This chart and the data that were cited previously present a picture of admirable corporate price behavior. According to researches by Professor J. Fred Weston of UCLA, he concludes that profit rates are not significantly higher in concentrated than in non-concentrated industry; that there is a relationship between efficiency and profits and nothing else; and that big companies are not only price leaders but also cost leaders. Continually subjected to the efforts of rivals to steal business away from them, they deal with this uncertainty by offering better quality and more productivity and/or lower prices by reducing their own costs. The process or production engineer plays a leading role in the ever-present drive to reduce costs. He is constantly probing into new developments conducted by the metallurgist, the chemist, the scientist and the mechanical engineer. He exploits to the fullest extent possible science and technology for the benefit of his company and society. It would be tragic to give him insufficient capital and subjugate him under bureaucratic regimentation. His activities demonstrate that market power in corporate pricing is an illusion and that mark-up pricing is the prevailing feature.

When economists of the Means and Galbraith strain propose to curb what they ill-advisedly consider as market power, their suggestions inspire charges of "predatory pricing." Their fallacious textbook picture was cogently refuted by that great transplanted Austrian economist Joseph A. Schumpeter in his incisive study, *Capitalism, Socialism and Democracy* (Harper and Bros., 1950). In discussing price competition, he wrote:

> But in capitalist reality as distinguished from its textbook picture, it is not that kind of competition which counts but the competition from the new commodity, the new technology, the new source of supply, the new type of organization (the largest-scale unit of control for instance)—competition which commands a decisive cost or quality advantage and which strikes not at the margins of the profits and the outputs of the existing firms but at their foundations and their very lives. This kind of competition is as much more effective than the other as a bombardment is in comparison with forcing a door, and so much more important that it becomes a matter of comparative indifference whether competition in the ordinary sense functions more or less promptly; the powerful lever that in the long run expands output and brings down prices is in any case made of other stuff. (Pages 84-85)

The close scrutiny of long-run data on price and profit behavior lends support to his thesis of the "powerful lever that in the long run expands output and brings down prices." This is further supported by the manufacturers' competition to develop new processes, skills and materials that result in more efficient manufacturing operations. To reduce production costs, each must constantly upgrade tools and methods.

Innovation competition is never mentioned by antibusiness liberal economists. Every manufacturer must be exceedingly alert or he will be out-innovated by his competition.

We also should not overlook the "competition of substitutability." As examples, a partial list includes the following:

—containers; metal vs. glass vs. paper
—auto components: steel vs. aluminum vs. plastics
—metal parts: rolled steel vs. forged steel vs. iron castings vs. zinc die castings vs. extrusions vs. investment castings.

This is a picture of market competition of capitalism. Truly, a far cry from the textbook fancies of Means and Galbraith, who in their naivete or bias consider the attainment of sales equivalent to market control. Every manufacturer worth his salt knows what some liberal economists seem to ignore, that current sales do not guarantee future sales. When a manufacturing concern has garnered a large segment of sales in its industry, it is proof that its product has appealed to the greatest proportional number of buyers, who in effect voted with their pocketbook. This is economic democracy at a high stage of development. To be sure it has its faults, but it is still superior to having a bureaucrat or a commissar decide what can be produced, how it can be produced and what you are forced to buy at what price. Also, bearing in mind the peccancies and proclivities of human nature, we are sure that most people would take their chances with capitalism rather than collectivization. Let us repeat: That in human nature which makes capitalism imperfect, makes socialism unworkable. We should also bear in mind the statement of Goethe: "Could we perfect human nature, we might expect a perfect state of things."

Hegel, another great German philosopher, was quoted in the following terms: ". . . people and governments never learned anything from history." It is obvious that this applies to economists of the strain of Means and Galbraith and politicians like Hart who deny or conveniently overlook the history of price and profit behavior and also ignore the testimony before another Senate antitrust and monopoly committee back in 1957 when economist Jules Backman testified as follows:

> The term administered price provides a useful description of the price making process in most segments of the economy. It does not involve a judgment that either the process or the price charged is wrong. The term does not indicate whether prices are fair or unfair, whether price behavior is good or bad, or whether prices are too high or too low. Unfortunately, some writers have used the term to describe a form of price behavior—usually one which they do not approve.
> It is useful to understand what administered prices are not. They are not monopoly prices. They are not prices set only by big business. They are not identical with inflexible prices.

All in all, administered prices are not the economic ogre portrayed by statists, the anti-liberalism liberals and radicals. As foreshadowed by the proper perspective on profits, price behavior in its long-term perspectives reveals the other important competitive factors that operate to the benefit of the worker as an employe and the worker as a consumer.

Price is but one vector of free market competition. The others of major significance are the competitions of:

quality
product
productivity
cost

innovation
substitutability

QUOD EST DEMONSTRANDUM: Administered, market power, oligopolistic, and predatory price theories are fallacious concepts. The long-term trend of declining profit margins is self-evident proof that the alleged market power of corporations is a fabrication of a wishful ivory tower fancy at variance with the hard facts of capitalist realism. Attention again is called to the sterling analysis by *Fortune* and the comment of Woodcock that a decreasing number of hours worked is necessary to purchase products, especially in durable goods. This is the other side of the coin that indicates that prices relative to wage rates are decreasing. By actions the manufacturers are disproving the words of the rhetoric that falsely present a picture of market power.

III

ILLUSIONS AND FALLACIES OF PRICE CONTROL

An incomes policy, that is a system of wage and price controls, has been advocated as a panacea for curing inflation. The arguments for controls have such an attraction of simplicity that they have indoctrinated a substantial segment of our public in their efficacy. A Gallup poll in November, 1974, indicated that 62% of Americans were in favor of controls. John Kenneth Galbraith, the *New York Times*, Senate Majority Leader Mike Mansfield and numerous Democratic candidates espoused controls. Flushed with victory, the Democratic party conference, meeting in December in Kansas City, supported an "across-the-board system of economic controls," to be administered by a new agency "whose members are confirmed by the Congress." This is sheerest naivete and misplaced confidence. Paraphrasing George Santayana, it can be stated that those ignoring economic and financial history are condemned to repeat it.

Such misplaced confidence in controls and planning is disturbing. It is shocking to contemplate the superficiality of economic wisdom exhibited by Myron E. Sharpe, the editor and publisher of *Challenge*. In an editorial in November/December issue of 1974, he opines that "an economic planning board can anticipate shortages before they occur." This is a wanton disregard of economic history, and a shocking ignorance of the workings of bureaucracies. Here we have politicians and a sample of intelligentsia advocating more bureaucracy to solve problems created and caused by politics, government regulation and regimentation. It is absurd to believe that all you have to do is to create a new government body with an impressive title like a *Planning Board* or a *Price Control Board* and its bureaucratic functionaries will in some mysterious way become endowed with an unprecedented amount of economic wisdom and foresight.

In this connection, Walter Guzzardi, Jr., writes in the March, 1975, issue of *Fortune*:

> The confidence [in controls] is badly misplaced. In principle, just about everything is wrong with wage and price controls. They constitute a surrender of our basic beliefs in the efficiency of free and competitive markets, and in freedom of action for business and labor. By garbling the vital signals usually conveyed by the free pricing system, controls misallocate resources,

create shortages and deter capital investment. Delicate price relationships that have gained wide social acceptance are upset by controls, impossibly difficult moral judgments by men are substituted for the neutrality and anonymity of the market place. Regulations become ludicrously complex, and business wastes energy and ingenuity devising ways to circumvent them.

In considering price controls, we will concern ourselves with two factors—the necessity and feasibility of price controls. The "New Socialist" of our era, John Kenneth Galbraith, is the arch-architect of controls. It is a major tenet of his belief that our economy is devoid of competition in the two aggregates of power—big business and big labor. He erroneously attributes more economic clout to big business than to labor. In his thesis, these giants "administer" prices upward, so they can increase their profits and wages at public expense. As a result he concludes that controls are necessary.

It is conceded here that while his thesis for wage controls is valid, his conclusions relative to price controls are not. In a forthcoming chapter, we will analyze union monopoly power, but here it will suffice to state that union monopoly power is a reality that is grossly underestimated and that business monopoly power is overemphasized and exaggerated. The analysis that was presented in the previous chapter invalidates conclusively the assumptions of Galbraith on the economic power of large corporations and that price increases come faster in concentrated industries. Professor Weston in his detailed researches has found that there is a negative relationship between degree of concentration and percentage of price change. In part because concentrated industries are in a better position to exploit research and development they are able to spur more rapid gains in productivity. As a result, Weston concludes that the role of concentrated industires is to blunt inflation. Thus, the evidence is conclusive that price controls are unnecessary and in effect would be counterproductive.

A convincing case against price controls was presented by C. Jackson Grayson, Jr., in the November/December, 1974, issue of *Challenge*. Grayson is Dean of the School of Business Administration, Southern Methodist University. He was chairman of the Price Commission during Phase II and is author of *Confessions of a Price Controller* (Dow Jones-Irwin, 1974). The facts are well marshaled and cogently presented, as attested in the following excerpts:

CONTROLS ARE NOT THE ANSWER

Governments have proclaimed price control programs for centuries, but "commanded cheapness" has never worked.

I will make one clear assertion at the outset: Wage-price controls are not the answer to inflation.

The lessons of history seem pretty clear. Centralized efforts to fight inflation were started before Christ was born. Rome, for example, fought inflation by various means for centuries. Finally, in A.D. 301, the emperor Diocletian imposed the first extensive price-wage control program. His edict (referred to as "commanded cheapness") set schedules for 76 different wage categories and for 890 different price categories (222 of which were for food!). The penalty for an offense was death. Thirteen years later, the program, in shambles, was abandoned. In the thirteenth century, the great Mongol, Kublai Khan, decreed maximum prices. And Medieval Europe had a "just price" code.

Not many people are aware of it, but the United States began some attempts at wage-price controls during its early years. The American Puritans imposed a code of wage and price limitations in 1636; those who violated the code were classed with "adulterers and whoremongers." The Continental Congress set price ceilings even before the Declaration of Independence. A few states enacted price control laws. Inflation became so severe that General George Washington complained in April 1779 that "a wagonload of money will scarcely purchase a wagonload of provisions." The attempts at control were sporadic, highly controversial, and not comprehensive. All efforts were largely abandoned by 1780.

Most modern nations have instituted wage-price controls during periods of war, but it was in Europe right after World War II that almost every nation tried some form of comprehensive peacetime controls (remembering the inflation that had torn apart European economies after World War I). Some European nations had succeeded with their "incomes policies" for a period of time. Some were started, stopped, and reinstated in another version. But none has lasted continuously.

As a result of my sixteen months as a price controller, I can list seven ways that controls interfere (negatively) with the market system and hasten its metamorphosis into a centralized economy.

First, wage-price controls lead to distortions in the economic system, which can be minimized only in the short run. The longer controls are in effect, the harder it is to discern real from artificial signals. No matter how cleverly any group designs a control system, distortions and inequities will appear. It happened in European control programs; it started to happen in Phase II.

Second, during a period of controls, the public forgets that not all wage-price increases are inflationary. In a freely competitive economy, wage and price increases occur because of real consumer demand shifts and supply shortages. The resulting wage and price increases signal to business, "make more," or to labor, "move here," or to the public, "use less."

Controls interfere with this signaling mechanism. An artificially suppressed price can eventually cause shortages; natural gas is an example. Similar examples can be found in the labor market, where suppressed wages do not attract labor to areas in which there are shortages of skills or workers. But with wage-price controls in place, the public believes that all increases are inflationary—almost antisocial—and the clamor is for no increases, or at least very small ones.

"You can eliminate the middleman, but not his function"— this old business saying applies equally to our economic system. We live in a world of scarce resources, and, as much as some would like to repeal the laws of supply and demand, it cannot be done. Some system must allocate resources, we hope to the most efficient use for society. If wage-price controls, other government regulatory rules, or business-labor monopolies prohibit the price system from performing its natural function, then another rationing system (such as central planning and control) must be used. You can eliminate the price system, but not its function.

Third, during a control period, the public forgets what profits are all about. Even before the recent wage-price controls, the public believed profits were "too high," though they actually declined from 6.2 percent of GNP in 1966 to 3.6 percent in 1970, and increased only to 4.3 percent in the boom year of 1972. And with profit increases raised to the top of the news during the recovery of 1972 and early 1973, the negative public sentiment against profits increased. Why? The control system itself heightened the public's negative attitude toward profits at a time when capital regeneration, the fuel of the capitalist engine, was already alarmingly low.

Fourth, wage-price controls provide a convenient stone for those who have economic or political axes to grind, particularly those interested in promoting a centralized economic system. For example, in 1972 Ralph Nader argued that the control system should be used to prohibit automobile companies from raising their prices to reflect style changes. Others argued that price increases should not be given to companies that employ insufficient numbers of minorities or pollute the environment. Nor should wage increases go to uncooperative unions. And so on.

Fifth, wage-price controls can easily become a security blanket against the cold winds of free-market uncertainties. They tell people what the limits are; they help employers fight unions; and they provide union leaders with excuses to placate demands for "more" from their rank and file. The controlled become dependent on the controllers and want regulations continued in preference to the competition of a dynamic market. At the same time, the controllers themselves can become so enamored of their task that they don't want to let go.

The public begins to fear what will happen when controls are ended and seeks continuance. Witness the fears of moving from Phase II to Phase III, and the public (and congressional) pressure for the freeze to replace Phase III. Even Wall Street seemed terrified at the thought of returning to supply and demand in the market. It is much easier to get into controls than to get out.

Sixth, under controls, business and labor leaders begin to pay more attention to the regulatory body than to the dynamics of the marketplace. They inevitably come to the same conclusion, summed up by one executive: "We know that all of our sophisticated analysis and planning can be wiped out in the blink of a Washington controller's eye."

Seventh, and most dangerous, wage-price controls misguide the public. They draw attention away from the fundamental factors that affect inflation—fiscal and monetary policies, tax rates, import-export policies, productivity, competitive restrictions, and the like. The danger is that attention will become permanently focused on the symptom-treating control mechanism rather than on the underlying problems.

In summary, perhaps the most dramatic way I can underscore my views is to point out the recent example of Britain, where years of successive stop-go economic policies and various types of controls (including guideposts) have led that nation to where it is today, economically and politically in a crisis state with one of the lowest income growth rates of modern nations and raging inflation.

Controls are not the answer.

It is important here to revert to a passage in Grayson's article in which he states that "the control system itself heightened the public's negative attitude toward profits at a time when capital regeneration, the fuel of the capitalist engine, was alarmingly low." Here we come back to one of our main themes of the success of the propaganda of the liberals and leftists in portraying our industrial leaders as profiteers and price gougers. In the face of facts to the contrary, the anti-bourgeois propagandists propose price controls. These economic highbrows, intellectuals educated beyond their intelligence, attribute to the bureaucrat more omniscience than he humanly is capable of possessing. In their misguided zeal they fail to perceive that prices perform a very important function. They provide a signaling system between buyers and sellers. Price controls break that communication. For samples of ludicrous efforts in exercises of futility just observe the bungling of the bureaucrats in attempts at controls as noted by Guzzardi in his *Fortune* article:

> Controls were also unable to cope with the complexities of the international economy:
> —At one juncture, the world price of zinc stood above the domestic price. To honor their commitments to their customers, domestic producers of zinc were selling at the lower price. But they had no incentive to expand the supply, and customers who didn't have commitments soon found themselves facing shortages.
> —Reinforcing bars, widely used in construction, are made from another internationally traded commodity, scrap steel. Controls on the bars were imposed at a time when the price was very low. But scrap was not controlled, out of fear that too much of it might be exported. Makers of the bars soon found the cost of their raw material shooting up and had no way to pass on the increases. Production was interrupted and construction hurt.
> —Baling wire is used by farmers to bundle crops. Before controls, much of the wire was imported from Japan. But prices were going up elsewhere, and the Japanese producers were withdrawing from the U.S. market when controls were put on. U.S. Steel found that the last price at which it sold baling wire, which was the controlled price, would bring a loss to the company of about $100 for every ton of baling wire it shipped. Under conditions so discouraging to production, the wire remained in short supply.

Price controls are notoriously counterproductive. In anticipation of controls, manufacturers raise prices, fearing that they will be saddled with costs that they may not be able to recoup. The subsequent distortions caused by price

Illusions and Fallacies of Price Control

controls aggrevate inflation by causing shortages that impinge upon stable economic growth. Price controls interfere with manufacturers' efforts to reduce costs by providing an incentive to do just the reverse. Companies could beat margin ceilings the same way they could beat an excess profits tax: By relaxing costs controls and finding ways to acquire unnecessary expenses and costs. According to Guzzardi,

> Corporate ingenuity also found other outlets, General Motors made some standard equipment into optional equipment on some models. Some companies introduced "superior" products at higher prices than the ones being replaced. Cheaper products were phased out, leaving only the more expensive available. Alternatively, many companies that kept their full line on the market achieved savings by allowing quality to deteriorate.

In his concluding chapters, Guzzardi says:

> For the devout, all the aberrations born of controls, and the bad record they made, proved only the inadequacies of the controllers themselves. Galbraith has expressed the view that "any controls program run by Republicans is bound to be fouled up." Arthur Schlesinger, Jr., remarked that "controls will work well only when administered by people who believe in them"—thus making it possible to explain every past failure, and every future one as well, by a shortfall of faith.
> Controls never bring gains that are more than fleeting and illusory. And the price of these gains is added inflation. But that cost is not the only reason to avoid controls. The more they are used, the more they acquire undeserved legitimacy as an anti-inflationary instrument. The idea is spread that somehow government can be grossly irresponsible in managing the economy, and then, by more intervention, save the country from the consequences. In this way too, price and wage controls make worse what they set out to repair."

As to price controls and economic planning, it would be most instructive if the radical economists, the liberals and their willful and naive lackeys would take off their blinkers, correct their economic myopia and observe objectively the developments in socialist countries. Fettered by blind allegiance to Marxist dogmas, they struggle ludicrously with controls and regimentation. The intelligentsia in literature, education and the media, whose falsifications about profits, prices and our system have engineered misconceptions and mistrust, should ponder the following excerpts from a dispatch from Moscow in the *New York Times* of April 5, 1973, by Theodore Shabad:

THE LONG SEARCH FOR EFFICIENCY

MOSCOW—"What, again?" That was the reaction of most Russians last week to the announcement of yet another economic reform—one that would consolidate the Soviet Union's 50,000 industrial plants into a system of large Government corporations, each combining a number of related factories. The people have been through so many reorganizations of Soviet industry that they tend to be skeptical of one more plan to correct the chronic problem of inefficiency and poor product quality.

The new reform and the public reaction raise a fundamental question: Why have repeated changes in Russia's planned economy failed to yield the objectives of effective management, an abundance of high-quality goods and rapid technological progress?

The Soviet leaders, who are adamantly opposed to a free-market economy and to any relaxation of controls over the key centers of national production, believe that central planning can be made to work. They contend that even under their system, prices, profits bonuses and other economic levers can be used to generate efficiency and technological progress. They see their new plan as a better way of using those levers.

But Western advocates of free enterprise believe that, for the most part, it is competition in an essentially free market that gives consumers a variety of goods of sound quality at a price they can afford. They hold that if competition is lacking, consumers tend to pay more for commodities and have less variety, and the flow of raw materials, labor and capital into different industries tends to be divorced from changes in demand. Western economists have serious doubts that an economy as big and complex as the Soviet Union's can be made to work efficiently by Government directives and without the stimulus and incentive provided by competition.

The Galbraiths, the Arthur Schlesingers and their ilk should study the experiences of another socialist country, Czechoslovakia. The inept bungling of bureaucratic empire builders is vividly portrayed in the following excerpts from a book review which appeared in the *Fortune* of December, 1972:

THE GRAYING OF CZECHOSLOVAKIA
by Dan Cordtz

A disturbing aspect of our experience with wage and price controls is the evident inclination of many Americans to accept them with equanimity. Price control, in particular, has come to be widely thought of as a benign institution, to be retained perhaps for years.

Anyone tempted to ignore the dangerous implications of price control, would do well to read a slim volume entitled *Czechoslovakia: The Bureaucratic Economy* (International Arts and Sciences Press, Inc.). The author, Ota Sik, is an economist who had plenty of opportunity to observe a controlled economy close up. Sik (pronounced Shick) was for twenty-eight years a member of the Czechoslovakian Communist party, and for ten of those years a member of its central committee. From April until August, 1968, when Soviet tanks rolled in, he was the leading architect of the country's economic policies.

Not so very long ago, some observers were predicting that the controlled economies of the Soviet bloc would outperform those of the West. But as long as the Communists insulate their plans from economic realities, the gap between living standards in Eastern and Western Europe can only continue to grow. As Ota Sik observes: "It is certainly no accident that orthodox Communists have stopped talking in recent years about catching up with and surpassing the capitalist economies."

We can state categorically that price controls are not necessary, that they are exercises in futility, and that they are counterproductive as they spawn shortages, misallocations and distortions.

The failures of bureaucratic economies point to three important economic lessons:

1. The limits of human intelligence.
2. The absence of self-corrective features.
3. The elimination of resource allocation.

Considering the first item, it should be recognized that bureaucrats are not endowed with any special capability to assimilate the multifarious economic and financial interrelationships of millions of goods and make decisions. Neither are they capable of foreseeing the possible secondary and tertiary effects of their decisions. As if the above are not enough to tax the mentality of a devoted human being, the bureaucrat is distracted in his functions by potential threats to his power and status. So, once ensconced in a position of power, party and economic ideology become secondary to his main objective, the preservation or growth of his little empire.

Regarding the second item, we find that under a collectivized economy the self-corrective feature of errors that is inherent in the free-market system is not existent in the socialist economy. Unlike the capitalist, who suffers losses, the bureaucrat can hide his mistakes for a long time.

When we examine the third item, it is obvious that the bureaucratic system cannot match the performance of free markets in resource allocation. Without a profit-price signalling system, the bureaucrat must make arbitrary decisions devoid of consumer preference and often at the mercy of power politics.

The inevitable conclusion is that, despite its deficiencies, the market mechanism of price and profit signals is far superior to a bureaucratic economy, which impedes economic growth and more often than not is conducive to economic stagnation.

Attempts to combat price inflation in a capitalistic system are no less defective. The usual scenario is as follows:

Tight controls on prices and wages are instituted. Shortages and dislocations start to develop. Because of the ensuing shortages and dislocations, controls have to be relaxed. The consequence is that you get all the price rises that you would have had in the first place compounded by those caused by shortages induced by controls. After this fiasco and any threats of further controls, you generate inflation caused by businesses trying to compensate for being left behind in the first go-around.

Because of strides in rapid communication and transportation, no group of controllers could possibly have the prescience and omniscience necessary to cope with the rapidity of changes in an increasingly integrated global economy. When they control natural gas, they mess up fuel oil, and when they fiddle with fuel oil they screw up gasoline. After they impose ceilings on U.S. prices for fertilizer and cotton, they suddenly undercut foreign prices so that foreigners denude the American supplies. The ensuing uncertainties bring down investment and plant expansion and end up with shortages of everything.

However, it should be pointed out that as far as individual prices are concerned, high prices are the only lasting cure for higher prices. Price controls treat only symptoms but are popular with the political demagogues because such short-range solutions pay off handsomely at the polls, but with baneful long-term economic consequences. The only real effective measures to get prices lower is to increase production through the incentive of adequate prices and profits. High prices are symptoms of several prime factors—excessive demand-pull forces of monetary and fiscal mismanagement and/or the cost-push factor of wage rate increases in excess of productivity gains. These causes of inflation and others and a system for its control will be treated extensively in chapters 10 through 13.

Lack of perceptiveness or sheer pandering to envy and prejudice are a cause of some fuzzy thinking concerning the energy crunch. This has to do with the clamor of politicians for rationing and price controls. They prefer compulsory rationing to rationing by the purse. They argue that the free market price is discriminatory and that it is not fair because the rich man will buy his gasoline and the poor man cannot. But this is true of the price of any product and this argument overlooks the fact that "moralizing" about prices in this fashion not only prolongs the period of shortages but may even deprive the poor man of a chance to get a job as investments are discouraged.

The analysis brought out in this chapter lead to the obvious conclusion that the free market system with its signaling system of prices as well as profits and losses, despite its lags and deficiencies, is the indispensable guide to producing the most goods at the most attractive prices responding to free choices by consumers. This system is not only the best allocator but also the best motivator for using and creating the most advanced technological innovations.

IV

PROFITS: THE ROAD TO WORKERS' CAPITALISM

"Truth is a powerful weapon," wrote Alexander Solzhenitsyn. Here we'll devote our attention to mobilize more facts and data about the true nature, roles and significance of profits and prices to counter the false propaganda of the Marxist and liberal intelligentsia who have inculcated a sizable segment of our students, the workers and the general public with contempt for profits and a distaste for our competitive system.

Profits are the most effective cost controllers ever devised, thereby providing the consumer with the biggest bargain of all. In their effort to maximize profits, managements utilize the latest in innovations provided by science and technology to reduce costs and thereby reduce prices on a relative and/or absolute basis, as evidenced by the history of prices of durable goods. Profits are the cheapest part of the dollar. Society in effect pays the manufacturer a service charge of 4 to 6 cents on the dollar. For this picayune charge, the management team provides quite a bargain in improving old products, in creating new products and new jobs. Here we will take the liberty of freely paraphrasing Winston Churchill—the manufacturer provides so much and gets so little in return.

Peter Drucker rightfully describes profit as a "necessary insurance premium for the real risks and uncertainties of all economic activity." In the *Wall Steet Journal* of February 5, 1975, he writes:

> The proper question for any management therefore is not: "What is the MAXIMUM profit this business can yield?" It is: "What is the MINIMUM profitability needed to cover the future risks of this business?" And if the profitability falls short of this minimum—as it does in most companies I know—the business fails to cover genuine costs, endangers itself and impoverishes the economy.

In this connection, it will be well to heed the words of Samuel Gompers, Mr. Meany's illustrious predecessor, who said: "The worst crime against working people is a company that fails to make a profit." Paraphrasing, we can add that the worst crime against our society is an industrial system that cannot make a profit.

In his perceptive analysis, Drucker further adds:

Profits: The Road to Workers' Capitalism

"Profit" is not peculiar to capitalism. It is a prerequisite for any economic system. Indeed, the Communist economies require a much higher rate of profit. Their costs of capital are higher. And central planning adds an additional and major economic uncertainty. In fact, the Communist economies do operate at a substantially higher rate of profit than any market economy, no matter that for ideological reasons it is called "turnover tax" rather than "profit." And the only economies that can be considered as being based on "profit planning" are precisely Communist economies in which the producer (state planner) imposes the needed profitability in advance rather than let market forces determine it.

There is no conflict between "profit" and "social responsibility." To earn enough to cover the genuine costs which only the so-called "profit" can cover, is economic and social responsibility—indeed it is the specific social and economic responsibility of business. It is not the business that earns a profit adequate to its genuine costs of capital, to the risks to tomorrow and to the needs of tomorrow's worker and pensioner, that "rips off" society. It is the business that fails to do so.

In paying a service charge of 4 to 6 cents on the sales dollar, the worker, consumer and society are paying for costs of cost and price control, costs of doing business, costs of staying in business, costs of today's jobs and costs of tomorrow's jobs and pensions. The most egregious "rip-off" artists and rapists preying on workers and consumers are the elitist intellectuals in literature and education who have deluded their servile lackeys in the media, unionism, politics and even the pulpit. In future chapters, we will demonstrate how they have deprived the worker and society of the full benefits of full employment with minimal inflation at steady economic growth.

Profits are the largest single source of capital formation for tomorrow's jobs. Profits are also the main fountainhead for funds for research and development, which are largely responsible for improving old products and creating new products and new industries for the ultimate benefit of worker and consumer. It would be tragic to see the 4 to 6 percent profit margin erode further or disappear, as the most deleterious consequences would accrue to the worker in the loss of job opportunities.

In this respect, let us consider what would happen if we confiscated all the profits away from corporations and gave them to the worker. He would at most save 6 cents on the dollar. His total pay would increase only a meager 10 percent. His 6 percent saving would equal his fringe benefits. It is also about equal to what the corporation pays in taxes—in effect, the corporation acts merely as a transfer agent as it takes money from the consumer and hands it over to the bureaucrat. For the 10 percent commission that the worker pays his employer, he in effect hires all the tools for his job, all the factory buildings, all the engineering, all the research, all the administration so that he can sell his own labor to persons who need and want his services.

By comparison he pays the Federal government three times as much. In reality profits paid to corporations who recycle the profits into more research, capital formation and new jobs and pensions are the biggest bargain that the worker buys. There is no need to hire the government to stop the businessman from making too much profit or charging too high a price. His competitors will gladly do that job for nothing. As we noted before, there is a quality war going on continuously. We will add here that there is also a continuous cost-control war in internal costs are well as in purchases. Purchasing agents are continuously looking for the best price, and occasionally it takes only one big discount to precipitate a price war. These facts of reality are a far cry from the myths of collusion conjured up by Gardiner Means.

The considerations of the limits to profit redistribution puncture illusions fabricated by the leftists about the enormity of corporate profits. The 10% gain in pay arithmetically derivable from confiscating "capitalist" profits is equivalent to four or five years' normal growth of real wages just before the inflationary binge.

Before delving further into the implications arising from the mischief perpetrated by the Marxist and liberal sham intellectuals, let us consider the feasibility of "soaking the rich" individuals to finance so-called transfer payments—the taking of money from people who have income coming in and giving it to people who have no money coming in. It has been indicated that we cannot tap the corporations, big and little. Let us now consider if we can tap the very wealthy individuals—the "rich bitches" and the "capitalist bastards," as they are portrayed by Marxists and their obsequious fellow travelers.

The accompanying table was constructed by the author from data furnished in *Statistics of Income, Individual Income Tax Returns* by the U.S. Internal Revenue Service. These were designed to show where the tax dollars are. The table reveals the percentage distribution of the significant income levels based on adjusted gross income before any deductions, including so-called "loopholes." The total of adjusted gross income of $746.6 billion is 93% of personal disposable income. Thus, we are dealing with a fairly true picture of personal income and its distribution among different income levels.

The table shows that the bulk of taxable income is in the $5,000 to $14,999 and the $15,000 to $24,999 income groups. Comparison of data between 1960 and 1972 shows some striking and significant shifts. In 1960 the bulk of taxable income was the $5,000 to $9,999 group, when income of that group represented 43% of total income, whereas the $50,000 and over income level class contributed only 3.7% of the total. So let us forget "loopholes" and confiscate all the income of our maligned "rich bitches" and "capitalist bastards" and what do we have? A paltry 3 to 7% to be distributed over all the other income groups. In 1960, the $10,000 to $14,999 class was 13.5% of the total. Now note the dramatic changes that evolved by 1972. The $5,000 to $9,999 group decreased from a 43% level to 20.3%, from first to third place. First place was taken over by the $15,000 to $24,999 group, surging dramatically from fourth to first place, with the $10,000 to $14,999 group holding second place but improving percentagewise from 13.5% to 25.2%, virtually doubling. Here we have dramatic proof that a basis for a "class struggle" does not exist.

It would be grossly unfair to tap the $5,000 to $9,999 segment for more transfer payments. So we are left with the $10,000 to $49,999 group to carry the burden because it represents 63.4% of taxable income. "Soaking the rich" cannot generate large amounts of transfer payments because the share of the groups grossing $50,000 and more was only 7.1% in 1972.

How can the average worker and individual know the

Table IV-1
WHERE THE TAXABLE DOLLARS ARE
Percentage Distribution of Adjusted Gross Income

Adjusted Gross Income Class	1960	Cumulation	Inverse Cumulation	1972	Cumulation	Inverse Cumulation
$ 2,999 and under	6.4		93.9	1.0		96.1
3,000 – 3,999	6.4	12.8	87.5	1.7	2.7	95.1
4,000 – 4,999	9.1	21.9	81.1	2.6	5.3	93.4
5,000 – 9,999	43.7	65.6	72.0	20.3	25.6	90.8
10,000 – 14,999	13.5	79.1	28.3	25.2	50.8	70.5
15,000 – 24,999	6.5	85.6	14.8	27.0	77.8	45.3
25,000 – 49,999	4.6	90.2	8.3	11.2	89.0	18.3
50,000 – 99,999	2.1	92.3	3.7	4.3	93.3	7.1
100,000 – 499,999	1.2	93.5	1.6	2.3	95.6	2.8
500,000 – 999,999	0.2	93.7	0.4	0.2	95.8	0.5
1,000,000 and over	0.2	93.9		0.3	96.1	
Taxable returns	93.9	93.9		96.1	96.1	
Non-taxable returns	6.1	100.0		3.9	100.0	
$ 4,999 and under	21.9			5.3		
5,000 – 14,999	57.2			45.5		
15,000 – 49,000	11.2			38.2		
50,000 and over	3.7			7.1		

Sources: Statistical Abstract of the U.S., 1974 (page 228, table 372).
 Department of Commerce.
 Bureau of the Census.
 U.S. Internal Revenue Service.

basic facts about our economic system when political demagogues and their cohorts in unionism, the pulpit, academia, literature and media pervert and prostitute the facts to screw the average man and shift the blame to the rich corporations and individuals? Their insidious and invidious propaganda against "profiteering" and "price gouging" has laid the basis for the emergence of "the revolution of rising entitlements." On this aspect, Daniel Bell had these cogent and thought-provoking comments in *Fortune* of April, 1975:

> . . . The promise of plenty has been transformed into a revolution of rising expectations . . . The promise of equality has been transformed into a revolution of rising "entitlements," claims on government to implement an array of newly defined and vastly expanded social rights. . . .
> Both revolutions have a lot of momentum behind them but there is no doubt that the entitlements have more. The increasing tendency of the Americans to turn to their government to solve their problems is reflected dramatically in some figures on spending by government at all levels. In 1950, spending by government to buy goods and services, and to effect transfer payments, represented 18% of gross national product. By 1974 the figure was 32%.

The revolutions of rising expectations and rising entitlements have been spawned by the propaganda of leftists and the intelligentsia and are the basic causes of two types of inflations. Labor is goaded into demanding wage-rate increases exceeding productivity gains in the mistaken belief that their extravagant claims can be paid for by profits. Here we have the origin of cost-push inflation that rapes every consumer. The voter and taxpayer is hoodwinked into believing that rising government expenditures can be financed by soaking the rich. Here we have the source of fiscal inflation. In truth, cost-push inflation is a tax on the consumer. The worker, in effect, is screwed twice by inflation caused by deficit spending—first when he is taxed to finance rising government spending; and second, when he has to pay more for goods whose prices have been increased by inflationary spending. Because there are limits to "soaking the rich," the average worker ends up being the "soakee" and the "screwee."

The rising tide in expectations and entitlements that have been so surreptitiously conceived and nurtured by the malefactors against working-class wealth, is threatening to engulf our economic and social system largely because it is impeding the formation of capital—the mainspring of current and future jobs and pensions. Another deleterious consequence is that it impedes the utilization of technology. Inadequate and low profits have led to insufficient plant capacity and shortages. In a letter to Senator William Proxmire from Arthur F. Burns, chairman of the Board of Governors of the Federal Reserve System, reprinted in the *Monthly Review* of November, 1973, of the Federal Reserve Bank of New York, Burns wrote: ". . . we have encountered critical shortages of basic materials. The expansion in industrial capacity needed to produce these materials had not been put in place earlier because of the abnormally low level of profits between 1966 and 1971 and also because of numerous impediments to new investment on ecological grounds."

Thus, we have fiscal and cost-push inflation further aggravated by shortages caused by insufficient capital formation, which, in turn, aggravate the problem by augmenting costs of capital formation by higher costs of plant and equipment and rising interest rates. A comparison of manufactured capital spending and personal income shows that manufacturing capacity in this country has not grown as fast as the overall economy for some time. This is especially so in the case of basic industrial materials—like steel, paper, copper, cement, aluminum and refined petroleum.

The record since the middle of last decade shows that capital spending was up 66% and personal income 100%.

Personal income is outrunning our capacity to produce, thus creating the condition of too much money chasing a limited amount of goods. There is another very important aspect in that plant capacity in the recent boom was not able to meet demand and was also too small to offer job opportunities required for reasonably full employment. Inadequate profits further cause economic damage to the worker and consumer as research and developments funds are restricted, leading to underutilization and underexploitation of technology. The process engineer and the product design engineer are restricted in their quest to endeavor to make new products and improve old products by making them stronger, or lighter, or quieter, or more compact, corrosion-resistant, easier to maintain, or to reduce manufacturing costs.

The point at issue is that, while the process engineer has done a very commendable job, he was in effect prevented from doing better in his job-creating functions.

With friends like the phony liberals and extremists of the left depriving the worker of reasonable prices and steady employment through their fiscal and economic extravaganzas, the average working man does not need any enemies. However, the highbrow elite left and their jerk lackeys hypocritically fabricate big corporations and business tycoons as enemies of the worker and the consumer. While raping the working man the intelligentsia and their subservient cohorts deceitfully and cleverly attempt to prove that not they but the rich are doing the screwing. Lenin and Goebbels were never that clever.

Shrinking profit margins and high interest rates, caused by an inflationary premium are restricting capital formation. According to *Value Line*, an investment sevice, the fact that profits have been shrinking in relation to total production is one reason why corporations are in a cash bind. They cannot sell stocks yielding 6-7% in competition with bond yields at 10%.

The growing reliance on external financing is clearly depicted in Chart IV-1, which is taken from the Chart Book of the Board of Governors of the Federal Reserve System as shown in the March, 1975, issue.

Chart IV-1 (Chart No. Added)
NONFINANCIAL CORPORATIONS

The charts in Chart IV-1 do not portray an affluent corporate structure with unlimited funds to absorb wage increases in excess of productivity gains and to finance through increased corporate taxes the governmental throwing money at problems. The dismal plight of corporate illiquidity is further corroborated by data furnished by the Internal Revenue Service and the U.S. Securities and Exchange Commission. In their tabulation of non-financial corporations assets and liabilities, they show that the current ratio of current assets to current liabilities has deteriorated from a ratio of 2.14% in 1950 to 1.64% in 1973. This ratio is calculated by ac-

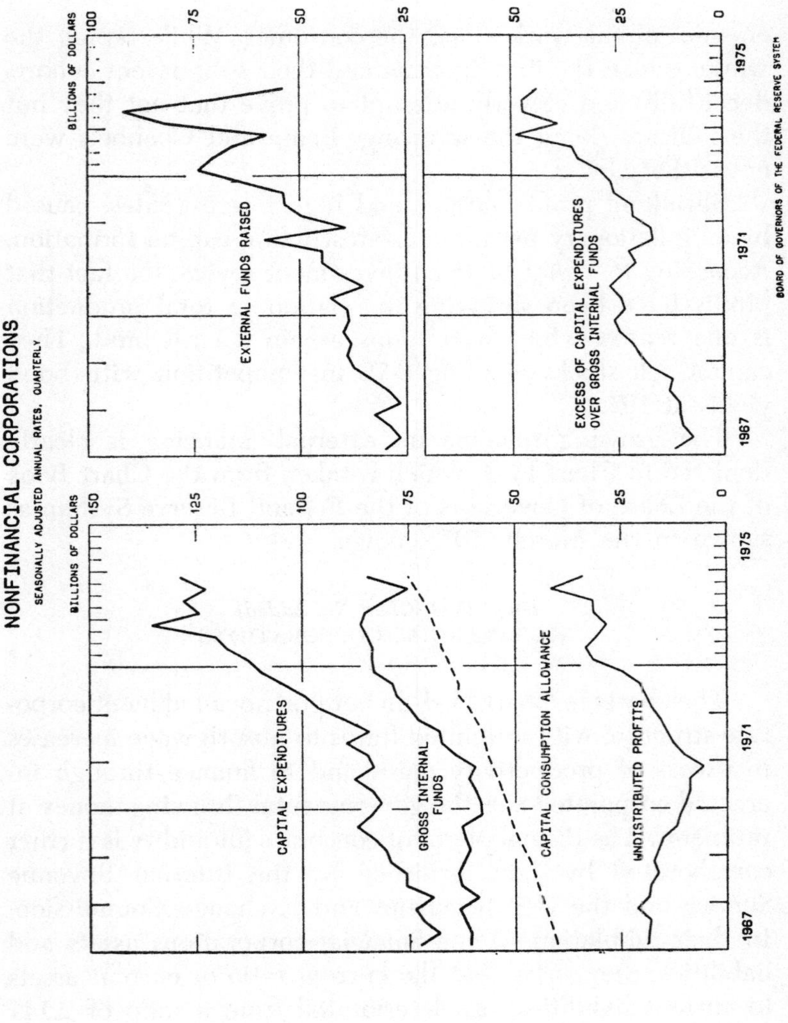
NONFINANCIAL CORPORATIONS
SEASONALLY ADJUSTED ANNUAL RATES, QUARTERLY
BILLIONS OF DOLLARS
150
125
100
75
50
25
0
CAPITAL EXPENDITURES
GROSS INTERNAL FUNDS
CAPITAL CONSUMPTION ALLOWANCE
UNDISTRIBUTED PROFITS
1967
1971
1975
BILLIONS OF DOLLARS
100
75
50
25
EXTERNAL FUNDS RAISED
50
25
0
EXCESS OF CAPITAL EXPENDITURES OVER GROSS INTERNAL FUNDS
1967
1971
1975
BOARD OF GOVERNORS OF THE FEDERAL RESERVE SYSTEM

Profits: The Road to Workers' Capitalism

countants to reflect the liquid position of businesses. A ratio of 2 to 1 is considered normal. Thus we have seen a decline from above normal to below normal. Witness the recent action of General Motors as it tapped the financial markets for $600,000,000 in notes. This was the first time in over 30 years that General Motors had to borrow.

We should consider carefully the impact of the havoc that the "real" enemies of the working man and consumer are wreaking. The Marxists and their subservient followers and dupes are undermining our economic system by subtly spreading miconceptions that culminate in extravagant expectations and entitlements that sap our economic foundations through inflation and taxes that fleece the consumer and worker. In the process, the lower income and middle class groups are screwed more than the rich. C. Lowell Harris, Professor of Economics at Columbia University, pertinently asks, "Can we free ourselves from obscurantists and obsolete prejudices?" Writing further, he says, "In applying the best of modern thinking to the search for better ways of taxing ourselves, let us look not only at the burdens business taxes impose upon us as consumers, workers and suppliers of capital but also at the effects on employment, production and progress."

Thus, the anti-bourgeois propagandists have created and fostered a climate of hostility and as a consequence are perpetrating rip-offs by fleecing workers and consumers through inflation and depriving workers of future jobs and pensions by impeding capital formation. By the same token they are putting back the possible arrival of a workers' capitalism, which we will discuss later in this chapter.

The true nature, role and significance of adequate or

increased profits become apparent when cognizance is given to the benefits that would accrue to the workers and the consumer.

> Higher profits would provide the means for replenishing the national supply of capital goods to replace equipment that is worn out or made obsolete by new technology. This would increase jobs in the machine tool and machinery industry and improve productivity, which is essential in reducing manufacturing costs.
>
> Higher profits would increase funds for research and development—increasing job outlets for scientists and technicians—thereby increasing our technological base for further growth in productivity.
>
> Higher profits would provide the incentive for such investments.

We can state categorically that there is no justification for a climate of hostility against profits and the market competitive system as workers, consumers and business managers have much more in common in nurturing adequate and reasonable profits than the phony do-gooders would care to or want to admit. After all, as small as they are relative to our Gross National Product, profits are the enzyme in the metabolism of our economic system—they are the fuel for the engine of our society where their by-products of beneficence far outweigh the objective. Hardly ever is so much done by so little. Would it not be better to risk paying a little too much in the short run than to deter investment and consequently pay too much in the long run?

Profits: The Road to Workers' Capitalism

In the previous chapter on price trends, we have cited compilations by *Fortune* showing that an ever-decreasing number of hours worked are required to purchase manufactured goods. In this chapter in Table IV-1, we presented tabulations to indicate where the taxable dollars exist. The long-term trends in taxable groups reveal the dramatic shift of the population to the middle income class. A close scrutiny of both tabulations in combination reveals an attribute of profits unsuspected and unappreciated by both protagonists and antagonists. Viewing the increasing purchasing power of an hour of labor simultaneously with the emergence of the majority of laborers into the middle class, we arrive at the conclusion that profits and the profit motive are great income equalizers.

Profits have created well-paying jobs and pensions and fringe benefits, providing rising incomes and security to an ever-growing labor force. The quest to maximize profits through cost reductions has resulted in an absolute or relative decline in prices in relation to each hour's purchasing power, thus providing not only the basics of life but also the amenities to virtually everyone. What once were luxuries to the rich only have now become necessities for most of the population.

Thus, profits have become an income equalizer, unappreciated and unacknowledged by elitists, moving the American worker into the middle class. This is a lesson for the pseudo-liberals to ponder. The equalizing was not accomplished by cutting up a fixed pie but by increasing the size of the pie. Unless we are alert and scotch the rhetoric of the left-wing distributionists, we will be confronted with a shrinking pie.

The name we accorded profits in the first chapter will bear repeating. We called profits a "commission" that the consumer paid to the manufacturer. For that commission of a meager 4 to 6 percent on average, the industrialist invented, designed a new product or redesigned and perfected an old one, assembled a staff of engineers and managers, constructed a plant, hired laborers and in many instances taught them a new skill and hoped that his efforts would result in a profit. It is wrong to call capitalism a profit system. It is actually a profit and loss system with rewards for success and penalties for failures.

As far as these commissions of 4 to 6 cents on the sales dollar are concerned, they are the biggest bargain that the consumer ever received, is getting and will continue to reap unless we allow the misguided and unsubstantiated anti-profit crusade to succeed too well. These commissions are the moneys earned over and above the expenses of operating our American business and industry.

Profits reinvested in the business could just as well be called "business savings" or "reinvested earnings." We would consider "recycled earnings" more descriptive in their function of the economy because these are the earnings recycled into the economy for research or plant expansion and/or plant renovation. This is important because it contrasts with the false picture of profits as clutched in the hands or bulging out of the pockets of a few potbellied, cigar-smoking tycoons. Neither are profits secreted away in some business vault.

A pertinent question logically arises: Who counts on the profits and dividends? There are over 30 million stockholders who depend on them. Over 33 million workers have

Profits: The Road to Workers' Capitalism

a stake in retirement funds that depend on dividends from stocks and bonds, the valuation of which is wholly dependent on the profitability and viability of the issuing companies; 369 million life insurance companies count on dividends that profits produce. Let's have a good look at each one of the three categories just mentioned.

A table on stock ownership in the U.S. Bureau of the Census, *Statistical Abstract of the United States,* 1974 (95th edition), Washington, D.C., 1974, shows the trend in stock ownership from 1959 to 1970. Table 759 indicates that the number of stock owners is increasing much faster than the population. From 1959 to 1970, the population grew from 178 million to 205 million, or 15%, while the stock ownership population grew 12.5 million to 30.9 million, or 147%. In other words, stock owners grew almost 10 times as fast as the population. This proves that the numbers attaining middle class status are growing at a prodigious rate. This view is further corroborated by noting the income distribution columns that indicate the accelerated growth of the $10,000-$14,999 and $15,000-$24,999 classifications.

The life insurance story is just as dramatic, as portrayed in Table 762 in the *Statistical Abstract* on life insurance in force. The number of policies increased from 134 million policies in 1940, with a per family coverage of $2,700, to 369 million policies in 1973, with a per family coverage of $24,400.

Last but of profound implications for the future welfare of the worker and the economy, we consider the private pension plans. In the first item, we called attention to the surging growth of stock ownership. But this does not end the story because a worker has a tremendous stake through indirect ownership of stocks and bonds, by far surpassing direct ownership. The stupendous growth of pension funds is illustrated by Table 452 in the *Statistical Abstract*.

The reader's attention should be concentrated on the surging rise in number of employees covered and the reserves which in 1972 totaled over $167 billion. These reserves are really the assets of the funds as outlined in the bottom table. Attention should be directed to the fact that, of the non-insured funds assets of over $124 billion, over $79 billion was in common stock. Herein lie potentials of dramatic significance. Workers' participation in management is a fact of life in Europe and especially in Germany, with benefits that have accrued to the benefit of the worker and the German economy. In recent decades, the inflation rate in Germany has been the lowest among industrialized nations. This success has been attributed to a degree to the workability of worker participation. In this country, this matter is in the talking stage. However, in our opinion, this may be just a prelude to the possibility of the emergence of worker control and eventual ownership via the pension funds. It is not too farfetched to contemplate that workers and union leaders would not make a bid to exercise voting rights accruing to common stocks in which funds are invested for their retirement. These funds have grown prodigiously and will continue to do so. Hence, profits may be the weld that will fuse together the interests of workers, middle class and management. All these groups now have a common interest in the profitability of free enterprise. Where this common interest is not so obvious now because of the new class rhetoric, it will strike home when cognizance is given to the fact of workers' control of industry.

Empirically, it has been established that profit margins are hardly adequate and in declining trends and that long-term price trends refute the market power theories of the dishonest or misguided critics of business enterprise. Profits and the profit motive have been proven as instruments that have produced economic and social progress. In the next chapter, we shall consider the philosophical aspects of profits.

V

PHILOSOPHICAL AND MORAL ASPECTS OF PROFITS

Profits are not anti-social or obscene if they have a redeeming social value. The pursuit of profits, characterized by an enlightened self-interest is a tremendous socio-economic force for the betterment of mankind. In this context, there is no longer anything to reconcile between the social conscience and the profit motive. If the quest for profits culminates in social progress by design or by accident, it has redeeming social values; otherwise, it does not. The ultimate criterion should be whether the contributions of the profit motive and profits to social progress outweigh the end result of alternate systems.

The themes listed above shall be amplified as we consider in this chapter allegations against and some fuzzy thinking about profits. We will depart from conventional presentations as we will quote verbatim from recent commentaries and interject our comments.

Irving Kristol, Henry Luce Professor of Urban Values at New York University authored an article entitled "Horatio Alger and Profits," in the *Wall Street Journal* of July 11, 1974: The article in its entirety follows:

> Over these past months, I have been attending many conferences of businessmen and it almost always happens that someone will intervene to inquire, plaintively: "What can we do to make the profit motive respectable once again?" Or: "Why, in view of the general prosperity which the free exercise of the profit motive has brought to our society, is it held in such low esteem—indeed, in contempt—by intellectuals, academics, students, the media, politicians, even our very own children?" Or: "Why is the profit-seeking businessman, who creates affluence for everyone, a somewhat less than reputable figure in American society today?"

Very simply because the Marxist and leftward leaning prevaricators have poisoned the minds of our citizens and students with falsehoods about the magnitude and true nature of profits.

> Whatever the precise wording, it's a fascinating and important question. In some ways, it may be the most important question confronting our liberal-capitalist society. There can be no doubt that, if business as an occupation and businessmen as a class continue to drift in popular opinion from the center of respectability to its margins, then liberal capitalism—and our liberal political system with it—has precious little chance for survival.

The drift in popular opinion will have to be arrested and turned around by a counteroffensive led by business leaders themselves to show profits in their true historical perspective and prove that profit is not a "dirty word."

But, as phrased, it is also the wrong question—in the sense that it reveals how antibusiness opinion has shaped the thinking and the language of businessmen themselves. For the idea that the businessman is ruled solely by "the profit motive," that he is simply an acquisitive creature lusting after the greatest possible gain, and that liberal-capitalist society is nothing more than an "acquisitive society," was originally proposed as an indictment of our socio-economic system, and is still taken by many to be exactly that.

There is no need to acquiesce in this indictment as our "acquisitive" society has contributed more socially redeeming developments in the basics of life and social amenities for our workers, consumers and voters without any political and economic oppression. This is in stark contrast to the economic bungling of a bureaucratic collectivism and the attendant loss of political freedom.

Indeed, if the description is true, the indictment is inevitable. Who on earth wants to live in a society in which all—or even a majority—of one's fellow citizens are fully engaged in the hot pursuit of money, the single-minded pursuit of material self-interest? To put it another way: Who wants to live in a society in which selfishness and self-seeking are celebrated as primary virtues? Such a society is unfit for human habitation—thus sayeth the Old Testament, the New Testament, the Koran, the Greek philosophers, the medieval theologians, all of modern moral philosophy. So if capitalism is what this indictment claims it is— if it is what so many businessmen today seem to think it is —then it is doomed, and properly.

But this is not what a liberal-capitalist society is supposed to be like, and it was only in recent decades that anyone thought it was supposed to be like that. As a matter of fact, if this had been the original idea of capitalism, it could never have come into existence—not in a civilization still powerfully permeated by Christian values and Christian beliefs. Certainly capitalism did free the spirit of commercial enterprise from its feudal and mercantilist fetters. It did legitimate the pursuit of self-interest— but the pursuit of self-interest rightly understood. And when this capitalistic ethic is itself rightly understood as an ethic, it turns out to be something quite different from a mere unleashing of "the profit motive."

When capitalism freed "the spirit of commercial enterprise from its feudal and mercantilist fetters" it performed a socially redeeming function. When the Bolsheviks outmaneuvered the Mensheviks, they unleashed a socio-economic system devoid of socially redeeming values. The Soviet bureaucrats cannot stand up to criticism of their floundering economic system and thus prohibit free speech and democratic elections.

Businessmen as Heroes

If one wants to appreciate the moral dimensions of the liberal-capitalist perspective, there is no better place to look than in the Horatio Alger novels—the only substantial body of American literature where businessmen are heroes rather than villains. These novels, of course, are no longer read today. But prior to World War II, they were still in wide circulation and were being avidly read by adolescent boys. They had by then been enormously popular for half a century, so presumably they corresponded to certain deep American beliefs. And what does one discover when one returns to a reading of Horatio Alger? Well, one discovers nothing like a celebration of "the profit motive," pure and simple. Indeed, one finds a moral conception of business as an honorable vocation for honorable men. A profitable vocation, to be sure. But profitable because honorable, not vice versa.

Philosophical and Moral Aspects of Profits

When our educators substitute avant-garde novels for Horatio Alger novels, they perform a socially unredeeming function.

The basic assumption of Horatio Alger is that the life of business is a good life because it helps develop certain admirable traits of character: probity, diligence, thrift, self-respect, candor, fair dealing, and so on—all those "bourgeois virtues" which no one quite believes in any more. A young man who enters the vocation of business must have these virtues latent within him, or else he cannot succeed honorably. And if he does succeed honorably, he will represent these virtues in their fullest form. Horatio Alger's success stories are also full-blooded morality tales.

It is also important to notice what Horatio Alger does not say. He does not say you cannot succeed otherwise—"speculators" and "freebooters" (wheeler-dealers, we should say) may indeed become wealthy, but such types are not honorable businessmen. They can become wealthy but are never "success stories," since they have only enriched but not "bettered" themselves, i.e., their characters have been in no way improved by their active lives. Nor does he say that success under capitalism is an analogue to the "survival of the fittest" in nature; the law of the jungle is not suitable model for human association in society. Nor does he say that "private vices" (e.g., selfishness, greed, avarice) are justifiable because they may result in "public benefits" (e.g., economic growth); he insists on a continuity between private ethics and the social ethic of a good society. All of these other apologia for liberal capitalism, which we are familiar with, are curtly dismissed by him as unacceptable to anyone with a more than rudimentary moral sensibility.

Now, it is true that Horatio Alger wrote fiction, not fact. But it will not do to dismiss him as a mere fancifier and mythmaker. To begin with, he would never have been so popular, for so long, if his conception of American society had been utterly fanciful. His readers understood that he was writing stories, not sociology—but they apparently perceived some connection between his stories and the reality of their socio-economic order. There was in fact such a connection, which even we can still dimly perceive. Some of us are old enough to remember that there was a time when the only thing more reprehensible than buying on the installment plan was selling on the installment plan —it encouraged "fecklessness." And we still have some business institutions which could only have been founded in Horatio Alger's world. Thus, on the floors of our various stock and commodity exchanges, transactions involving millions of dollars take place on the basis of nothing more than mutual trust: there, a businessman's word is his bond. Imagine trying to set up such institutions today! A thousand lawyers, to say nothing of the SEC, would be quick to tell you that such confidence in the honor of businessmen is inconsistent with sound business practices.

What the 20th Century has witnessed is the degradation of the bourgeois-capitalist ethic into a parody of itself—indeed, into something resembling what the critics of liberal capitalism had always accused it of being. These critics, intellectuals and men of letters above all, never did like modern liberal society because it was "vulgar"—i.e., it permitted ordinary men and women, in the marketplace, to determine the shape of this civilization, a prerogative that intellectuals and men of letters have always claimed for themselves. This is why so many intellectuals and men of letters naturally tend to favor some form of benevolent despotism, in our time called "a planned society." But their criticism was relatively ineffectual so long as liberal capitalism was contained within a bourgeois way of life and the ethos celebrated by Horatio Alger. The common man has always preferred bourgeois capitalism to its intellectual critics; in the United States he still does, for the most part.

But the trouble is that capitalism outgrew, as it were, its bourgeois origins and became a system for the impersonal liberation and satisfaction of appetites—an engine for the creation of "affluence," as we say. And such a system, governed by purely materialistic conceptions and infused with a purely acquisitive ethos, is defenseless before the critique of its intellectuals. Yes, it does provide more food, better housing, better health, to say nothing of all kinds of pleasant conveniences. Only a saint or a snob would dismiss these achievements lightly. But anyone who naively believes that, in sum, they suffice to legitimize a socio-economic system knows little of the human heart and soul. People can learn to despise such a system even while enjoying its benefits.

A system of purely materialistic conceptions cannot exist as it does not operate in an ethical vacuum. Acquisitiveness is ethical or unethical. The one has socially redeeming attributes, the other does not. However, the ultimate result governs social redeemability. The capitalist profit motive, governed by ethical standards, can be accepted as inherently containing socially redeemable values. However, a collectivized, bureaucratic system, although guided by purported ethical standards, but culminating in an inefficient economic system and political oppression, cannot be accepted as such.

"People can learn to despise such a system," because the critique of pseudo-intellectuals has appealed to envy and pandered to prejudices. Hence, they concoct the theory of exploitation without offering empirical evidence, which really refutes their charges. Long-run perspectives on profit margins and prices do reveal exploitation—the kind that taps technology for improving human existence.

Placid Acceptances

Nothing more plainly reveals the moral anarchy that prevails within the business community today than the way in which it can placidly accept—indeed, participate in—the anti-bourgeois culture that is now predominant. How many businessmen walked out indignantly from a movie like *The Graduate*, which displayed them (and their wives) as hollow men and women, worthy of nothing but contempt? Not many, I would think—the capacity for indignation withers along with self-respect. How many businessmen refuse, as a matter of honor and of principle, to advertise in a publication such as *Rolling Stone* or even *Playboy*—publications which make a mockery of their industry, their integrity, their fidelity, the very quality of their lives? The question answers itself.

If businessmen are nothing but merchants of affluence, then their only claim to their rights and prerogatives is that they can perform this task more efficiently than the government can. This assertion is unquestionably true, but it really is irrelevant. Efficiency is not a moral virtue and by itself never legitimizes anything. It is the culture of a society—by which I mean its religion and its moral traditions, as well as its specific arts—which legitimizes or illegitimizes its institutions. For decades now, liberal capitalism has been living off the inherited cultural capital of the bourgeois era, has benefitted from a moral sanction it no longer even claims. That legacy is now depleted, and the cultural environment has turned radically hostile.

The legacy need not be considered as depleted. That the cultural environment has turned radically hostile is the outgrowth of an anti-business propaganda based mainly on the misreading or deliberate misrepresentation of profit and price history. It is distressing that a man of Kristol's competence and perceptiveness should fall prey to insidious propaganda.

Today, businessmen desperately try to defend their vocation as honorable because profitable. Without realizing it, they are standing Horatio Alger on his head. It won't work. That inverted moral ethos makes no moral sense, as our culture keeps telling us, from the most popular movie to the most avant-garde novel. This culture is not, as it sometimes pretends, offended by some bad things that some businessmen do, it is offended by what businessmen are or seem to be—exemplars of the naked "profit motive." Businessmen, of course, are unaccustomed to taking culture seriously. They didn't have to, so long as it was mainly a bourgeois culture, with anti-bourgeois sentiments concentrated on the margins. Today, unless they start trying to figure out a way to cope with the new cultural climate, they are likely to catch a deathly chill. It may be a bad time for businessmen to sell stock (or buy stock) but it would seem to be a good time for them to take stock.

Yes, it would seem to be a good time for businessmen to take stock and start fighting back vigorously and aggressively and demonstrate that the profit motive is ethically legitimate, has socially redeeming values outweighing by far any alternates conceived by the theoreticians and Utopian dreamers of the left.

To requote Kristol from his last paragraph: "That inverted moral ethos makes no moral sense, as our culture keeps telling us, from the most popular movie to the most avant-garde novel."

Here Kristol betrays three misconceptions. First, our moral ethos is not inverted; second, it does make moral sense. These two principles gain credence when viewed objectively by the criterion of social redeemability. In the third place, it is unnecessary and imprudent to acquiesce in the acceptance of the leftist-spawned "anti-profit culture." The avant-garde culture, created by anti-business (and, in the end, anti-worker and anti-consumer) propaganda, in itself is not only devoid of redeeming social values but also is in effect if not in purpose a conglomeration of socially unredeeming elements. The tacit acceptance of the highbrow culture in itself is a mark of "social unredeemability."

To requote Kristol from his concluding paragraph: "It [the avant-garde culture] is offended by what businessmen are or seem to be—exemplars of the naked profit motive."

Here again, Kristol betrays victimization by the extravagantly specious rhetoric of the Marxist and liberal charlatans. An "ethical naked pursuit of profit" does not require any moral or philosophical sanctions as long as it culminates in social betterment, thereby bearing the stamp of social redeeming values. If a businessman strives for profits with a conscious awareness of social responsibility, so much the better. However, the businessman, pursuing naked profits ethically, need not subject himself to philosophical, moral, ethical or psychological conversions, just to kowtow to the whimsies of a sham avant-garde culture which is spawned by socially unredeemable propaganda of lies, distortions and perverted rationalizations, intentional or unintentional.

We have stressed the importance of capital formation as an engine toward providing the amenities as well as the basics left for worker and consumer, and as such it is characterized by redeeming social values. Whether it be primitively naked or civilized with moral aspects, profit becomes distinguished in redeeming social values as it performs its function of the most effective and productive allocator of capital resources.

Profit also gains stature in social redeemability as it performs its function as the most productive cost controller as it provides an ever-increasing supply of basics and amenities of life to workers and consumers at lower costs, expressed most significantly in terms of hours worked to acquire goods and services.

If profit results in ecological or environmental damage, where costs outweigh benefits, it loses its status of social redeemability. Here it behooves the governmental agencies to create a socially redeemable means for redressing the balance. However, when policies of overreaction and overkill of eco-freaks and sham consumerists, spawned by

Philosophical and Moral Aspects of Profits

misconceptions and vindictiveness, culminate in costs outweighing benefits, they must be adjudged as unleashing unredeeming social activities. A program of moderation in reasonable time schedules and attainable objectives contains redeeming social values; otherwise, it does not.

If our people working for corporations and being educated for positions in business were permeated with a sound philosophical approach toward profits as socially redeeming, their objectives and expectations of a personal sense of satisfaction and accomplishment of personal meaning and fulfillment would be attained. That they are uneasy and that they may have doubts is not the fault of our profit system but the fault of its irresponsible detractors.

People can achieve their potential when they work for a purpose they believe in, and profits in the context of social redeemability provide a purpose worth believing in.

Four ingredients have to be considered: consumer needs and wants, a free market that signals his needs and wants, the capacity to fulfill his preferences and profits. They all coexist, but profit becomes paramount because without profit there is no incentive to respond to consumer choices and no future base to fulfill consumer preferences. A capitalist society based on profit and a free market can best respond to needs and wants of consumers, whereas in a socialist society the inefficient, dogma-fettered bureaucracy ineptly attempts to make the myriad decisions.

Adam Smith saw profit as a means to an end not as an end in itself. Profit can stand up to examination in either and both senses as long as the pursuit is ethical and the end result contains redeemable social values.

Profits will be maximized and society will benefit most

when employees operate in an environment of true perspectives about profits and work in an atmosphere of socially redeemable functions. This entails a redressing of a false culture relative to profits propagated by misleading sham intellectuals and misled servile followers.

In our social philosophy, profit as a purpose, means or end stands up under scrutiny in the light of social redeeming values.

The critics of capitalism overestimate the quantity factor of profits and underestimate the manifold profit by-products such as jobs, pensions, new products that make life more convenient and more pleasurable for an ever-growing number of people. The by-products of profits by far outweigh the by-products of bureaucracies, whose by-products engender economic regimentation and political oppression. The free market detractors have been so obsessed with "how much" that they neglected to see "how useful" profits have been in quantifying not only quantifiable but also unquantifiable things (*Economist* June 15, 1974, page 130).

Leftist ideologues have long nurtured the notion that the economic and political freedoms of capitalism are but a subterfuge for exploitation. In their theory, exploitative profit is the main culprit that underpays the worker and overcharges the consumer. Our empirical data has shown the hollowness of these charges. However, the story does not end here. The myth of exploitation has fathered the explosion of expectations and entitlements.

In their crescendo against the free market system, the radical and sham liberals scream that something is wrong with human societies based on capitalism. It is admitted by

Philosophical and Moral Aspects of Profits

us that capitalism has its faults, but these are due to the imperfections of human nature. Again we quote Goethe: "Could we perfect human nature, we might expect a perfect state of things." With perfect human beings, we could expect a perfect state of things under capitalism as well as socialism or even under the utopian society of anarchism. But with human nature conditioned for thousands of years by acquisitiveness, the constitutional governments and free markets of capitalism provide the most effective safeguards against the excesses of human nature. The excesses of the tycoons and the wheeler-dealers of capitalism are no match for the atrocities perpetrated by the tyrants of collectivized societies. There are no restraints whatsoever for the lust for power. The quest for power in socialist societies is devoid of redeeming social values, while the quest for profits in capitalist societies is a fountainhead of socially redeeming by-products.

Whatever is wrong under capitalism is redressable. However, there is more wrong in the rhetoric of radicalism and sham intellectualism that is misleading and packed with lies and loaded with Marxist clichés and hackneyed themes of pseudo-liberalism.

We will conclude this chapter with a quote by Henry Ford II, who in 1966 told a Chicago audience, "As I see it, there is no longer anything to reconcile, if there ever was, between the social conscience and the profit motive. It seems clear to me that improving the quality of society is nothing more than another step in the evolutionary process of taking a more far-sighted view of return on investment."

This is in line with our opinion that the corporation's

job is to provide what the public wants at the lowest price. Profits, ethically pursued, have been a tremendous force in meeting the wants of consumers, expressed in a free market with no need of an imprimatur from ivory-tower intellectuals. Thus, profits must be accorded the attributes of redeeming social values.

VI

THE PROPAGANDA AND THE RHETORIC

Marxists, intellectuals, economically myopic union leaders and demagogic politicians have conspired, naively or intentionally, to form a hardcore cadre to mount an unwarranted attack on profits. To serve their own purposes, they have exploited the economic illiteracy of workers and consumers.

The Marxists equate profits with worker exploitation. But, as we have shown, profits in their historical time perspective are not only non-excessive, but more recently even inadequate, thereby, stunting capital formation and in turn economic growth, preventing the formation of new job opportunities. Furthermore, we have demonstrated that profits, not unethically pursued, have redeeming social value.

Elitism is the mental block that prevents the intellectuals and men of letters from accepting a profit- and market-oriented economy. In the previously quoted words of Kristol:

> . . . these critics . . . never did like liberal society because it was "vulgar"—i.e., it permitted ordinary men and women, in the marketplace, to determine the shape of this civilization, a prerogative that intellectuals and men of letters have always claimed for themselves.

And so as the Marxists orchestrate, the intellectuals, consciously or in naive stupidity join the chorus. As a consequence they brainwash our youth. That explains their misconception about profits, alluded to before, that profits of corporations average about 28 cents per sales dollar rather than the meager recent range of about 5 cents on each dollar of sales. This diabolical dissemination of falsehoods has had a profound effect on our youths' attitude toward work. In a most revealing and thought provoking book, *The Real America: A Surprising Examination of the State of the Union* (Doubleday, 1974), Ben J. Wattenberg cites the following report on a query by Daniel Yankelovich to students (page 268):

Hard work will always pay off: Percentage agreeing:

1968	69%
1969	56%
1971	39%

No doubt, a catastrophic deterioration. As the siren song gains in intensity, the union leaders chime in with their diatribes and fulminations against "excessive" or "unconscionable" profits. They mislead their members into the belief that higher wages can be financed out of profits and that the subsequent inflation is only further proof of profiteering and price gouging. Here the union worker is being screwed, not by the "capitalist bastard," as he is led to believe but by his own "best friend," the union leader.

Here a disturbing question arises: In the present condition of such pervasiveness of misinformation about profits, can a union leader exercise farsighted economic statesmanship?

While the crescendo surges louder and louder, let us not forget about "friend of the common man," who is in the wings eager to get on stage for his contribution in his grandstanding. Of course, it is the demagogic politician. He chirps in with his "malefactors of great wealth," "economic royalist," ad nauseam. Eager to outpromise other votes-at-any-price politicos, he has to put on a grandstanding play of showing that he is "doing something." So he throws money at problems and if a bureaucracy that he creates causes further problems he simply mandates another bureaucracy. Witness the fiasco of the I.C.C. relative to its overregulations of the railroads. Now he adds the Federal Railway Administration. In creating new agencies, he may be setting up a means for spreading political largess in jobs for his political hacks, but perversely he saddles business with chores that distract the attention of businessmen from their main responsibilities. According to the office of

Management and Budget, individuals and business firms spend 130 million man-hours annually filling out 5,146 different types of government forms. This awesome paper-shuffling paradise has grown from 200 social programs in the Kennedy adminstration to over 1,100 at the present time. However, this motley crowd of radical and liberal economists and social scientists, with their attendant do-gooders, have perpetrated and are perpetrating a gigantic cruel hoax on the worker and the public when they spread the erroneous belief that these friends of the common man are soaking the rich to pay for all this transfer of income from rich to poor. They will not admit that a dispassionate analysis will reveal that the funds available from the rich individuals and corporations are limited and that in the final end the productive worker and consumer pay for this largess in taxes and inflation.

Don't worry, we did not forget about the media in this respect as they get special honorable mention.

Relative to TV, in his book (p. 95), Wattenberg makes these pertinent and perceptive comments:

> Does television present a fair and balanced portrait of America? and the second question is: Can it?
> It doesn't really, and it probably can't. The operative fact in the news business—and television we are now teaching and talking about is part of the news business—*is that good news is no news.*

On pages 315 and 316, he adds:

> A case can be made that a good part of our domestic malaise can be laid precisely at the feet of a media system that under-

reports progress. Consider the two attitudinal bedrocks discussed earlier in this volume. Americans say their own lives are fine and they say America is in trouble. There is another way of putting that! What people know of first-hand they think well of. What people know of second-hand, information gathered through the transmission belt of our system of communications, they think ill of.

After all this case could be made about American attitudes. If Mr. Smith and Mrs. Jones and Mr. Green and Mrs. Brown all say their lives are pretty good, thank you, and if society, or "America," is only a collection of Smith, Jones, Green, Brown and their friends, then America is not on the wrong track at all, but is in fact a whopping success, and the only reason that Americans think things are lousy is because they are given a bum steer by the media system that lives by one cardinal rule, "good news is no news."

This writer cannot recommend Wattenberg's book too highly, as a perusal of his exhaustive and timely researches reveal the real essence of American economic, social and cultural progress. His studies and commentaries parallel and complement the topics in this discourse.

In researching to discover what really has been going on inside America since the obstreperous rise of what Wattenberg calls the "failure and guilt complex" (fabrications of various vested interests whose themes are calamity and reform), Wattenberg has surveyed three areas: (1) objective data, facts and figures culled from reports of the U.S. Bureau of the Census; (2) attitudinal data as reported by such scientific pollsters as Gallup, Harris, Roper, Yankelovich and Opinion Research; and (3) what Wattenberg calls "the rhetoric"—the mouthings of the intelligentsia, politicians and TV pundits and the superficial and specious outpourings of "advocacy" journalism. What he discovers is a gap between fact and fancy, between the objective data and the lurid rhetoric which exploits the doubts and economic illiteracy of the average Americans.

In the writer's opinion, *The Real America* should be accorded wide publicity and circulation so as to gainsay the irresponsible rhetoric and brazen propaganda. The media can be faulted on counts of failing to report constructive economic developments while overstressing the evils and dangers in our economic situation. They overdramatize the long-run inconsequential trivia and are devoid of historical perspective. As a result they must be adjudged as largely responsible for the conflict between fact and fancy.

The media have been the transmission line that has spread anti-profit and anti-bourgeois propaganda to a point where they have unleashed a momentum of rising expectations and rising entitlements that are affecting the functioning of our economic system. How so?

Because they have engineered a psychological momentum of rising expectations. Witness the construction worker, the teamster, and our public employees. Wage raises in double-digit figures predated by far double-digit inflation. Any raises now below former rate advances are or would be considered inadequate. It is one of the proclivities of human nature to extrapolate into the future what has been occurring currently.

This psychological momentum in expectations as well as entitlements can be held largely responsible for the dilemma of stagflation of 1969-70 and the slumpflation of 1974-75, which are the inevitable results of the convergence

The Propaganda and the Rhetoric

of the demand-pull inflation and wage-tax-cost-push inflation. Demand-pull inflation can be defined as that arising out of a condition when more dollars chase a limited amount of goods, when more dollars are being paid out in purchasing power by the private and public sectors of our economy than can be matched (without raising prices) by the producers of capital equipment, consumer goods, foods and raw materials.

Wage-and-tax-cost-push inflation occurs when wages, taxes and prices take off on a one-way uphill road and become flexible only in an upward direction. The resultant momentum renders inoperative the efficacy of the conventional tools of fiscal and monetary policies—the fine tuning that appeared to be reasonably successful from about 1960 to 1969.

We have arrived at a critical juncture in our economic society as the public sector has become greater at ever-increasing increments to a point where it is encroaching upon the ability of capital formation to serve in its function to provide a growing base for fulfilling basic needs and amenities. The explosion in deficit spending, arising from the psychological momentum of expectations and entitlements, is a prime cause of demand-pull inflation, because deficits not met by savings are monetized, thereby increasing the money supply that chases a limited amount of goods as supply in the short run is inelastic—that is when supply cannot respond immediately to a rise in prices. It is nothing but sheer economic stupidity to run a budget deficit when the economy is operating at *full physical plant capacity*. Please note that we are stressing *full physical plant capacity,* because a much better trade-off would be less rhetoric and misconceptions about profits, the limits of income distribution and the limits of the tax base of the rich and more adequate profits and higher capital formation to utilize more fully human productive capacity. In plain words, this would mean more jobs. Deficit spending also contributes to cost-push inflation as the politicians and demagogues attempt purportedly to soak the rich corporations, resulting in increasing the tax factor in cost-push inflation. These arch-swindlers don't admit they in reality have conned the average worker and consumer in paying through the nose in higher prices and higher taxes. In Chapter Twelve, a much fuller consideration will be given to deficit spending and government expenditure inflation.

The market economy is inherently endowed with admirable qualities of corrective forces that operate through fluctuations in interest rates, provided there is a minimum of interference from the government sector. The government should confine itself to moderation in its actual roles in monetary policy and fiscal stimulation. However, to get back to the present juncture, fiscal irresponsibility has had tragic economic consequences in two respects. First, it played a major role, aside from cost-push inflation, in causing inflation of such a magnitude that it resulted for the first time in our financial history of an inflationary premium in our interest rates. Second, in the ensuing what would be a normal disinflationary period, interest rates on bond and mortgages have not been allowed to decline substantially as they normally do because of competition for funds in the money market by the government to meet deficits. High interest rates and high construction costs impede corporations from tapping the equity and bond markets to obtain funds for expansion and job creation. The potential home buyer is priced out of the market. The demagogues all of a sudden in this respect lose their rhetoric. But, don't worry; they will find a scapegoat while they continue swindling and screwing the common man.

Cost-push inflation, which has its basis in wage-rate increases exceeding productivity gains, has a ratchet effect in only one way—upward. This has been true since the New Deal gave unions virtual monopoly power. In the judgment of the writer, it was humane and just to free wage rates from the discipline of a market economy rather than leave wage-rate determination to the vicissitudes of economic fluctuations. Here, as in other aspects of life, labor responsibility would exhibit redeeming social values, if excesses did not generate deleterious consequences. As long as wage-rate increases exceeded productivity gains by a moderate amount and profits were reasonably adequate, the ingenuity of managers and engineers in exploiting technology was able to cope with the challenge. The result was the greatest improvement in human welfare in the history of mankind. We have cited corroborative evidence before, but will add here a table and commentary from a timely, informative and sparkling book, *Two Cheers for the Affluent Society*, by Professor Wilfred Beckerman (St. Martin's Press, New York, 1974):

Getting back to our analysis of cost-push inflation, we must interject an economic caveat. We have arrived at a critical juncture in our economic system. The unwarranted rhetoric and spurious propaganda against important elements in our economic system—such as profits, the limits of

Table VI-1 (Table No. Added)
Table 4.1
SAMETZ ESTIMATES OF U.S.A. NATIONAL PRODUCT
ADJUSTED FOR LEISURE, COSTS OF URBAN CIVILIZATION,
AND OTHER ITEMS: 1869-1966
(billion dollars at constant prices, and indices)

	(1) GNP	(2) Leisure	(3) Total GNP plus leisure	(4) Index of Col. (1)	(5) Index of Col. (3)
1869-78	9.4	1.2	10.6	100	100
1929	97.0	60.0	157.0	1,033	1,481
1966	315.0	240.0	555.0	3,250	5,235

Source: A. W. Sametz, "Production of goods and services: the measurement of economic growth," in E. B. Sheldon and W. E. Moore (editors), *Indicators of Social Change: Concepts and Measurement* (Russell Sage Foundation, New York, 1968), p. 83, Table 2.

Contrary to the assertions of those who constantly complain that, on account of various omissions, the growth of conventionally measured GNP overstates the "true" rice in welfare, the above figures show that one of the omissions from GNP, namely leisure has shown a spectacular rise over the last century, and has hence made an enormous contribution to the rise in economic welfare of the U.S.A.

income distribution and the tax base—have created and fostered such an uncontrollable momentum in expectations that our managerial and technological ingenuity is no longer able to compensate for double-digit wage rate increases. Wage-rate increases exceeding productivity gains in industry in the aggregate have been moderately excessive, but not so in the construction industry, where double-digit wage rates increases have been the rule rather than the exception since 1965. As a result we have this distressing development, as reported by Lewis Beman in an article in *Fortune*, May, 1974, captioned "Why Business Ran Out of Capacity":

The Propaganda and the Rhetoric

> *The cost of construction—a much larger part of the bill for adding to facilities than for streamlining them—has risen three times faster* than equipment prices; in fact, construction costs have risen faster than manufacturing wages. Except for situations in which the pace of technology has produced dramatic gains in efficiency, expansion projects that were marginally worthwhile in 1969 would not typically look very appealing in 1974.

The arrant rhetoric as applied to the construction industry has led to a psychological momentum in expectations, leaving in its wake economic consequences that are sickening to behold. First, it has caused unemployment in the construction industry. Second, it has caused capacity shortages which not only limit the supply of goods, but also prevent the utilization of surplus labor that was eager to be employed. Finally, it has caused a horrendous GNP gap with consequences that injure most those who least can afford it. The most tragic victims of the swindling and screwing, caused by rhetoric and radical and pseudoliberal speciousness, are the destitute, the handicapped and the aged living on fixed incomes.

VII

THE HARVEST OF THE WHIRLWIND

It is plausible to attribute a host of social and economic consequences to the wanton rhetoric and propaganda regarding profits and our culture. Among the social consequences we can list crime, drugs, embezzlement, welfare cheating, shoplifting, etc. In the economic area, we can enumerate undesirable consequences such as stagflation, slumpflation, lower profits, lower productivity, a deteriorating work ethic and losses in capital formation, job opportunities, etc.

A strong case can be made for ascribing the social consequences to misleading information about profits. The inflation caused by the psychological momentum in expectations and entitlements inevitably leads to unemployment, creating fertile grounds for discontent, disenchantment and envy. The drug pusher flashing new clothing and sporting luxury cars becomes an object of emulation. Given a false picture of profits, the criminal, the would-be criminal, and the underprivileged are provided with grounds for rationalization. Welfare cheating is held justified. Stealing, embezzling, shoplifting, burglary, etc., appear as a justifiable response to alleged obscene, excessive and unjust profits. Among our youth in the educational system, our college professors erroneously justify disrespect for law, order and authority. Witness Marcuse justifying violence, and Commoner intolerance toward free speech for ideas that do not conform to left-wing ideology. In an article on one of the three "Pillars of the American System," Joseph Adelson, professor of psychology at the University of Michigan, wrote on education in *Fortune,* April, 1975. Excerpts, significant to the thesis of this book follow:

> Just ten years ago, American education could look back upon a period of prodigious achievement. With some strain but with remarkable vigor, the nation had been able to educate the children born in the postwar baby boom. Even more impressively, it had democratized higher education, more so than any other nation, recruiting to the campus an ever growing proportion of the college-age young. These were achievements of scale; but the most admirable accomplishment of all, though the least widely remarked, was the development in the elite universities of a superb system of graduate education and scholarship.
>
> Each of these triumphs, it would ultimately appear, carried some hidden costs; in particular, there was a growing tension between the mass and class directions that higher education was

taking, between egalitarian aims and meritocratic claims. But given the euphoric mood of the moment, these problems, even when recognized, were held to be either minor or manageable.

Then came a precipitous tumble, from those high spirits to our current malaise, that peculiar mixture of cynicism, fatigue, and sadness with which we now view education. Why the fall, and why so very rapid?

The proximate cause, and certainly the most dramatic, was the debacle in the universities. A much-celebrated, much-publicized generation of the college young—the brightest, the best educated, the most idealistic, etc.—suddenly gave itself over to riot, fanaticism, and occasional thuggery. What was worse was that the university authorities were revealed as unable to govern, indeed unable to cope. By and large, administrations were simply too paralyzed to act, and when they did, they found themselves abandoned by confused and often cowardly faculties. Worse still was the recognition, when the disorders were past, that the universities were no longer able to defend or inculcate certain values central to their purpose: academic freedom, rationality, and merit.

As to freedom, the university has now become the most unpleasant and at times the most dangerous place in America to venture unfashionable opinions. As to rationality, an astonishing number of students now believe, or profess to believe, in the occult, witchcraft, astrology, and the more simple-minded forms of mysticism, and an even larger number cling to magical or conspiratorial ideas about economics, politics, psychology and sex. As to merit, many institutions have felt compelled to adopt what amount to racial and sexual quota systems in the hiring and promotion of faculty. The erosion of these central values is far more advanced than most nonacademics recognize, since the situation has been poorly reported by the press, which seems to imagine that the campuses are returning to "normal."

It was to emerge, in time, that the technology gap, like the missile gap later on, was to put it politely, a fiction. American science and technology were not falling behind, as both the space program and the continuing American domination of Nobel science awards (and much else) were to make entirely plain. Yet given the temper of the times, one could not take a prudent position on science education without seeming dangerously complacent—an enemy of progress, indeed an enemy of the people.

The furor over Sputnik, now so far behind us, foretold remarkably well the pressures education was to face in the decade to follow: a society facing problems, some genuine and some illusory, some manageable and some essentially intractable; a spasm of hysteria; recriminations directed toward education; and education itself chosen to be the agent of reform.

* * *

The country had become intensely aware of poverty and race, and it became the program of the Great Society to erase poverty and to reduce the disadvantages associated with race. New or expanded social and economic programs were to do much toward these ends, but education was to be the ultimate solvent. This expectation was initially placed upon the schools without rancor and with some expectation of success.

But success soon proved to be elusive, and as it did, a mordant and then hostile tone crept into much of the published commentary about the schools. They had failed; they were mediocre, incompetent, incorrigibly bourgeois and thus alien to the aspirations of the poor. They were not the solution, but part of the problem, not merely the arena but in fact the very instrument of educational failure among the dispossessed.

The verbal assault upon the schools on issues of poverty and race was a blow from which education has not yet recovered. Even now, after much contrary evidence has become available, it is widely believed that the schools, through failures in sensibility or effort, or at least in techniques, are to be held responsible for the educational difficulties of the urban poor. The repetition of these charges during the Sixties led to a serious loss of moral authority, and lent impetus to other and quite different demands being made upon education.

There emerged, in the left-liberal commentary on education, a sort of warmed-over, vulgarized progressivism, which took the doctrine of human perfectibility in a rather different direction—toward the unchaining of character, and beyond that, toward the ideal of ultimate self-realization. It was held that Jack was a dull boy—apathetic, conformist, intellectually stagnant, but above all, constrained and unfulfilled—because, among other things, the schools were dreary and enervating at best, and at worst sheer prisons of the human spirit. It was said that the best and brightest of our young were the particular victims of these coercions, as witness their frequent ennui and alienation. Hence the schools were to be remade—again.

* * *

". . . The adversary culture, having worked its mischief upon education, has now turned to larger, choicer targets—sexual identity and marriage, and so far with alarming success."

Let us not forget that the adversary culture was able to achieve a measure of success because they were able to brainwash our youth and a segment of our population with a subtle and seductive propaganda based on falsehoods and distortions about profits and alleged inequities and inequalities of income distribution. This is tragic because all this is done in the name of offering us as an alternative a utopian society where life is so pleasurable that walls and guns are necessary to restrain their objects of Socialist beneficence from escaping to the "decadent West." The sham high-brow intellectuals offer us as an alternative a utopian egalitarian society where everything is so sublime that they restrict the freedom of expression so that the recipients of the Socialist cornucopia would be restrained from heaping fulsome paeans on their benefactors. These elitists offer us the benevolence of a society where people are denied freedom of expression lest they pray that God bestow His Graces on the leaders.

In another article on the "pillars," Tom Alexander makes these pertinent comments relative to science:

> Historians have begun to toll the end of the "Era of Progress" —the remarkable two-century episode that moved the mass of Western people from hand-to-mouth subsistence to nutritional abundance, automation, two-car garages, instant-on TV, and

off-and-on dismay. By now, the very word "progress" has come to taste of irony.

Historically speaking, it was an odd notion anyway, at least until after the emergence of scientific method in the seventeenth century proffered a powerful means of adding to the store of human knowledge. It was a mere step from there to viewing ordinary people as potentially perfectible creatures who could not only govern themselves but improve their condition. Out of this line of thinking came the American, French and Industrial revolutions.

No finer laboratory existed for working out the consequences of this proposition than North America with all its space and novelty. What emerged was a characteristic American attitude toward hardships as "problems" rather than acts of God, a characteristic history full of inventor heroes, and a characteristic elan: whatever could be done, would be done. The sequence flared to supernova in the glorious irrelevance of Project Apollo and began to gutter out with the cancellation of the SST.

By then a small cadre of intellectuals who for years had been sniping ineffectually at the flanks of the onrushing technological columns were reinforced by legions of students, politicians, journalists, and—unkindest cut—men from science itself. The acts and artifacts of the bewildered engineers and scientists were all at once being called "inhuman," "irrelevant," "profligate," and "dangerous."

* * *

From case histories of such affairs as the nuclear-safety debate, it's pretty clear that adversary science generally leads to distortion and concealment of the all-too-wispy information upon which decisions must be based. Truth tends to fall between the cracks, and it becomes hard to discern the case for moderation. Given the peer pressures within the scientific and academic communities, it's not always possible to find the expert willing to stand up in defense of, say, a little more pollution or a little less safety.

Probably a more fruitful course than adversary science is a rededication by the scientific community to its own internal standards of honesty and rigor, and an extension of these to its discourse with the public. A ringing denunciation of lopsided science comes from Harvey Brooks, dean of Engineering and Applied Physics at Harvard. "I believe," Brooks has written, "that the highest allegiance of science must continue to be truth as defined by the validation procedures of the scientific process itself, and that the distortion of scientific results or the selective use of evidence for political purposes, no matter how worthy, is unforgivable insofar as it is presented cloaked by the authority and imputed objectivity of science."

In another article of three on the "Battered Pillars of the American System" in the *Fortune* Special Bicentennial Issue, Peter Berger, Professor of Sociology at Rutgers University, wrote on the machinations and fabrications of leftist intelligentsia relative to religion:

> It is quite possible to argue that the notion of a crisis in American religion is an invention of intellectuals. Recent surveys show that some 40 percent of the population is in church every week; religious books make up one of the most expansive sectors of the publishing industry; and college students continue to crowd religion courses.
> In recent decades, religion in America has been characterized by an accelerating accommodation to nonreligious culture. The effects of this secularization of the churches have been most obviously devastating in mainstream Protestantism. Many of its thinkers and church leaders responded to the deepening secularity of the society by celebrating it. The huge success of Harvey Cox's *The Secular City*, published in 1965, did not initiate the celebration (indeed, the book was singularly unoriginal), but did ratify and broadcast it.
> The situation came to be redefined in an interesting way. Not only was secularism no longer to be seen as the enemy of the churches: in a total reversal of tradition, accommodation to secular culture was to be the true realization of the churches' faith. The comic, and indeed masochistic, aspects of this redefinition were not very widely perceived; but if ever there was an ideology of rape produced by the rapee, this was it. An especially grotesque manifestation of this attitude came along about a year after Cox's book, in the media-promoted "death of

God theology"—the ultimate fulfillment of any religion editor's prayer for a good man-bites-dog story.

Those who followed Cox's lead had learned to take their cues from a rather small elite of fashionable intellectuals, who, supposedly, knew where things were at. In the late Sixties, many churchmen jumped on every bandwagon announced as important by intellectual fashion. By and large, these bandwagons were either politically left or counter-cultural in character.

Needless to say, this did not mean that most members of the mainstream Protestant denominations joined the political left or the counterculture. What did happen was that there developed a widening gap between the leadership and the man in the pew, who often was not prepared to follow the ecclesiastical avant-garde in either its theological or its politico-cultural extravaganzas. The outcome of this tension between leaders and members was not so much a rebellion as a sour hangover following the turmoil of the late Sixties—a whimper rather than a bang. There have been of late some signs that out of this misadventure may come a new seriousness about the theological content of mainstream Protestantism, but the costs of the years of frantic accommodationism will be felt for a long time.

Until Vatican II, the Roman Catholic community in this country was in a situation of cultural isolation not greatly dissimilar from that of evangelical Protestantism. The rapid tumbling of the walls since then has been all the more remarkable. This process too has a comic aspect. The progressive reformers believed that their actions would make the church a more vital force in the society. Instead, these actions have plunged the church into its most severe crisis of credibility in recent history.

Every theological, cultural, and political folly of the Protestant avant-garde was enthusiastically embraced by its Catholic counterparts, who jumped on bandwagons with all the fervor of teenagers newly released from the strict discipline of school—those tight-lipped teaching nuns finally got their comeuppance.

* * *

The late Sixties made manifest a virulent anti-Americanism in precisely those circles on which the society depends for its metaphors, its "definitions of reality," and the legitimations of its values—broadly speaking, in the intellectually most active groups. These, of course, are the same circles from which the

The Harvest of the Whirlwind

religious avant-garde has been taking its cues.

The most turbulent expressions of this anti-American mood seem to have passed, both in their political and cultural forms. They may or may not recur. But what has remained is ultimately much more dangerous than riotous students with Vietcong flags—a quietly spreading belief that there is something intrinsically rotten about the American System and that its political ideals are a sham.

These days there is another kind of "of course statement"—about the intrinsic "sickness" and "oppressiveness" of the American System.

* * *

The same modern developments that have weakened the credibility of religion have also weakened the other value-generating institutions of society—family, local community, regional and ethnic culture, and even that peculiarly American institution, the voluntary association. Increasingly, the political state has confronted an amorphous, atomized mass of individuals.

The state has, in the end, only two basic options: It can rely on other institutions for the values required for political health; or it can try to generate such values itself. The second option is, in essence, the totalitarian one. It is profoundly offensive to the instincts of American democracy and pluralism. But if the first option is to be taken, there is a depressing scarcity of relevant institutions to look to. And the churches are, without much doubt, the most important.

* * *

What is more, recent trends have come perilously close to a new "establishment of religion"—to wit, the legal establishment of the quasi-religion of secularism. This would be a violation of the religious liberty of large numbers of Americans. Even more seriously, though, it would be an act of social suicide on the part of the American System.

Has the American System lost the capacity to survive? A negative answer is overwhelmingly plausible if one looks at the immense capacities of the American economy, the inventiveness of American science and technology, the resilience of the country's political institutions, and the human qualities of its population. All of these resources—material, human, and institutional—will not prevail, however, without a resurgence of the American spirit. This will require political and intellectual leadership of a sort that has been painfully lacking in recent years. It will also require a revitalization of those institutions that have always been the matrix of beliefs and values in the society. Among those institutions the churches occupy a central place.

In the foregoing considerations of social consequences and the following analysis of economic consequences, we do not imply that these groups are distinct and disparate, as there are interrelationships. The propaganda of sham high-mindedness creates envy among the unfortunate besides providing justification in the potential criminal. Likewise affluence increases the number of targets. Now, we shall proceed to enumerate some of the economic consequences of the nefarious dissemination of lies, distortions and sophistries about profits and income distribution engendering an adversary relationship that has no basis in facts and statistics:

STAGFLATION AND SLUMPFLATION: These were discussed before.

PROFITS: The erosion in real profits and profit margins is causing a shortage in plant capacity that not only limits output, causing shortages, but also limits job opportunities currently and in the future.

CAPITAL FORMATION: Profit erosion and the price inflation of capital equipment and especially of plant construction have a terrific impact in reducing the purchasing power of the profit dollar for job creating capital formation. The machinery and machine tool industries are more labor intensive than mass-produced durable goods, consequently wage rate increases in excess of productivity gains are of necessity fully passed on in price increases.

TECHNOLOGY: Inadequate profits and capital formation lead to limits on utilization of technological improvements and innovations. It is a pity that spokesmen for Marx's stagnators put shackles on Schumpeter's innovators.

PRODUCTIVITY—WORK ETHIC—LABOR ATTITUDES: Here we will repeat what was said in our chapter "Myths and Realities of Corporate Profits":

This myth of the 28% profit margin also has a deleterious effect on productivity. When Gallup pollsters asked a cross section of American adults last year, "Could you accomplish more each day if you tried?" One half said, "Yes." They did not accomplish more because 80% believed "companies benefit from increased productivity at the expense of workers". This attitude also arises from union encouragement in the adversary relationship to get "more and do less." After all, "more" was the perennial exhortation of Gompers.

Here also we will repeat the results of a query made by Yankelovich TO COLLEGE STUDENTS:

a. Hard work will always pay off:
Percentage Agreeing
1968   69%
1969   59%
1971   39%

Truly, this is an astounding decline. Why? Textbooks formerly extolled the dignity of labor and the joy of hard work. Today this approach to education is considered not only corn but also dangerous. All this arises because our educators are infected with or deliberately contribute to the misinformation about profits and income distribution. Thus they contribute to the false grounds for the justification of featherbedding and of "dogging it." This is in striking contrast to the youth educated in the "old-fashioned way." They did not dynamite or burn schools, disrupt lectures not conforming to their warped views, mug teachers in the halls and require remedial reading courses as college freshmen.

The tragic part of all the loss in the potential productivity gains is that it does most damage to the worker and the consumer. He is led to believe that he is screwing the company, but in the end result he is shortchanging himself and his own family as well as other workers and consumers.

GOVERNMENT INTERVENTION: The rhetoric and propaganda of the intelligentsia, abetted by educators, political charlatans, the media and labor leaders, have caused economic and political dislocations, blamed big business for them and have as a consequence concocted a host of government restraints. They have foisted on the public as well as business a huge government bureaucracy that is supposed to solve all problems and redress all inequities and inequalities. The worker is hoodwinked into believing that the rich corporations and individuals will pay costs of the bureaucracy, which once installed, has only one purpose—to perpetuate itself. The paper-shuffling bureaucracy, with a vested interest in increasing its activities in the interference on the private economy, is evermore shackling business in its endeavor to cut costs and create job opportunities. More and more they interfere with the market economy in the discharge of its function as the most effective allocator of resources to the betterment of the human race. The utopian visionaries should recognize that you cannot sweep under the rug mistakes made in a free market economy as well as you can in a collectivized economy.

This does not imply that all government regulation is bad and unnecessary. The market economy is not 100% infallible. In many areas, such as environmental protection, government restraints are necessary and would be salutary if pursued to attain reasonably sound scientific objectives, not hobbled by "instantitis." As Charles G. Burck writes in *Fortune*, issue of April, 1975, "The Intricate 'Politics' of the Corporation":

> . . . Markets do not set out to reward participants on the basis of "social justice," although in fact they often do produce a "leveling up" effect. (More than a quarter of U.S. black families have attained incomes above the national median.)

We will add that Americans have become the first massive middle class society under an economic system which operates well when left alone and which could do better with less government intervention and, where necessary, with government regulation operating in an atmosphere of optimal social redeemability and not shortsighted bureaucratic vindictive and counterproductive interference largely motivated by self-perpetuation.

In our judgment, it is sheer economic stupidity to underwrite or subsidize poorly managed or mismanaged private businesses. They should not be spared the penalties of bankruptcies. The free market system is a system of rewards and penalties. So be it. The rescue of failing, mismanaged businesses does not involve redeeming social values. The sustenance and transplantation of the subsequent unemployed, according to principles to be proposed in a forthcoming chapter, do contain such values. It is one of the admirable qualities of a free market economy to weed out high cost and inefficient operations, a quality sorely lacking in collectivized economies.

ECONOMIC GROWTH: The havoc inflicted by the irresponsible rhetoric takes a heavy toll in inhibiting economic growth. Thus, it impedes capital formation, the exploitation of technology and, most important of all, job creation in this country and in developing countries. In the next chapter, fuller consideration will be accorded economic growth, its necessity and feasibility.

The articles in *Fortune,* alluded to in the foregoing paragraphs, were well researched and admirably presented. However, it appears as if the editors were remiss in furnishing a summary of the activities of the adverse culture, the unwarranted propaganda, its origins, the consequences and especially for proposals for a counteroffensive. In our opinion the editors should have researched into the origins of the propaganda. They would have discovered that the basis rests on misconceptions about profits and income distribution. They would have discovered that the premises as well as conclusions of the radical and pseudo-liberal elitists are based on untenable myths, such as the following:

> The myth that profits are excessive and of such magnitude that you can finance throwing money at problems by taxing the rich corporations.
>
> The myth that corporations should be able to

absorb tax increases without passing them on to the consumer in the form of higher prices.

The myth that corporate profits cause inflation.

The myth that incomes of the rich, those making $50,000 a year or more, constitute such a large portion of total income that they can be taxed to finance social welfare programs.

The myth that the lower-middle income classes in the $10,000-$25,000 range and the upper-middle income classes in the $25,000-$50,000 range can escape the follies of the demagogic politician.

The myth that corporate profits are so excessive and of such magnitude that wage increases exceeding productivity gains can be absorbed by corporations without the necessity of increasing prices.

The myth that wage increases exceeding productivity gains do not cause inflation.

The myth that corporate "administered pricing" gouges the public in unnecessarily high prices and profits.

The myth of the Failure and Guilt Complexes that account for the alleged desire to atone for inequities and inequalities.

As George Orwell said, "You have to belong to the intelligentsia to believe things like that: no ordinary man could be such a fool." However, the sad fact is that too many have been bamboozled into believing the above-enumerated myths through repetition, repetition, repetition, etc., ad nauseam.

The motives of the leaders in the rhetoric against profits is hard to pinpoint. It could be envy, as Kristol opines. It could be sympathy for the underdog to such an extent that gullibility to the speciousness and blandishments of Marxism was a natural consequence. Whatever the reason, there is no excuse for failure to ask for substantiation of serious charges. If profits are excessive, by how much? What is the criterion for adjudging profits excessive and exploitative? There should be no condoning the creation of myths and illusory problems when real problems exist. It is flagrant stupidity to seek solutions for illusory problems and neglect real problems. An open mind is required to observe imperfections on both sides of the fence. It is not in the spirit of intellectual honesty to exaggerate imperfections of one system and gloss over the egregious faults of the other. Myth fabrication should not be condoned but should be labeled as a reprehensible act, wholly inconsistent with redeeming social values.

It is not difficult to pinpoint the motives of a union leader. He has a vested interest in the adversary relationship. It appears that he must forever yell, "MORE." Otherwise, it appears that the reason for his existence will be eroded. It also should be noted that internal union politics seem to indicate that he has no other choice, as there is always a militant just too eager to outpromise the leader. It behooves our best minds in economics, sociology and psychology to come forth with ideas for the retention of worthwhile union attributes while eliminating this cancer in our economic system.

To condone the demagoguery of the politician would be an act of rank social unredeemability. He is in a most enviable position to enlighten the economic illiterate. But what does he do? He stoops low abjectly and panders to their ignorance, envy and prejudices. He espouses proposals that look appealing in the short run to make himself look good, even if these irresponsible concoctions hurt the economy in the long run. Witness the advocacy of rolling back oil prices, of holding down utility rates and of labeling accelerated depreciation charges as "giveaways" to corporations.

The intelligentsia is an assortment of evil schemers, conscious conspirators and a host of gullible fellow travelers. Their sympathy for the unfortunate poor is to be commended, but their arousal of false unrealizable goals is to be condemned. It is difficult to fathom their need to concoct fabrications and myths. They may be misguided in their zeal to help the poor with visions of an utopian society in which human nature instantly will change to their liking. They fail to see that human nature has not changed in 800 generations through 50,000 years. Their own conduct of willful distortions, lies and myth creation is living proof that wishful thinking can blur the powers of reasoning. They fail to perceive that capitalism, like socialism, has its merits and demerits, but that the proclivities of human nature make capitalism imperfect and socialism unworkable. They consider their motives noble and sublime but they treat motives of the Establishment with suspicion and hence create the Failure and Guilt Complexes.

VIII

ECONOMIC GROWTH: ITS NECESSITY, DESIRABILITY AND FEASIBILITY

"A failure to maintain economic growth means continued poverty, deprivation, disease, squalor, degradation and slavery to soul-destroying toil for countless millions of the world's population," wrote Wilfred Beckerman in his preface to his cogent presentation for economic growth in his *Two Cheers for the Affluent Society*. This book is recommended for gaining insights and perspectives on such vital issues as economic growth, pollution and other related factors of significant concern in domestic and international areas.

Beckerman identifies "two basic anti-growth camps"—those who claim that "growth is impossible" (page 2). Before going on to give our listing of the necessity and desirability of economic growth and later an analysis of the feasibility, here we will interject some comments to correlate some of Beckerman's analysis and conclusions with some of the conclusions outlined in the foregoing chapters of this book. This has to do with propaganda.

In his second chapter beginning on page 24 and entitled "Passengers on the Anti-Growth Bandwagon (Including Some Who Have Been Hijacked)," Beckerman zeroes in on the propagandists and their fellow travelers. He writes that "it will be argued that much of the case against economic growth is based on major errors of logic, distortions or ignorance of the facts, and special pleadings of various kinds" (page 24). Here we will state that it is no mere coincidence that virtually the same group that distorts facts on profits and the free market system is in the forefront of those denigrating economic growth. In our judgment there is a suspicion that certain sham intellectuals of extreme radicalism are envious of the strides in growth made by capitalistic-oriented economies of the U.S., Germany and Japan as compared with the ineptness exhibited by socialist societies and, therefore, are attempting to throw monkey wrenches into the mechanisms of our societies.

Wattenberg's view of the media is buttressed with this opinion by Beckerman:

Catastrophe is always good news. The public as a whole likes to hear about the imminence of disaster and about the fact that they are living on the edge of a precipice. . . . Bad news has always been better for publicity than good news.

Some of the media of mass communication, therefore, exaggerate the magnitude of environmental problems or obstacles and objections to sustained economic growth.

It is our contention that economic growth is needed and desirable for the following reasons. It is needed to:

Provide jobs.
Control inflation.
Increase capital formation.
Enhance and exploit technology.
Finance alternate energy resources.
Redress pollution.
Decrease population growth.
Uplift economies of developing countries.

The above list does not purport to be complete and the sequence presented is only a rough approximation of priorities. The ideas listed above are not to be construed as existing in tight compartments as there no doubt is a measure of overlapping. Following is a brief treatment of each item but of sufficient magnitude consistent with the themes propounded in this book.

1. Jobs

Below is a table reconstructed by the author on the labor force (persons 16 years old and over) and participation rates, 1960 to 1973 and projections to 1990.

Table VIII-1

	Labor Force (Millions)	Participation Rates (Percent)
1960	72.1	59.2
1970	85.9	60.3
1971	86.9	60.0
1972	89.0	60.2
1973	91.0	60.5
1980	101.8	60.8
1985	107.7	61.3
1990	112.6	61.5

Source: U.S. Bureau of Labor Statistics, *Special Labor Force Reports*, as reported in *Statistical Abstract of the United States*, 1974, table 543, page 337.

Now if we adhere to the spurious exhortations of the economic growth stagnators and carefully observe the foregoing table, we must ask where are we going to find employment for over 20 million persons who will enter the labor force from now to 1990. The intelligentsia of liberalism and radicalism espouse movement so far removed from reality that it is incompatible with sober reality. Stop economic growth and embrace a collectivized, bureaucratically controlled economy and the millennium will arrive! What rubbish! What a tantalizing dish they attempt to serve us: a collectivized economy that reeks with inefficiency in the attempt to control the economy; a collectivized socialpolitical system that *is efficient* in controlling minds.

Pertinent to the above table and commentary was a news item in the *New York Times* of May 5, 1975:

> Observing that in recent years, the average cost of creating each new job in the United States has been estimated at more than $40,000, the President's economic adviser, L. William Seidman, said in Washington yesterday that over the next five years

Economic Growth

some $400-billion in new capital must be generated to accommodate an estimated 10 million persons who will be entering the work force in this period

Below is a table reconstructed by the writer from table 43, page 59, from the previously cited *Facts and Figures of the Tax Foundation*.

Table VIII-2
CAPITAL INVESTED PER WORKER
IN MANUFACTURING

1939	$ 5,188
1949	8,089
1959	17,528
1963	20,426
1970	37,079
1974	40,000 plus

Please observe that while the Consumer Price Index rose 180% from 1939 to 1970, capital required per worker increased 619%. More will be said later on various implications of foregoing figures; but here, it will suffice to conclude that a prodigious amount of capital will have to be generated via the profit route to ensure economic growth. Assuredly, the worker and would-be worker do not need the phony friendship of the elite who would screw them out of a job they need and will need for a fulfilling life.

2. INFLATION CONTROL

Economic growth is desirable and will be needed to enhance technology and increase its exploitation to assure constant improvement in productivity to at least maintain if not decrease costs of production. Economic growth, spurred on by the incentive for profit, will provide the profits required to avail ourselves of the technology so significant in cost reduction. What a lovely, benevolent circle! The epitome, the apotheosis of social redeemability!

3. Capital Formation

Capital formation is the process of saving and reinvestment of earnings that results in spending for capital goods, or goods used in the production of goods and services for the consumer. Hence, it is related to technology and job creation as well as other factors. Thus, it takes no stretch of the imagination to perceive its significance in economic growth.

4. Enhancement and Exploitation of Technology

Economic growth is of paramount importance relative to technology. Our technological base must be nurtured to grow at a constant and if possible at an increased rate. This will require huge funds which can come only from savings and profits. These funds cannot come from pie-in-the-sky and rainbow-chasing fantasies or from secret coffers of corporations presumably in existence as per theories of profiteering and price gouging concocted by specious special pleaders of sham liberalism and radicalism.

Economic growth is also advisable and logically inevitable to tap the technological base to improve productivity, to provide new jobs, to control inflation and so technology will breed more technology. Another salutary circle! The innovators of capitalism by far outperform the stagnators and standpatters of socialist bureaucracies.

5. Alternate Energy Resources

This is a special case of item 4. The interrelations and interreactions are numerous, but it should be stressed that it will require a substantial dose of ingenuity and funds from economic growth going into economic growth and into the exploitation of existing and as well as creation of new technology to develop new sources of energy. It is imperative to reduce our dependence on foreign oil and eliminate the threat of geopolitical blackmail.

6. Redressing Pollution

Economic growth causes pollution. However, the solution is not economic stagnation or even retrogression, as the eco-doomsayers and eco-dumbsters would have it. The ideal solution will be found in more economic growth to provide the funds and the technology to redress the pollution caused by economic activity. It is not hard to envision a salutary denouement in which industry may even be able to compensate for some of the pollution caused by nature itself. This can only be achieved in a milieu of government control within the context of reasonable and scientifically realizable objectives within a reasonable time schedule. The objectives of clean air and water can be achieved only through unhampered economic growth and not in an atmosphere of vindictiveness, demagogic pandering to prejudices and ignorance and economic stagnation or retrogression.

7. Decreasing Population Growth

It has to be recognized that for the destitute in developing and primitive societies a large number of children provides a form of old-age insurance, particularly where infant mortality rates are high. In all instances where infant mortality rates were reduced, as a result of economic growth and as a result of higher incomes accruing from economic growth, incentives to have large families were reduced.

8. Uplifting Economies of Developing Countries

There is no conflict between growth and the "quality of life" for developing countries. And yet, when multinational corporations invest in natural resource ventures in developing countries, provide jobs for local people and develop export markets, the intelligentsia unleash a propaganda against "capitalist imperialists" with charges of "exploitation." The sham premises and unwarranted conclusions of this spurious, elitist rhetoric were convincingly refuted by Wattenberg in the following presentation:

> The Claim: Because America is so affluent, because Americans are so numerous, because we need so many resources, we are exploiting other, poorer nations and we're using "more than our share" of the finite resources of "spaceship earth." (The common figure used is that Americans are only 6% of the world's people, but consume 30% of the world's resources.) This, it is stated, will cause animosity, war, tragedy and catastrophe.
> Rebuttal: Try flying that one in Bolivia. Tell the tin miners that America, in order not to "exploit" Bolivian nonrenewable natural resources and in order not to use "more than our share

Economic Growth

of resources, will cut tin imports by 90%. Of course, this will mean that Bolivia will lack the dollars to buy certain things American produces, like penicillin—but so be it. Tell a peasant in Zaire that America will cut copper imports by 90% in the years to come in order not to be economic imperialists. Of course, this will deny the government of Zaire the funds to build schools, hospitals and roads, but it will have a great redeeming feature: It will lighten the self-inflicted guilt load on the shoulders of some affluent environmentalists in America who slept through their college courses in economics.

In fact, the complaint that "we're using more than our fair share" can be described, more accurately, in fewer words: "international trade." America imports tin, and oil, and cocoa, and copper, and rubber, and bauxite and transistor radios assembled in Taiwan. With the monies received from such items, foreign nations buy penicillin from us, and computers, and airplanes and X-ray machines and wheat and also pay for an agricultural geneticist who can help double rice production. The nations that sell resources to America, in short, get a marvelous commodity in return. It is called "money" and with it they can buy all sorts of wonderful things that have, in the last three decades, revolutionized the underdeveloped world so that health, education, life expectancy and communications standards, to name just a few, are at a level that—while low by American standards—are unprecedented in their own national histories.

America's "use" of resources does not "rob" anyone. The proper analogy might be with the nuclear breeder reactor, which creates more energy than it uses. Tin ores in the Andes are just rocks—unless someone wants to buy them. Once someone buys them, those rocks turn into penicillin, schools and food. That is a healthy process—not an imperialist, unfair or necessarily exploitative one. (Pages 179-180)

In essence, underdeveloped countries need dollars to buy industrial and pharmacological products more than they need to leave their raw materials in the ground. They can obtain the wherewithal only through trade. Let us not forget the important role played by multinational corporations in this process. They have been rightly called the transmission belts of progress (A. James Reichley, *Fortune*, April, 1975). However, it behooves us to monitor their abuses without impinging on their effectiveness in their vital function. A slowdown in American growth and the activities of multinational enterprises would simply mean reduced American demand for most of the products of the world's poorer nations. Nothing would do more harm to their exports than a prolonged stagnation in the industrialized countries of the world.

In the foregoing consideration of eight items relating to economic growth, by no means exhaustive or all-inclusive, one obvious fundamental factor should become apparent. Quite simply, growth is essential to reduce poverty in America, the industrialized nations and, especially, the developing countries.

In the foregoing paragraphs of this book, it has been proven conclusively that all propagandist charges against the necessity and desirability of economic growth are untenable and that they were based on illogical extensions, misrepresentation of facts and sheer ignorance. Next, follows an analysis of the second claim, that economic growth is impossible because resources are limited. It is the objective of the rest of this chapter to prove that the natural-limit theory of growth is unadulterated intelligentsist buncombe. This theory is the basis of elaborate computer simulations by the Club of Rome, which feeds the computer erroneous assumptions and the computer dutifully spits out egregiously false conclusions. In terms of a cliché of recent vintage—hackneyed but significantly true—"Garbage in—garbage out." Erroneously endowed with the mantle of scientific methodism, the computer mistakenly predicts economic collapse within a few generations. The computer's unquestioned readouts impress the scientific and economic illiterates. Witness this exemplary bit of econonsense in the words of Anthony Lewis of the *New York Times*: "Growth is self-defeating. . . . the planet cannot long sustain it. . . . To ignore that tendency, to predict that growth can go on forever, is like arguing that the earth is flat. Only the consequences are more serious."

This a perfect example of an eco-dumbster's claptrap. The diametric position is true. The consequences of no-growth would wreak incalculable harm. The fallacies underlying the reasoning of eco-doomsayers and eco-dumbsters are the assumptions that raw materials will always be used in the future as they are today, that technology will be as sterile as their minds and that an economic phenomenon known as elasticity of supply does not exist.

Supply is considered as elastic when an increase in price creates an increase in supply. The expansion may not be immediate; thus, it is temporarily inelastic. But, eventually, it becomes elastic, with a time-lag of several to as much as five and ten years. There is an immediate technological response in this phenomenon of elasticity of supply that has been grossly underestimated and unappreciated. The technology of substituting plentiful materials for scarce ones grows every day.

To this effect, the London *Economist* made these pertinent comments in the January 4, 1975 issue:

> When the world price of most raw materials soared to absurd heights during the Korean war in 1951, America's Paley report and other pundits forecast that raw materials would for the rest of our lives be very scarce and expensive. Instead, for the next

two decades they were relatively cheap and in glut. The high prices of 1951 stimulated almost immediate oversupply and also overdue economising and substitutions in raw material use. The terms of trade for primary producers (i.e., export prices divided by import prices) did not return to 1951 levels until 1972.

Towards the end of those 21 years, the relatively depressed prices were naturally beginning to stimulate undersupply and extravagant use of materials. The question became whether material prices would correct this by rising steadily through the 1970s, or whether there would be another Korean-type crunch year of suddenly far too high prices which would be likely to lead through overinvestment and oversubstitution back very soon into glut.

This last, surely, is what has happened. In the two years to March, 1974, energy and raw material prices went far above production costs even from new sources. As in 1951 there has now been a worldwide rush towards overinvestment and oversubstitution. It is a fair bet that the terms of trade for energy and raw material producers will be below first quarter of 1974 levels through most of the period 1975-95.

The history of this century is quite largely a history of men's astonishing mental deficiency in always underestimating the elasticity of supply. Japan itself went to war in 1941 because it thought that it could not prosper without physical possession of what it imagined was always going to be scarce oil. To this end it had built up by Pearl Harbor Day a supposedly massive military stockpile of 19m barrels, and launched itself against the civilised world because it believed its own fears that it would never again be able to get so much oil unless it could become the dominating power over Indonesia and Burma. Thirty years later, having lost the war, and with rather bad relations with Indonesia and no oil from Burma, Japan was buying on the free market that amount of oil every three days.

Our present underestimates of the elasticity of supply of energy, although probably on something like the same apocalyptic scale, is presumably not going to send armies marching across the world, unless America invades Saudi Arabia or something. But most industrial countries are committing huge resources to building congenitally limbless ducks (digging new conventional coal mines in the area dominated by the Yorkshire branch of the coalminers' union, drilling oil beneath storm-tossed seas) which will come out quacking as a defence against permanent sellers' markets just at a time when the appearance of buyers' markets is much more likely. Meanwhile Japan is, mostly by accident, spending equally large sums putting itself into a posture where it may dominate through two critical decades that much more probable buyers' market for all other mined materials as well as imported energy.

Economics of Gluts

There is a long lesson from history and very elementary economics why oversupply and advantage to the buyer are especially likely in energy. Ever since the 1770s energy has been in most elastic supply, because technology is always on the verge of bringing new ways of releasing energy from matter in less labor-intensive and more transportable ways than the way which is in fashion as the cheapest and most easily transportable now (coal through most of the British century of 1775-1875, oil through most of the American century of 1875-1975, obviously some newer form through most of the Pacific century of 1975-2075).

It is difficult to account for the schizoid approach of the eco-doomsters and the intelligentsia toward the potential of the computer. They feed rubbish into the computers and become apoplectic about the unscientifically ominous projections. On the other hand, they fail to appreciate the potential of the explosive growth in the information-processing industry. It may be that their prejudices and wishful thinking, colored by dogmata of Marxism and phony liberalism, do not allow them to differentiate between limits to exponential growth in use of resources and the unlimited exponential growth in knowledge and technology. John Diebold, President of Diebold Group, Inc., international management consultants, and expert on automation, presented this bit of insight in an article in the *New York Times* on June 25, 1972:

> Scientific knowledge is now increasing at an annual rate that must be something like 4 to 5 percent, too. If this goes on, by the time today's baby dies 80 years hence, about 97 percent of the scientific knowledge then existing will be knowledge that nobody today has thought of.
>
> The pace of advance of scientific knowledge is surely likely to quicken. Because of computers, the efficiency with which we can make mathematical calculations has already increased by a factor of more than 10,000 in the past decade and a half. We have not yet begun to realize the revolutionary powers that this is putting into our hands and minds.

The factors of raw materials and food were treated brilliantly in an article in the London *Economist* of June 29, 1974. Excerpts follow:

A Little More Time

> Even if there are no improvements in existing technology the world is not likely to be threatened with a physical shortage of raw materials until about A.D. 100,000,000.

A Prolific Mile

> The prophets have assumed four limiting factors on the world's economic growth, in ascending order of respectability: they say the world will run out of raw materials, will suffer ever-increasing pollution, will have too large a population, and too little food.
>
> On raw materials, the Club of Rome reached its equations by assuming that actual reserves of any material cannot be more than two to five times "known reserves," with nil elasticity of supply and substitution after that. It then asked the computer what would happen if demand for precisely these things went

on expanding exponentially. The computer replied, naturally, that everything would then break down.

This mode of argument could always have proved that world production of most things stopped long ago, because "known reserves" of most materials all through history have been only a few decades' worth of demand.

The world's food problem has nothing to do with physical limits on food production. Even if there were no new discoveries in food-growing technology from now on, and we continued to cultivate only the very small proportion of the earth's surface now used as farmland, a raising of all other countries' efficiency of cultivation to that of the Netherlands would already suffice to feed 60 billion people (today's world population is 3.7 billion). Those who say that more intensive cultivation always ruins the soil should note that the land in Holland has been farmed with increasing intensity for 2,000 years.

If the rate of growth of rice yields in India and Pakistan in 1965-71 were continued for a century, all of mankind would indeed die, because the surface of the earth would be covered with rice to a depth of three feet. But this should not obscure the world's two real agricultural problems. First, about 60 percent of the world's workers still labor on farms; with modern techniques, every country will soon be able to feed itself with under 10 percent of its workers there; this rather imminent threat of technological unemployment for half the world's workers is a major turning point in history. Secondly, the flock away from agriculture to the towns will be handled least well in the poorest countries, from which the biggest flight from the land is still to come.

Crusades That Are Needed

The middle classes who interpreted environmentalism to mean that other people should not disturb their peace and solitude, radical youth eager to condemn materialism, the newspapers and clergymen and academics who told what some must eventually have known to be untruths because this inflated their importance, the alarmingly intemperate scientists. Yet there was a real passion for doing good among very many of those who interested themselves in these issues. Those who prefer to stick to facts rather than fancies should consider why they fail to attract this potential force for doing good to the crusades that are needed—such as the devising and financing of performance contracts for all who will bring re-employment opportunities, modern urban management systems, and nutrition programmes (of which transport, not cultivation, will be the key) to the world's growing urban poor. Such things, however, need action, not just nice spine-chilling calls for inaction.

What does economic growth and technology hold for the future? For answers we again turn to the London *Economist*. In an article in the January 4, 1975 issue we get this look-see into the future. Significant excerpts follow:

The New Quarter-Century

At the end of this quarter-century of unexampled improvement, and at the gate of the last quarter-century of the second Christian millennium, conventional opinion is again feeling very gloomy indeed. On past form, this suggests that 1975-2000 should instead be a period of great advance. Technological commonsense suggests the same thing. In the next two-and-a-half decades the computer, telecommunication and automation revolutions will come of productive age. The spin-offs are fairly predictable. They make it overwhelmingly likely that we should be able to enjoy at least another trebling of real gross world product in 1975-2000, provided we again increase world money supply and again permit a sufficiently intelligent free market system in at least some countries to keep bringing that new knowledge into productive effect. Our small economic problem at the gate of the new quarter-century is that the management of world money supply and the operation of market mechanisms have been temporarily disrupted, because one commodity, crude oil, whose sales until 1973 accounted for about ½ percent of gross world product, has been quintupled in price, to a price incidentally 10 times its marginal cost: this has shifted 1½-2 percent of gross world product out of people's spending power into sheikhs' and shahs' savings which they hold in very liquid form.

It seems improbable that we will not solve this 1½-2 percent of a problem eventually, by the automatic operation of the high elasticity of substitution for overexpensive oil if by nothing else. If that can be achieved, mankind should turn its unexampled intelligence to curing the acute problems of food shortage, people surplus and resource profligacy, all of which it has rather stupidly ignored in recent years.

Prosperity will not increase evenly, now that knowledge, which is transferable between nations, moves fastest to those countries which have the most innovation-oriented business system.

The Cost of Going Slightly Wrong

In the 1920s and 1930s, inflation and then depression so poisoned tribal instincts in Germany that civilised men sang hymns to a mass murderer who was self-evidently mad. In the 1950s and 1960s a continuing capitalist boom so addled some rich intellectuals' tribal instincts that they now regard it as progressive to call for zero economic growth, although this would mean that infant mortality rates in poor countries would not then once again fall by two-thirds in the next 25 years. In the fourth quarter of this century, we face the probability of the present fairly bad inflation giving way to fairly bad world depression followed by opportunities for faster economic growth than ever. The main dangers of the new quarter-century will lie in the erratic and emotional folly which can be a deadly characteristic in educated tribes when rather easy economic problems are handled slightly wrong.

Our eco-doomsters and eco-dumbsters and our radical and sham liberal highbrows are as prescient relative to economics and technology as the three characters mentioned in the following three anecdotes:

The first Commissioner of Patents, Henry L. Ellsworth, states in his annual report for 1843, while commenting on important inventions which have been made, that "the advancements of the arts, from year to year, taxes our credulity and seems to presage the arrival of that period when human improvement must end." This rhetorical flourish is probably the origin of the unfounded story of the Patent Office official who resigned because everything had been invented.

(*The Story of the United States Patent Office*, Pharmaceutical Manufacturers Association and U.S. Department of Commerce, 1965, page 9)

210. Before the turn of the century, a bishop, paying his annual visit to a small religious college, was discussing the state of the world while a guest at the home of one of the professors. He ventured the opinion that because everything about nature had been discovered and inasmuch as all possible inventions had been made, the world was on the verge of the millennium. The professor disagreed. He said the next fifty years would produce many discoveries. "Many!" cried the bishop. "Name one." The professor replied that in the next few years man would be able to fly like the birds. "Nonsense," exclaimed the bishop. "Flight is reserved for the angels."

The bishop's name was WRIGHT—he had two sons, Orville and Wilbur.

211. One afternoon Mark Twain, who lost more than one hard-earned fortune by investing it in harebrained schemes described to him in glittering terms, observed a tall, spare man with kindly blue eyes and eager face, coming up the path with a strange contraption under his arm. Yes, it was an invention, and the man explained it to the humorist, who listened politely but said he had been burned too often.

"But I'm not asking you to invest a fortune," explained the man. "You can have as large a share as you want for $500." Mark Twain shook his head; the invention didn't make sense. The tall, stooped figure started away.

"What did you say your name was?" the author called after him. "Bell," replied the inventor a little sadly, "Alexander Graham Bell."

—Vansant Coryell

(From *The Complete Speaker's and Toastmaster's Library Human Interest Stories*, Prentice-Hall, 1965)

Paraphrasing Ralph Waldo Emerson's well-known dictum that "invention breeds invention," we can say that knowledge breeds more knowledge. Here, we are not speaking of the highbrow knowledge of elitists and anti-bourgeois propagandists who stand in the way of exploiting our knowledge and technology for the betterment of mankind. All we need is to unleash private business, the most effective resource allocator ever invented by man, to tap and to add to this huge reservoir of knowledge and technology. The potential of the information banks boggles the mind as they furnish the means for most effective utilization of scientific and technological knowledge. They will reduce unnecessary duplication and transfer research time of our scientists and technologists to more significant and rewarding tasks. Through a judicious application of spending, taxation and competitive policies, governments should unshackle the innovators so that they can operate in an environment where demand and costs approximate as nearly as possible social demand and costs, where companies are rewarded by profits and growth when they make a profit under these conditions, and where companies are rightly toppled if they fail to make a profit in these conditions. A prime example of social redeemability. Attacks on size attained through redeemable social values should not be condoned.

The main arguments of this chapter have been directed to disprove the myths of the ecological lunatic fringe that growth is deleterious and that growth is impossible. We have presented conclusive evidence that growth is necessary and feasible. We should divert our attention from the counterproductive and sterile arguments of growth versus no growth to creation and sustenance of stable growth. After all, even allowing for inflation, the average income of the bottom tenth of the population has increased about 60% since 1950. Twenty more years of growth could do more to increase that income than all the palaver of politicians and bureaucratic attempts at redistribution.

Reconstructing the concluding sentence of the *Economist* article on "The New Quarter Century," we can say that we should avoid and/or counteract the main dangers of that new quarter century that lie in the erratic and emotional folly which can be a deadly characteristic when rather easy economic problems are handled slightly wrong.

Here we can single out the emotional folly that attends profits and their impact on capital formation and the exploitation of technology. In order to show that they are doing something, politicians vote for government spending to solve problems—some real and some just fabrications—by throwing money at them. Also, in order to show that they are doing something against big business and the rich, they soak the rich corporations with high tax rates and impose unrealistic depreciation guidelines. While posturing as benefactors, they actually inflict economic damage on the lowest income segments of the population because they inhibit the job creation function that resides in profits as they are recycled into capital expenditures that exploit the newest technology. The scientific aspects of the newest technology are wondrous to behold but let us not forget the significant economic aspects—job creation and cost reductions.

The folly of politicians is causing tragic economic consequences because in effect they deny or stupidly overlook the fact that long-term growth depends upon investment. The rate and importance of investment in long-term growth were perceptively outlined by the London *Economist* in its issue of July 26, 1975, in its commentary on "A World of Slow Growth." The editors opined that "economic growth over the next 10 years will be slower than the world is accustomed to unless politicians dare sharply to increase the rewards for risk taking."

Other excerpts from the article follow:

> Long-term growth depends upon investment. It can never be consumer-led or social-service-expenditure-led. A temporary boost to output and demand can be obtained from higher budget deficits. But the effect of this quickly wears off unless (a) the dose is repeated; or (b) investment responds to temporarily higher consumer spending, taking over the work of creating extra demand (and the capacity in the longer term to meet it).

It is economic folly not to be able to differentiate between the effects of government deficit spending and private investment spending on economic growth and inflation. Higher budget deficits give a temporary boost to output and demand, while private investment spending out of profits is permanent. Deficit spending to be effective over a longer period must be repeated, but this results in losing control over the money supply, leading to inflation. No such problems arise from private investments, as these increase the supply of goods to match the rise in incomes. It behooves all of us to think in terms of allocating less to the bureaucrat and more to the businessman. A rise in profits through tax reduction would result in a greater and steadier rate of growth. The resultant profits would still be small in relation to the GNP, but they sure would have a big impact on economic growth, with the lowest-bracket income earners becoming the biggest beneficieries.

Before concluding this chapter on economic growth, it is necessary to clear up some loose and fuzzy thinking about capital formation.

One such instance was provided in an editorial, "More Capital Formation," in the *New York Times* on July 31, 1975. According to the *Times*, there is not a shortage of capital but a surfeit. This, says the *Times*, is due to the fact that the economy has scarcely begun to recover from its slump. American industry is therefore "operating far below capacity and does not need to expand its plant in order to increase production." The *Times* cites figures showing that the rate of operation of all durable goods industries is 64.5 percent of capacity, while a year earlier this rate was 82.5 percent.

The usually discerning *Wall Street Journal* contributed this booboo in an editorial, "The House Tax Cut," on March 5, 1975:

> Nor do we understand why a Republican administration, a Democratic Congress, business and labor—and especially labor —believe that an increase in the investment tax credit to 10% from 7% will do this economy any good. It's clear why liberals go along with it: Because President Kennedy first proposed it as an alternative to a single cut in the corporate tax rate, the ITC is an acceptable bone to throw to business. But there's never been any evidence that it acts as a positive stimulus to production; it's merely a subsidy to capital accumulation.
>
> The AFL-CIO should be aghast at the implications of a further hike in the investment tax credit; instead, it is actually supporting the idea. Here we have an economy with more than 8% of the work force unemployed, a figure that no doubt will

rise, and unemployed fixed capital probably in the range of 20%, and everyone thinks it would be dandy to give business an incentive to buy new machines instead of using old machines and unemployed workers.

Both editorials miss the essential point of capital formation. Capital formation is as important in plant and equipment replacement and renovation as in plant expansion. New technology is always available waiting to be exploited. What matters most is the availability of funds and confidence. Once the fear of operating at even a lower rate of capacity is overcome, the process engineer is ready to see his controller and manager and propose spending money on new technology to reduce costs to compensate for the take of the bureaucrat and the union worker who demanded and exacted a wage increase in excess of productivity gains.

Here it would be appropriate to analyze just what the productivity gains are that every one talks about but doesn't seem to know what they really are. Productivity gains are advances made by the application of new technology, new processes and new materials. This means expenditures of time and money. Current expenses cover only a small portion. Thus, the bulk of the funds must come from retained profits and depreciation allowances. Here is where inflation hurts not only the corporation, but the worker or would-be worker even more. When depreciation reserves are figured in terms of costs without regard to inflation, they are inadequate and interfere with the cost reduction function of the process engineer and with the most admirable function of job creation.

We alluded to the *Wall Street Journal* editorial of March

5, 1975, in which we found to our surprise some sloppy economics. However, the editors regained their bearings on April 8, 1975, when they wrote more cogently with their usual acuity the following editorial which is presented in full:

Cutting Corporate Taxes

If Congress were to vote on a reduction in the corporate tax rate to 40% from the current 48% there's not much doubt the proposal would be resoundingly defeated. But if the vote were by secret ballot, we suspect such a bill would be approved, even by a comfortable margin. Our belief is that a majority in Congress understands that much of the weakness in the U.S. economy is due to the heavy tax on capital, magnified by inflation, and that the most direct way to stimulate expansion, employment and tax revenues would come through a reduction in the corporate tax rate.

But Congress does not vote in secret, and members of Congress do not usually stray very far from their perception of "political practicality." Democrats who might vote for such a tax cut in secret have to worry about being characterized as captives of big business, thence unseated by more liberal Democrats; Republicans have the same problem, worrying about more liberal Republicans and all Democrats. So Congress labored for more than two months on a tax bill to charge the crumbling economy without even considering a reduction in the corporate tax rate.

Why this sorry condition? Is President Ford to blame for doing so little to sell the public on the economic benefits of such a tax cut? Are the liberal Democrats to blame for acting like liberal Democrats? Is the press corps to be accused of contributing to an atmosphere of hostility toward business, thereby making it politically impractical for politicians to vote their convictions? Is the problem more basic, in that perhaps the schools have not been selling the role of the corporation in a free economy?

While these are generally the excuses offered up by the business and financial community, the truth is American businessmen have done a pitiful job in making the arguments for a cut in the tax on capital. Indeed, they've done no job at all. The deeply rooted assumption is that to call for a cut in corporate taxes is a waste of breath, so why bother?

Instead, businessmen will try the back door of tax relief. They will lobby furiously for handouts from Washington, knowing Congress rather likes dealing in special-interest legislation that involves giving away money that doesn't belong to it in the first place. They'll push for gimmicks, like the tax-loss carryback, which even liberals can support in the certain knowledge that their constituents don't understand what it means. Or they'll go for a hike in the investment tax credit, which the liberals regard as their very own bone for busines, which can be thrown out and recovered on a short string.

If the business community is not going to make the case for corporate tax reduction, who will? We have even heard an economist for organized labor say privately he'd prefer cutting the corporate tax rate to the assorted gimmicks lately considered, but why should labor make the case for something the National Association of Manufacturers only mentions in perfunctory fashion? Can you imagine the shop steward at the blackboard, the rank-and-file gathered 'round, while the boss peers through the window hopefully?

Most Americans who are working still work for corporations. Why is it that they were not being advised that the swiftest, neatest way to move the economy back toward full employment is to reduce the government bite out of corporate profits? It should not take much to persuade the most educated work force in the world that it would suddenly be more profitable to do business in the United States, that instead of sending out capital, the U.S. would be attracting it. And competition would prevent corporations from retaining higher nominal profits to somehow spend on wine, women and song; prices would fall relative to what they would otherwise be, and thus real wages would rise.

As it is, inflation has been magnifying all three of the taxes on capital. Dividends paid with cheap dollars push recipients up the progressive tax ladder. Capital gains taxes must be paid even though the gain is only nominal, the result of inflation. And the government doesn't absolve companies from paying taxes on illusory inventory profits. The real culprit, of course, is inflation, but that inflation is throttling the economy through its tax effects on investment and production.

U.S. economists of the left, right and center may have their differences on how genuinely competitive American corporations are or on the distribution of incomes between rich and poor. But not many of them seem prepared to argue that there is a more effective way to spur output and employment than through a reduction in corporate taxes. Why isn't anyone saying so? The silence from the corporate community for some reason has us recalling Casey Stengel's comment about his New York Mets: "Can't anybody here play this game?"

It is one of the main tenets of this book that profits are the most effective spur to output and employment. Tax cuts to corporations would be of immediate benefit in increasing profits. What the *Journal* overlooked is that the propaganda and rhetoric have made it impossible to vote these cuts because the distortions about profits have left the people with the impression that big business gouges the public by ripping-off the consumer with profit margins of 33¢ on the sales dollar. It should be mandatory for businessmen and the media to present the true facts that business normally gets about 4 to 5% on the dollar on average. It would be fitting for all businessmen to insist that all press releases and reports to stockholders should mention the profit margin in the very first paragraph if not in the very first sentence. The *Journal* could make a most salutary and meaningful gesture by insisting that all corporate reports conform to this principle before their profit reports are inserted in the columns of the *Journal*. The Dow-Jones news ticker service should insist on the same criterion.

If this practice won't start with the businessman, the *Wall Street Journal* and Dow-Jones, where will it?

In the next chapter, we will consider the distribution of income and an applicable social philosophy.

# IX

THE DISTRIBUTION OF INCOME AND A SOCIAL PHILOSOPHY THEREOF

"The rich are getting richer and the poor are getting poorer." So goes the claim of anti-business propaganda. Rubbish! Another myth conjured up by irresponsible rhetoric of radicalism and intellectually dishonest liberals.

It is the objective of this chapter to refute the above claim. We will consider various aspects of income distribution and income inequality, the alleged inequities in income distribution as well as a social philosophy that is applicable. We will demonstrate that the poor are gaining in absolute income, in their relative share and that their numbers are decreasing.

At the outset, we wish to stress that aggregates at times conceal more than they reveal. We call your attention to the following commentary and table by Wattenberg in his previously cited fine book *The Real America* (page 63):

> The poor, then, are becoming fewer and somewhat better off when measured against the absolute standard of the poverty line. But what about the relative standing in the society? The claim has been made, after all, that "the rich are getting richer and the poor are getting poorer." This is an argument about how the pie is split, not about the size of the slices, about income distribution and not necessarily poverty as such.
>
> Is there statistical validity to back up the claims that we have today a less-fair America, a system in which the poor have even less of a break than they did twenty years ago?
>
> No, not according to most recent Census numbers. The numbers, in fact, show that a modest amount of favorable redistribution of income has taken place to the poorest and away from the very richest Americans. As the table shows, the "lowest fifth" of the income distribution was the only one to make even a minimal gain. And only the "top 5%" showed a substantial decline.

Table IX-1 (Table No. Added)
PERCENTAGE SHARE OF INCOME RECEIVED
BY EACH FIFTH OF FAMILIES

	1960	1970	Change
Lowest fifth	4.9%	5.5%	+ .6%
Second fifth	12.0%	12.0%	
Third fifth	17.6%	17.4%	− .2%
Fourth fifth	23.6%	23.5%	− .1%
Highest fifth	42.0%	41.6%	− .4%
Top 5 percent	16.8%	14.4%	−2.2%

Bravo! Here, we have statistically historical proof that the poor are not getting poorer. This is not an isolated case. An analysis of Census Bureau and Internal Revenue Service

The Distribution of Income

statistics show that this has been an ongoing process for decades. The above tabulation indicates what has occurred in the relative shares. However, it would be interesting to find out what is happening in the absolute numbers. In other words, the above data indicate about how the pie is split and now our attention is to be focused on the size of the slices.

In a tabulation from the U.S. Bureau of the Census, *Current Population Reports,* Series P-60, No. 97, "Money Income in 1973 of Families and Persons in U. S." (United States Government Printing Office, Washington, D.C., 1975), Table 22 showed income at selected positions and percentage share of aggregate income in 1947 to 1973.

Close observation of the table on the upper limit of each fifth reveals many significant features. We cannot look with complacency on the great disparity between the whites, blacks and other races. The eco-doomsters should go among the less privileged and preach to them the panacea of no-growth that will lead them to utopia. However, let us not overlook that the percentage increases for blacks are increasing faster as their absolute income rise in magnitude. In considering the upper limit of the lowest fifth, we find the Negro category increasing 362% from 1947 to 1973 as compared with 279% for the white group.

Bearing in mind the upper limit of each fifth as shown in "Population Report Table 22" at roughly $6,000; $10,000; $14,000; $19,000; and, $30,000, and observing Table 9 in the same report, the shift in the number of families from the lower income groupings toward the higher is significant. In other words, the poorest of the poor made the most striking advances.

Let us cumulate the bottom line for 1947 and progress from the lowest to the highest group and do likewise for the top line of 1973.

Table IX-2
CUMULATIONS IN INCOME GROUPS

	1947		1973	
Under $1,000	17.6		2.7	
1,000- 1,499	8.7	26.3	2.1	4.8
1,500- 1,999	9.1	35.4	2.8	7.6
2,000- 2,499	11.0	46.4	3.4	11.0
2,500- 2,999	9.9	56.3	3.1	14.1
3,000- 3,499	10.0	66.3	3.0	17.1
3,500- 3,999	7.3	73.6	2.7	19.8
4,000- 4,999	10.0	83.6	5.7	25.5
5,000- 5,999	6.5	90.1	5.2	30.7
6,000- 6,999	3.4	93.5	5.0	35.7
7,000- 7,999			5.0	40.7
8,000- 9,999	4.1	97.6	9.6	50.3
10,000-14,999			21.8	72.1
15,000-24,999	2.4	100.0	20.7	92.8
Over 25,000			7.2	100.0

A close scrutiny of the above cumulation will show that, in 1947, the greatest concentration was in the group of $3,500 and under, as 66.3% were in that classification, compared with only 17.1% by 1973. It should be borne in mind that the tables cited are in current dollars so that there is an inflationary bias. Nevertheless, allowing for inflation, considerable progress has been made. Also, please note that despite the inflationary bias, only 7.2% of the families were in the $25,000 and over segment. That the above detailed data were not distorted by inflation is indicated in a more compact tabulation by the Tax Foundation given in constant dollars, adjusted for inflation, and shown below:

Table IX-3
MEDIAN FAMILY MONEY INCOME AND DISTRIBUTION OF FAMILIES BY INCOME CLASS IN 1973 DOLLARS[a]

Selected Calendar Years 1947-1973

Total Money Income (1973 dollars)	1947	1950	1960	1965	1970	1973
Median money income	$6,032	$6,146	$8,436	$9,792	$11,277	$12,051
	Percentage Distribution					
Total	100.0	100.0	100.0	100.0	100.0	100.0
Under $3,000	18.6	19.5	13.0	9.8	7.2	6.0
$3,000 to $4,999	20.3	17.8	11.9	10.6	8.8	8.6
$5,000 to $6,999	22.1	22.1	13.6	11.0	9.8	9.4
$7,000 to $9,999	19.9	21.1	23.6	20.1	16.8	14.9
$10,000 to $14,999	19.1	19.4	23.7	27.3	27.6	25.5
$15,000 and over			14.4	21.4	30.0	35.5

[a] A "family" is defined as a group of two or more persons related by blood, marriage, or adoption, residing together.
Source: Department of Commerce, Bureau of the Census. Numbers of families by income class calculated by Tax Foundation.

Let us first cumulate the 1947 and 1973 data from the lowest to the highest brackets

Table IX-4 (Cumulation from Table IX-3)

	1947		1973	
Under $3,000	18.6	3	6.0	
$ 3,001 to $ 5,000	20.3	38.9	8.6	14.6
$ 5,001 to $ 7,000	22.1	61.0	9.4	24.0
$ 7,001 to $10,000	19.9	80.9	14.9	38.9
$10,001 to $15,000			25.5	64.4
	19.1	100.0		
Over $15,000			35.5	100.0

Let us now perform a reverse cumulation from the highest to the lowest classifications

Table IX-5 (Inverse Cumulation from Table IX-3)

	1947		1973	
$15,000 and over	19.1		35.5	
$10,000 to $14,999			25.5	61.0
$ 7,000 to $ 9,999	19.9	39.0	14.9	75.9
$ 5,000 to $ 6,999	22.1	61.1	9.4	85.3
$ 3,000 to $ 4,999	20.3	81.4	8.6	93.9
$ 1,000 to $ 2,999	18.6	100.0	6.0	100.0

An analysis of both above tables indicates that, in 1947, 61% of the families were in the $7,000 and under group, while, in 1973, 61% were in the $10,000 and over group.

Here we have in all the foregoing cited facts and figures, the incontrovertible evidence that the numbers of the poor are declining, that their incomes in absolute numbers as well as in relative shares are increasing. They are getting a bigger slice of a bigger pie. This refutes the myth of the "trickle-down theory." In essence, we have attained middle class status for the great majority. It is also of paramount importance to note that the majority middle class was increasing at a steady pace. A strong case can be made for the assertion that instead of allowing money to trickle down from the rich and the middle classes, these much maligned economic groups are pulling the less fortunate to a higher income group. In effect, there is a leveling up as more and more of blacks, Chicanos, and less fortunate are given a chance to attain middle class status.

It is strange that such success should be spelled f-a-i-l-u-r-e by the intelligentsist visionaries as they attempt to fabricate and pin failure and guilt complexes on innovators and producers. HOGWASH! As the less fortunate arrive at the gates of middle classdom, their self-styled friends slam the gates in their faces and proclaim, "No Growth—Zero Production Growth." Again, we ask, "Who is screwing whom?"

Having refuted the myth that the "rich are getting richer and the poor are getting poorer," we turn our attention to clearing up some misconceptions about numbers of the rich and their taxable base as well as a corollary myth of income distribution feasibility. Career reformers and income redistributionists perpetrate a cruel hoax on the working man, the consumer and the destitute when they hoodwink them into believing that the big uncle in Washington can soak the rich to pay for the outrageous growth in government expenditures. They don't tell their victims that the victims also pay a big price in higher taxes and in the hidden taxes of inflation.

To get a clear picture of the rich, their numbers and

magnitudes of their incomes and taxes, we delved into Table 1.1 of the U.S. Internal Revenue Service, Statistics of Income, *Individual Income Tax Returns,* 1972.

Let us first consider the millionaire. We find that, in 1972, there were 1,030 receiving gross income in excess of $1,000,000. They were less than one-half of one percent of the total returns. 1,024 returns were taxable. Evidently only six were not taxable. The adjusted gross income of this group was $2.29 billion. This group paid just over $1 billion in taxes, paying an effective rate of 45.7%. It is evident that not much can be generated here in distributional income through confiscation.

About 600,000 returns were made by those earning $50,000 or more. This group comprised 7.4% of all returns and generated incomes totaling $53 billion. This segment paid about $16.5 billion in taxes, leaving about $37 billion for confiscation for distribution or financing wild spending sprees.

Here we have ample substantiation for our contention that there is no great class of "rich bitches" and "capitalist bastards" and that their income does not aggregate a total that would be able to finance goodies from Uncle Sam without the necessity of tapping the working and middle classes. Here we have evidence that the career reformers actually screw the worker and perpetrate a horrendous and cruel hoax.

The facts and figures cited in the foregoing paragraphs show it would be absurd and dishonest to deny the inequalities in our system. Likewise, it behooves the vociferous and insincere critics of our system not to overlook the inequities of the alternate systems they espouse.

The Distribution of Income

Before presenting our pragmatic approach to a social philosophy of equity in terms of redeeming social values or useful social purposes, we offer a list of definitions to be used in the context of this work.

Equality: state of being equal.

Inequality: social disparity; disparity of distribution or opportunity.

Equity: justice according to natural laws or rights; impartiality.

Inequity: injustice; unfairness.

Egalitarianism: a social philosophy advocating the removal of inequalities among men.

Pragmatism: a philosophy in which the meaning of conceptions is to be sought in their practical bearings; that truth is preeminently to be tested by the practical consequences of belief.

In our concept, equity is being served when there is movement toward the attainment of the goals of equality. This implies a recognition of the imperfections of human nature because human beings are not born equal and that imperfections in human nature will hinder the execution of policies toward our goals of perfect equality and perfect equity. Considered in this light, capitalism is more productive and more efficacious than socialism. It is absurd to expect and hope that total equality can become a reality. As Spinoza said, "He who seeks equality between unequals seeks an absurdity." Equity will be served as long as progress is being made toward equality. In this context, social redeemability is being pursued in its function of a useful social purpose.

A social philosophy of equity based on redeeming social values and useful social purposes is based on the following principles:

1. Equal rights to basic liberties such as voting, assembly, freedom of expression and belief and thought and equal rights to possession and disposal of goods and property and protection under the law.

2. Equal rights to justifiable inequalities that arise from exercise of equal rights to basic liberties, such as inequalities of income, wealth, power and authority, provided that these do not contravene the rights of others.

The principle of equal rights to basic liberties means that every person has rights to the most extensive pursuit of liberties, provided that these pursuits are consistent with the liberties of others. These liberties encompass the rights of assembly and free speech, and to vote and run for public office; the liberties of thought and conscience; the liberty to hold property; and the right to equal protection under the law.

The rights to inequalities that arise out of natural forces are compatible with the basic rights as long as there is no inequity. Inequality is not necessarily conducive to inequity. Equality governs opportunity, while equity governs end results. Voltaire hit it right on the head when he said that equality is natural when limited to rights and unnatural when it attempts to level goods and powers. He wrote that

The Distribution of Income

not all citizens can be equally strong but all can be equally free.

It is important to understand that men are not born equal. This is a natural phenomenon and should be accepted as such. It is neither equity nor inequity that men are born with different natural endowments into social positions that are unequal.

Our concept of social redeemability recognizes the unplanned difference in natural capacity and the unplanned unfavorable starting point in society. The egalitarian proposes to redress these differences and the end results thereof. However, his choice of a mechanism is ultimately counterproductive if the end results of the basics and amenities of life and the basic freedoms are compromised. The egalitarian's authoritative state sets up a huge bureaucracy to carry out the leveling process. Once ensconced in power, the revolutionary idealism that got them into power is compromised to keep them in power. They cannot tolerate criticism of the ineptitudes and gross inefficiencies of the economic mismanagement and hence control all means of expression of speech and ideas. However, the ends of equity are better served when the natural abilities of the better endowed are harnessed and put to work through the mechanism of the free market. The inequalities of income distribution, wealth and ability are justified when, through the invisible hand of enlightened self-interest and the signaling apparatus of the market system, they redress to a degree the position of the social group that was shortchanged by nature.

This process of redressing is in no way to be construed

as an admission of failure because some inequality still exists. Thus, this does not justify the fabrication of the failure and guilt complexes. These are inventions of the hypocritical egalitarians. This redressing activity is a natural process. It could be the result of conscious effort but is not necessarily so.

In our view a man is justified in doing what he pleases with his holdings as long as he did not impinge upon the basic rights of others in his prior acquisition and does not compromise the liberties of others in his use or disposition of these holdings. History has shown that, on balance, in spite of the proclivities of human nature, the invisible hand of enlightened self-interest and free markets have tended to work toward improving the lot of the worse off. This fulfills our criterion of redeeming social values.

The egalitarians point to the inequalities in our society and claim that they are excessive. They also call attention to what they term the power element in economic transactions and holdings. They exaggerate on both counts. The data cited in the forepart of this chapter show that there are inequalities of income, but not to the degree suggested by the irresponsible rhetoric of the intellectuals, some of whom may be honestly motivated while others sow confusion and mistrust because they have a vested interest in discontent. We also provided data in historical perspective indicating that progress is being made toward greater equality at the same time that absolute figures are showing a tremendous improvement. What the overzealous egalitarians overlook is that their proposals to equalize the size of the slices will in effect decrease the size of the pie. The rate of progress does not satisfy the misguided egalitarians

The Distribution of Income

and they propose to install a system that they believe would hasten the process. They are led astray in their belief that a bureaucracy would be more prescient and more omniscient and more effective than the invisible hand of enlightened self-interest operating in a relatively free market where producers and innovators respond to the signals of free choices of consumers.

Enough of abstractions. Let's get down to some specifics. Our concepts are based on a pragmatic approach in contrast to the ivory tower speculations of intelligentsist egalitarians. We had been influenced to a great extent by Spinoza, Voltaire, Kant, William James and by the more recent studies of John Rawls' *A Theory of Justice* (Harvard University Press, 1972) and Robert Nozick's *Anarchy, State and Utopia* (Basic Books, New York, 1974). However, our approach is more pragmatic in that we get down to the more mundane world of reality. In the chapter on "The Moral and Philosophical Aspects of Profits," it was our contention that profits had redeeming social values, refuting the changes that profits were obsessive, excessive or exploitative. Here, we enlarge our thesis to include the whole gamut of an economy—prices, the market mechanism, equity, equality as well as profits.

In his philosophy, Kant called for equality: not of ability, but of opportunity for development and application of ability. Kant insisted that the function of government is to develop the individual, not to abuse or use him. We would say it is the function of a social system to develop the individual by means of mechanisms operating as naturally and automatically as possible to achieve the best optimum balance of equity and equality. It is sheer folly to propose and expect perfection. Human beings are not perfect and any institution or social system of human beings, by human beings and for human beings cannot operate in perfection. To attain the optimum practical balance, we need a signaling system that best allows the choices and preferences of millions of individuals and consumers to be registered. The pricing system of capitalism reflects the desires and choices of buyers much better than any guesses of the bureaucrats of socialist economies. Profits, we have shown, are the incentive to the innovator, in their role of a response mechanism and also serve their function as the best resource allocators. To be sure there are mistakes, but they are not as costly as under socialism, where economic inefficiency is dominant and attended by political and intellectual oppression.

One of the greatest contributions of a capitalist economy, one greatly overlooked, to the betterment of mankind is its cost control mechanism. Historical perspective has shown that manufactured prices have fallen in terms of buying power under the impact of the efforts of engineering know-how to reduce costs. Historical perspective also indicates that the American farmer in his drive to reduce costs can outperform any system of collectivized farming. Here social equity is best served as the basics and amenities of life are available to more people than ever before. Under the free market system, guided by a price mechanism and spurred on by profit incentives, American business and agriculture have provided more food, more manufactured goods and more leisure time to more people than any socialist economy. The balance sheet shows such a preponderance of assets over liabilities that the net worth accruing to society and each individual is the highest ever attained. And yet, the intelligentsia, blinded by Marxist ideology, cannot see the benefits, which they grossly minimize, but see costs, which they maximize out of proportion and reality. We cited articles in our chapter on "The Illusions and Fallacies of Price Controls" in which the economists and bureaucrats of socialist states are going through ridiculous rituals in their efforts to find substitutes for the free market mechanism, with no success. The sham intellectuals, who have spawned and fostered a phony rhetoric against business and profits, ignore these exercises in futility and absurdity.

In an industry as simple and as basic as agriculture, collectivism has produced ideological disasters that are a monument to human folly. This is perceptively reported and analyzed by Irving Kristol in an article in the *Wall Street Journal* of January 20, 1975. The article, entitled "Food, Famine and Ideology," follows in part:

> Why is there a food shortage in the world today? The usual answer one will hear is that it is the result of population growth outstripping the growth of food supply. Now, that is a terribly interesting answer. It is interesting to begin with, because it is patently and demonstrably false: Over the past quarter-century, the world food supply has been growing almost twice as fast as population. It is perhaps an even more interesting answer in what it reveals about the state of mind of those who offer it—i.e., a deep ideological reluctance to make certain kinds of elementary judgments in the realms of economics and politics.
>
> There are three main reasons for the current food shortage and the threat of world famine which it evokes. These three reasons are: (1) Russia, (2) China, and (3) India. More specifically, it is the conditions of agriculture and of agricultural productivity in these nations that is at the root of the matter—a condition that has only a little to do with economics, and everything to do with politics.
>
> Ever since the Russian Revolution, but especially since the forced collectivization of the early 1930s, agriculture in the Soviet Union has been a Communist disaster area. The literature on

this subject is voluminous in extent and unanimous in its conclusion: The application of Communist dogmas has been ruinous to agricultural productivity. Peter Drucker, in his *Age of Discontinuity,* has pointed out that an economist in 1912, simply by projecting ahead the rate of economic development in Russia for the previous decades, could have accurately predicted that Russian industry would be pretty much at today's levels. (In that respect, the Russian Revolution can be deemed to have been superfluous.) But the same economist would also have predicted a far higher level of agricultural productivity than now exists in the Soviet Union. The only—repeat: the only—reason the Soviet Union is importing large quantities of food rather than being a food exporter is that its political regime, for ideological reasons, has made it necessary.

And the same is almost surely true for China. One has to use the qualifying "almost" because one knows so relatively little about conditions inside China.

Every country—e.g., *Chile, Peru, Mexico*—which has launched experiments in collectivized agriculture has quickly witnessed a decline in agricultural productivity.

If the Soviet Union and China were not importing food, and if the Soviet Union were instead exporting food (which it is inherently and easily capable of doing), a significant portion of today's world food shortage would simply not exist. Which leaves us with India—a special case in some ways, though not nearly so special as is popularly thought.

India's Prospects

Moreover, only a few years ago India was close to self-supporting in food, indeed, official Indian economists were predicting a gradually improving condition in the years ahead, even taking population growth into account. True, Indians would continue to be poor—but there was no foreseeable reason why they should be on the verge of starvation. And it was further assumed that economic growth and eventual industrialization in India would gradually reduce the birth rate, as it has practically everywhere else. The outlook for India, in short, was not exactly bleak, though it would be an abuse of language to call it optimistic. India would be very poor for decades to come, but it would, with each passing decade, become somewhat less poor.

What happened to these forecasts and expectations? Well,

what happened is that the Indian government mucked them up, by a stubborn and doctrinaire insistence that the nation's economy be subordinated to a vague set of "Socialist principles." Agricultural prices at all levels were fixed so as to provide "cheap food for the masses"—with the inevitable result that the farmers lost any incentive to grow more food, distributors lost any incentive to market food, etc. Added to this has been an elaborate system of controls over business generally, so that all forms of economic enterprise are being smothered to death by a huge and vastly inefficient bureaucracy, and a xenophobic hostility to foreign capital that prevents other enterprises (e.g., fertilizer plants, oil refineries, agricultural equipment manufacturing) from ever being born.

In the *Washington Post* for January 11, India's food minister points out in an interview that, even now, the quantity of food that India can produce is sufficient to avoid famine. His explanation as to why famine is nevertheless a real threat is that the wealthy Indians are eating too much leaving too little for the poor. In view of the relatively small proportion of Indians who are wealthy, and of the universal limitations of the human stomach, this interpretation is clearly preposterous. But that is the way Indian officialdom thinks. And, it must be said, their silliness is matched only by their arrogance. Even at this moment, negotiations for American aid are being held up because India will not agree to a "no export" clause—apparently because it wishes to send much of the American aid to Russia, to whom it "owes" two million tons of wheat!

Nor do I wish to suggest that you have to be some kind of Socialist to ruin your agriculture. It helps, as the case of Burma proves beyond all doubt—once a major rice exporter, it now can barely feed itself. But, in truth, any kind of detailed government intervention and regulation will do. Argentina, for instance, which should in all logic be the Canada of South America, is on its way to poverty and perhaps even famine because of a political philosophy which is closer to fascism than to socialism. But the basic truths remain: (a) Whatever the situation with regard to industry, agriculture is most productive when individual incentives prevail and the free market for agricultural produce predominates. (b) The existing threat of famine in various parts of the world is largely the derivative of a political ideology that thinks otherwise.

The intriguing question is why our scholars and scientists

and journalists so resolutely shy away from these truths, and why they prefer to think and talk about an apocalyptic crisis in world history rather than a quite mundane and vulgar crisis in a particular ideology. I think the answer is not so hard to guess at. There really are a lot of intellectuals in this world for whom the prospect of saying—or even seeming to say—a few kind words for capitalism is a fate worse than death.

It behooves all intellectuals to view honestly and objectively which system provides the best balance in equity and equality. They should ask these questions:

1. Do the benefits of capitalism operating under a system of signaling in a free economy outweigh the costs?
2. Do the benefits of a collectivized society operating under a system of bureaucratic edicts outweigh the costs?
3. Which system provides the best means for developing the potentials of the greatest number of individuals?

We will close this section of this chapter with a question and an answer.

Question: In our capitalist society, what factor, though very small in magnitude in relation to the total economy, has been the most instrumental in achieving a significant balance of equity and progress toward equality?

Answer: PROFITS.

A war of words has engulfed philosophers and social scientists as they argue among themselves the relative merits and demerits of the two recent books that we mentioned before by Rawls and Nozick. For the sake of perspective, let us outline the positions of the antagonists. Rawls is the new darling of the leftists and pseudo-liberals because he brings forth ideas that provide the rationale for their redistributionist and interventionist theories. Nozick is the

The Distribution of Income

new fair-haired boy of the libertarians because he promotes ideas consistent with the theory of the minimal state.

First, a summary of Rawls' theses. According to Rawls, justice is the basic attribute of social institutions, comprising rights to personal liberty and rights that arise from the distribution of wealth. Rawls asserts that each person has a right to the most widespread basic liberties, provided that they do not contravene the like liberties of others. These entitlements include the right to vote and to run for public office, to hold and dispose of private property, and to exercise freedom of speech, thought and religion.

As to distribution of wealth, Rawls condones inequalities of wealth, power and authority, provided they work to the advantage of those who are worst off. In his view, such inequalities are permissible if they enhance the living standards of lowest stratum of society. No one is entitled to natural advantages arising from birth or a more favorable social position. Rawls claims that "no one deserves his greater natural capacity nor merits a more favorable starting place in society. But it does not follow that one should eliminate these distinctions. There is another way to deal with them. The basic structure can be arranged so that these contingencies work for the good of the least fortunate" (Rawls, *Theory of Justice*, page 182). Rawls considers "the distribution of natural talents as a common asset" (page 102). In other words, justice requires that natural fortune and the luck of social position should be assayed as a collective resource and put to work for the common benefit. Justice does not require equality, but it does require that inequalities are utilized to improve the lot of the fate of the least advantaged.

These philosophical abstractions are embraced by

some of the pseudo-liberals as justification for the welfare state that utilizes transfer payments. However, neither Rawls nor any of his adherents cite statistical data. They operate under the illusion that the "rich are getting richer and the poor are getting poorer." The data that we have presented categorically refute the long-nurtured myth. In all this a significant point is missed. The intellectuals of the left are so engrossed with the concept of wealth that they overlook, through ignorance, naivete, wishful thinking or deliberate intellectual dishonesty, the fact that most income and more and more income derives from work rather than from wealth.

The following table was compiled from data appearing in *Historical Statistics of the U.S.* and more recent Department of Commerce series on national income to show what percentage compensation of employees comprised of national income.

Table IX-6
COMPENSATION OF EMPLOYEES, 1900-1974
(% of National Income)

1900-1909	55.0
1905-1914	55.2
1910-1919	53.2
1915-1924	57.2
1920-1929	60.5
1925-1934	63.0
1930-1939	66.8
1935-1944	64.4
1940-1949	64.3
1947-1952	64.5
1959-	69.8
1969-	73.9
1973	73.8
1974	74.9

The Distribution of Income

We now turn to pragmatism, where the meanings of conceptions are to be sought in their practical bearings and where truth is preeminently to be tested by the practical consequences of belief. With these in mind, an observation of the above table reveals that the "invisible hand" is working to such an extent that Adam Smith would be exalted at the relentless and inexorable distributive success of a neutral market. On the other hand, bureaucratic transfer payments impede the job-creating function of a free economy. Thus, they create injustice. This is contrary to our concept of social redeemability.

Bureaucracies and politicians pandering to envy and prejudice also contribute to the diminution in income inequality. They may aid the very few at the lowest statum of income. However, their lot can be improved with more desirable social goals and consequences through a negative income tax. Welfare has encouraged family disintegration, which, in turn, combined with the misleading rhetoric against profits, has contributed to the creation of a crime pathology.

The table shows the remarkable growth in employee compensation. It is important to ascribe this growth not so much to income distribution, but to the growth in jobs. Thus, in helping the poor, economic growth has proved itself to be far more effective than wealth or income distribuiton. In fact, unrealistic income transfers are counterproductive. As an example, take Chile, Uruguay or Argentina. Perón took a nation of untold natural resources that should have been the groundwork to make Argentina the Japan of South America, but he flouted economic laws to keep prices down, increase wages and guarantee everyone a job.

Argentina adhered to this beguiling panacea by increasing the government payroll and subsidizing inefficient state and private industries. The consequences are economic ineptitude and massive deficits financed by the printing presses, leading to three-digit inflation. The cost discipline of profits and the free markets were not permitted to function. The cost discipline of the free market economy isn't always painless, but it is important to take note that misguided efforts by autocracies to avert consequences of human error are at times economically deleterious and thus lacking in social redeemability.

Even though our empirical data in historical perspective fulfill the requirements that justify Rawls' criterion for the rationale for the existence of inequality, we do not accept his theory, for fundamental reasons. Who is to measure an acceptable inequality and by what criterion? If you surrender this function to a central authority, you entrust these functions to a bureaucracy, which inevitably encroaches on personal freedoms and which also leads to economic inefficiency and bungling. Thus, in the end, the pie is divided more equally, but it is a smaller pie. It is an economic absurdity to appease envy and suffer the consequences of economic deterioration. Personal and economic freedom is a criterion of higher social redeemability than unattainable equality. No useful socially redeemable function is served in striving for the unattainable and rendering impossible what can be realized. The neutrality of the invisible hand of profits in a free economy in providing income growth is no match for the biases and bunglings of bureaucracies.

The Distribution of Income

However, the equalitarians are not satisfied with Rawls' acceptance of inequality as long as it works for the good of the least fortunate. They want to go whole hog and collectivize natural talents and to arrogate to themselves the determination of the life style of society.

The equalitarian critique of Rawls' theories was presented by Marshall Cohen, professor of philosophy at the City University of New York, in his review of Rawls' book in the *New York Review of Books* of July 12, 1972.

Cohen appears to accept the theory of "the rich getting richer and the poor getting poorer." Truly, a conclusion unrelated to reality. This is an example of the tendency among theorizers to draw conclusion from insufficient data or by ignoring data that does not fit their theories or wishful thinking.

"Our high culture" may not "enjoy the extravagant support" of Cohen and his "new class" intellectuals, but Wattenberg has proven empirically that "Real America" is satisfied with its personal status.

It is never pleasant to contemplate inequalities, but they are facts of life. However, the psychological impact is exacerbated by pandering to envy, and it would be more humanitarian to point out that the inequalities are not as great as portrayed and that acceptance of nature's roll of the dice can lead to a larger absolute slice of a growing pie. "The impairment of liberties" of which Cohen speaks is one of those half-truths, the promotion of which does more mischief than good. A man of Cohen's intellect should know that absolute freedom can exist only in an anarchical society and that the degree of freedom is less prevalent in any alternate system to the free market and personal freedoms of a capitalist society. But please observe the contradiction. Just a few sentences before, Cohen was willing to sacrifice some freedom to you know what. This recalls the well-known statement of Orwell.

It should be noted that the kind of claptrap purveyed by Cohen and his like of cohorts appears to have contributed in a major degree to the mistrust and discontent amongst our student body. We were not objecting to his right to say what he desires, but the point that we are raising is that unless there is someone at his lectures to present a rebuttal, the brainwashing of a large segment of our students is inevitable.

Now, we turn to Nozick's book, *Anarchy, State and Utopia*. He succinctly states his theme in the opening sentence, when he writes that "individuals have rights, and there are things no person or group may do to them without violating their rights." This leads to his thesis of the "minimal" state whose function is severely limited to protection against fraud, force and theft, and to enforcement of contracts. According to the jacket of the book, Nozick brilliantly demonstrates that any more extensive activities of the state will inevitably violate individuals' rights. The jacket concludes by summarizing the book as an integration of ethics, legal philosophy and economic theory into a profound and unified position in political philosophy.

Nozick's concept of the inviolate individual is cogently presented in his final paragraph:

> The minimal state treats us as inviolate individuals, who may not be used in certain ways by others as means or tools or instruments or resources; it treats us as persons having individual rights with the dignity it constitutes. Treating us with respect

The Distribution of Income

by respecting our rights, it allows us, individually or with whom we choose, to choose our life and to realize our ends and our conception of ourselves, insofar as we can, aided by the voluntary cooperation of other individuals possessing the same dignity. How *dare* any state or groups of individuals do more. Or less." (Italics in original)

The two main objectives of the book were to provide the rationale for the "minimal" state and to refute the concept that the state should enlarge its functions to redistribute wealth and advantages arising from differing natural abilities and differing social positions.

Nozick delineates his principle of "entitlements" in the following passage:

1. People are entitled to their natural assets.
2. If people are entitled to something, they are entitled to whatever flows from it. . . .
3. People's holdings flow from their natural assets.

Therefore,

4. People are entitled to their holdings.
5. If people are entitled to something, then they ought to have it (and this overrides any presumption of equality there may be about their holdings). (Page 225)

In the last part of the book, Nozick gives his outline of a "utopia" which would embrace a minimal state furnishing a framework within which individuals may form any free and restrictive groups they wish.

Now let us observe a critique of the book by an intellectual of the "new class." This was provided by Sheldon S. Wolin, professor of politics at Princeton University, in his analysis in the *New York Times* of May 11, 1975. He berates Nozick for his failure to tell us something about "real politics."

We wish, Wolin were a bit more consistent. In his review of Wattenberg's *Real America* in the *New York Review of Books*, Wolin appeared to have gone through extraordinary mental gymnastics in his futile attempt to discredit the "hard" data and attitudinal surveys quoted by Wattenberg. He saw no merit in the "real economics" and "real politics" in *Real America*.

We call attention to Wolin's comments about the "power element in economic transactions and holdings." In his review of Wattenberg's book, he made references to power in the following terms:

> . . . "existing structure of control" . .
> . . . "structure of power" . . .
> . . . "exert great power" . .
> . . . "power and control" . . .
> . . . "powerful groups" . . .

All these references to power are made relative to corporations and individuals, implying that the establishment wields undue economic and political power. We may ask Wolin:

"How come that the powers have not been able to control excessive government spending?"

"Why have corporations been unable to counteract the monopoly power of unions?"

"Why has the establishment power been unable to control the false rhetoric about profits, prices and market power?"

To quote Wolin himself from his attack on surveys in his review of *Real America*, "The hypocrisy of the situation is stunning."

It appears that the controversy between the equalitarians

The Distribution of Income

of the Cohen and Wolin and quasi-egalitarians of the Rawls genre, on the one hand, and the neo-laissez-faire doctrines of Nozick can be summarized as an ideological war of words on the status of the individual relative to the state. The egalitarians view the state supreme and would use the state to exploit the more advantaged to improve the lot of the least advantaged. Under the minimal state doctrine of Nozick the "individual is considered supreme."

However, the philosophical exercises of the egalitarians seem to overlook pragmatic economic consequences per se and the economic consequences arising from the interplay of human psychology.

As we have illustrated before, the profit motive, through cost control disciplines and recycled profits, has improved the condition of the poor to a larger degree than any state or collectivized society, and with less infringement upon personal freedoms. Humans are not only acquisitive but also possessive and the minimal state provides the best environment for the operation of those attributes in a free market economy to improve the economic and social conditions of all classes without penalizing any particular class. Thus, social redeemability would be served to its highest degree. If human nature were perfect, we could obtain a perfect state of conditions under any system. But we have to accept the imperfections of human nature and the inequalities of natural assets as natural facts.

From the foregoing analysis an important question emerges:

What system utilizes natural assets and guides psychological attributes to the highest degrees while minimizing the effects of human proclivities?

We cast our vote for the individual and the minimal state.

We cast our vote against the authoritarian state where power does corrupt and breeds more irresponsible and tyrannical power.

Our concept for social redeemability is based on the following premises:

1. Every person is born with natural assets arising from natural genetic factors.
2. Every person is entitled to his natural assets.
3. Every person is entitled to an unobstructed development of his natural assets.
4. Every person is entitled to whatever flows from his natural assets and developments of his natural assets, provided he does not impinge on the entitlements of others.
5. Every person is entitled to dispose of the results of his natural and developed assets.
6. The minimal state can be expanded only to the point of aiding to educate the less advantaged to develop their natural assets.

Thus the disparity of end-result inequality would be reduced by improving the equality of opportunity.

Under the foregoing concepts, everyone is free to develop his natural assets and is entitled to any distribution in accordance with service as perceived by others in a free market.

It is not to be overlooked that the above conditions would exist in an ideal state. Because of human proclivities and lags in a free market economy, developments may arise that will require rectification. Thus, people should be allowed by free association to formulate means for redressing inequities. It would be undesirable to control appeals to envy, demagoguery and sham intellectualism. However, as strong a case can be made for Truth in Teaching (Stigler) and Truth in Media as can be made for Truth in Advertising.

The distributive effects of natural differences should be not nullified when we recognize that most income derives from work and not wealth; education and recycled profits will reduce the disparity more effectively than any other state intervention. We agree with Nozick that excessive transfer payments are a form of taxation that in effect is forced labor. We would judge it as confiscation. It is ironic that egalitarians promote transfer payments to help the least advantaged, but in reality decrease the corporate function of job creation. Thus, misguided egalitarianism promotes inequality.

Egalitarians justify the redistributive state, but the historical data on employee compensation, profits and dividends indicate that the market was slowly and inexorably decreasing the disparity in income. But with the advent of the Great Society and unbridled union power, the redistributive effort went too far and is now impeding profit recycling into capital formation and hence new jobs. As we shall illustrate in future chapters, budget deficits and excessive union power have spawned unemployment with inflation as stagflation and stumpflation.

In reality, efforts at redistribution through excessive transfer payments and wage-rate increases in excess of productivity are counterproductive because taxes and inflation decrease the purchasing power not only of the consumer but more importantly of the entrepreneur and the innovator, who create new jobs.

Egalitarians err in focusing on income from wealth because most income derives from work not wealth. The illusions and fallacies of redistributing wealth create more problems than they solve because they impede the creation of incomes that accrue from jobs, which in turn are formed from recycled profits.

In conclusion, it is our contention that distribution as perceived for service to others in the milieu of the neutrality of the free market is far superior to any state-controlled authority. Under capitalism, differentials in entitlements arising from differentials in contribution are best perceived and best accepted. Hence, social redeemability is allowed to develop to the highest degree as the least advantaged are helped to the highest degree.

X

TAX LOOPHOLES: RHETORIC VERSUS REALITY

The conspiracy theory of tax policy, often repeated to the point that it is widely accepted, charges that special interest lobbyists for the rich have either bribed or fooled congressmen into writing tax loopholes and permitting tax shelters that allegedly enable the rich to avoid paying their fair share of taxes or not even paying any taxes.

It will be proven by the record that this rhetoric, like that concerning profits, is patently false. These charges may yield dramatic publicity to the demagogue but any attempt to close tax loopholes will not yield the funds to finance deficits and enlarged federal government spending. This is another example of a hoax concocted by the "new class" elitists to justify throwing money at problems and also to create class envy.

To the records again, this time to see if the rich pay no taxes. The claim has been made that the rich do not bear their proportionate share and that the middle class is burdened with a disproportionate share. The following table is from *Tax Loopholes: The Legend and Reality*, by Roger Freeman, published by the American Enterprise Institute for Public Policy Research (Washington, D.C., 1973):

Table X-1 (Table No. Added)
SHARES OF THE FEDERAL INDIVIDUAL INCOME TAX
BY MAJOR INCOME BRACKETS, 1970

Adjusted Gross Income Bracket	Shares of Adjusted Gross Income	Share of Tax Liability
Under $7,000	19.5%	10.5%
$7,000 to $19,999	59.2	54.0
$20,000 and over	21.3	35.5
	100.0%	100.0%

Source: Internal Revenue Service, *Statistics of Income, 1970, Individual Income Tax Returns* (Preliminary), 1972; hereafter cited as IRS, *Statistics of Income, 1970.*

As proven by the table, the middle classes do not bear a disproportionate amount as compared with the affluent groups.

By referring to the IRS tabulations, the reader will find interesting data, especially in the cumulations from the

Tax Loopholes: Rhetoric Versus Reality

smallest income groups and then the cumulations in reverse from the largest income groups.

Table X-2
TAXABLE AND NONTAXABLE INCOME TAX RETURNS, 1972

Income Class	Total Number Returns	Number Taxable	% Taxable of Total	Income % of Total
$1,000,000 or more	1,030	1,024	99.4	0.3
500,000 "	3,696	3,676	99.5	0.6
200,000 "	22,929	22,821	99.5	1.3
100,000 "	114,636	114,211	99.6	3.0
50,000 "	598,313	596,298	99.7	7.4

Source: IRS, *Statistics of Income, Individual Tax Returns,* 1972.

Two important conclusions are derived from the above data. It can be observed that the numbers not paying taxes are infinitesimally small. We are not condoning loopholes or tax shelters, which justifiably should be removed, but it should be noted that the dramatics attending the fulminations against such practices may produce publicity but nothing tangible in revenue. In the second place, it is tantamount to conjuring up a mirage to dangle before the uninformed that goodies from Washington can be financed by skinning the rich.

Just how ludicrous the conspiracy theory is can be illustrated by forgetting about closing loopholes and considering confiscation.

What the table indicates is the amount that could be given each of 55 million families if all income after taxes were confiscated and distributed. In other words, if all income after taxes were taken away from those making a million dollars or more and given each family, the amount would equal a "whopping" $23.64. If all income were taken away from those making $500,000 or more, including the millionaires, the amount would be $40 for each family.

Table X-3
CONFISCATORY POTENTIAL

(1) Income Class	(2) Gross Income $ bn.	(3) Taxes Paid $ bn.	(4) Net After Taxes $ bn.	(5) (4) ÷ 55 Million
$1,000,000 or more	2.3	1.0	1.3	$ 23.64
500,000 "	4.1	1.9	2.2	40.00
200,000 "	9.5	4.1	5.4	98.18
100,000 "	21.5	8.2	13.3	241.82
50,000 "	53.5	16.7	36.8	669.09

Source: Columns (1), (2) and (3), IRS, *Statistics of Income.*
Columns (4) and (5) derived by the author.

And yet the intelligentsia persist in peddling the claptrap that there is a bottomless bonanza in soaking the rich. "The hypocrisy of the situation is stunning."

Freeman in his book (page 26) cites Joseph A. Pechman and Benjamin A. Okner, both strong proponents of top reform, as having estimated that closing several loopholes would yield from $3.1 to $10.2 billion.

An incalculable volume of rubbish is disseminated by pseudo-liberal politicals and utopian-blinded intellectuals in their loose treatment of accounting depreciation. In seeking cheap votes or sowing the seeds of class hatred, they often bring up the charge that "accelerated depreciation is a bonanza to big business" or "a giveaway to big business." This is preposterous and the reverse of the truth.

There are several accelerated depreciation methods. The one that can be most easily explained to and understood by the average reader is the declining balance method, which we will illustrate here in comparison with the straight-line method to refute the rhetoric. However, first, it would be appropriate to define and illustrate depreciation. According to the dictionary, depreciation is an act or process of depreciating or a decline in value. It is also the state of being depreciated. However, the accountant looks upon depreciation from two aspects. He recognizes the fact that a new machine, for example, will depreciate in value as a result of usage and age. In addition, the accountant attempts to allocate the cost of the new machine over its useful life so as to avoid distorting the profit and loss statements over the years.

Assuming that a new machine costs $100,000, will have a useful life of 10 years, and will have no salvage value, it would be ridiculous to charge the full $100,000 as an expense for the first year and nothing for the remaining nine years. It is obvious that earnings would be understated the first year and overstated the following nine years. Under the straight-line method the accountant would allocate $10,000 to each of the 10 years.

Accelerated depreciation connotes a more rapid early depreciation. And it is here where dishonest anti-business critics get their apopletic "conniptions" because business is permitted to allocate higher depreciation charges in the early years. Either they are stupid or conveniently and dishonestly forget to mention that lesser amounts are charged in later years.

This is illustrated in the table of depreciation schedules. Under the declining-balancing method, you are permitted to deduct twice the 10% of the straight-line rate of 10%, or 20% of the remaining balance. An observation of the table will show that by the end of the fifth year, you have been allowed to write off more than two-thirds of an assets' value rather than one-half as under the straight-line method. However, later in the life of the asset, the declining-balance method allows less generous allowances in order to compensate for the early generosity. This belies the envy-pandering rhetoric of cheap politics.

The table of depreciation schedules shows that the declining-balance method is favorable to the taxpayer for the first eight years. The favorable gap is most pronounced in the fourth year, when the cumulation reaches its peak, and then declines progressively when it becomes negative in the ninth year. According to Commerce Clearing House in their "Depreciation Guides," it is permissible to change from the declining-balance to straight-line method. If the declining-balance method were followed through the life of an asset, the asset would not be fully charged off as indicated in the table for the tenth year. As a result, it is a common practice to change over to the straight-line method where this method would give a larger deduction than the declining-balance method over the later years.

Again referring to our schedule, we find that the asset starts the sixth year with an adjusted remaining basis of $32,768. The straight-line rate is 20% based on the remaining useful life of five years. The depreciation charge is $6,554 for each year of the remaining five years. The total cumulation for the first five declining-balance years and second five straight-line years is $100,002. So, we must be fair with our left-wing and pseudo-liberal critics that business gained a windfall of $2 on a $100,000 machine investment. By their words (figures) you shall know them!

Table X-4
DEPRECIATION SCHEDULES

(1) Year	(2) Remaining Basis	(3) Declining-Balance Rate	(4) Depreciation Allowance Per Column (3)	(5) Depreciation Allowance: Straight-Line Method	(6) Cumulation: Declining Balance Method, Column (4)	(7) Cumulation: Straight-Line Method, Column (5)
First	$100,000	20%	$20,000	$10,000	$36,000	$20,000
Second	80,000	20	16,000	10,000	48,800	30,000
Third	64,000	20	12,800	10,000	59,040	40,000
Fourth	51,200	20	10,240	10,000	67,232	50,000
Fifth	40,960	20	8,192	10,000	73,786	60,000
Sixth	32,768	20	6,554	10,000	79,029	70,000
Seventh	26,214	20	5,243	10,000	83,233	80,000
Eighth	20,971	20	4,194	10,000	86,578	90,000
Ninth	16,777	20	3,355	10,000	89,262	100,000
Tenth	13,422	20	2,684	10,000		

When the economic aspects of depreciation are considered, it will be discovered that, contrary to the false notions fabricated by phony liberals, generous depreciation allowances work to the benefit of the worker. The increased cash-flow is recycled into new equipment that is more productive and hence conducive to cost reduction. It is asinine to promote policies that would handicap manufacturers in the quest for cost reduction. That is what the rhetoric against liberal depreciation policies is all about.

U.S. industry operates under the least liberal depreciation policies and as a result U.S. industry is losing its competitive positions. The National Machine Tool Builders Association and *The American Machinist* have repeatedly shown that the United States has the highest percentage of overage and obsolete machine tools and the lowest percentage of machine tools under 10 years of age. West Germany and Japan have the most generous cost recovery policies. Hence, it is no surprise that fixed capital formation as a percentage of GNP is the greatest in those two countries and that productivity gains are also the highest. This, combined with a productivity-oriented work ethic, makes the West Germans and the Japanese such tough competitors in world markets. Let us not forget that a prudent depreciation policy protects the current jobs, while profits create future jobs. With such counterproductive and phony friendships of pseudo-liberalism, does labor need any enemies? The sham benefactors in effect impede job sustenance and job creation and delay the advent of worker capitalism.

Despite the importance of depreciation in economic growth, its history has been woefully neglected. Deductions for depreciation have been permitted since the introduction of the Federal income tax system in 1913. For the first 20 years, until 1934, the Treasury Department gave taxpayers a considerable amount of freedom in the choice of determining useful life. For 20 years, the Treasury Department operated under the assumption that the advantages gained in the early years by high depreciation rates would be offset by no depreciation charges in the later years of useful asset life.

It was a prudent policy and should have never been altered. It is humanly impossible to forecast useful lives of equipment, especially sophisticated machinery and machine tools. Accelerated technological innovation renders the forecasts of useful lives even more difficult. It would be more conducive to economic growth to give the manufacturer more freedom. The alternatives are very simple:

> More liberal treatment of depreciation allowances fosters economic growth, utilizes and stimulates technological innovations, reduces costs and creates more jobs.
>
> More restrictive allowances work in reverse of the above-enumerated benefits.

In essence, an unrestricted treatment of depreciation charges permits market forces to determine utilization and stimulation of technology, while restrictions permit the bureaucrat to interfere with economic forces. As usual the result is the reverse of the intended goal.

The course of depreciation took on a strange twist in

1933 and 1934 because of a misreading of monetary events from the end of World War I to 1933. This tragic event occurred because monetary developments were misinterpreted by pseudo-liberal and radical economists on one side and the ultra-right-wing "wringer" economists on the other.

According to Milton Friedman and Anna Schwartz in their exhaustive and scholarly *A Monetary History of the United States, 1867-1960* (National Bureau of Economic Research, New York, 1963), the 1929-1933 economic debacle was a crisis in banking illiquidity that was brought about by an inept monetary policy that caused the money stock to decline by one-third from 1929 to 1933. They wrote that the "monetary system collapsed, but it clearly need not have done so" (page 407). One main conclusion can sum up the gist of the book: All major economic crises, and a majority of minor declines, can be accounted for in monetary developments or more specifically in money supplies. This is considered significant because in 93 years of monetary history, encompassing a variety of industrialization, money stock emerges to be the preponderant determinant of economic expansion and contraction.

In our opinion, the two main unstable factors that triggered the stock market crash were to be found in excessive credit in stock speculation and the precarious conditions in international monetary affairs spawned by the stupid economic exactions of the Versailles Treaty. John Maynard Keynes' prophetic warnings in *The Economic Consequences of the Peace* were ignored, and the uneconomic terms imposed on Germany by France and Italy created an unstable international banking situation and economic hardship in

Germany that laid the groundwork for the rise of Hitlerism. France further aggravated the situation by machinations in the foreign exchange markets.

In their analysis of the 1920s and the early 1930s, Friedman and Schwartz write:

> The economic collapse from 1929 to 1933 has produced much misunderstanding of the twenties. The widespread belief that what goes up must come down and hence also that what comes down must do so because it earlier went up, plus the dramatic stock market boom, have led many to suppose that the United States experienced severe inflation before 1929 and the Reserve System served as an engine of it. Nothing could be further from the truth. By 1923, wholesale prices had recovered only a sixth of their 1920-21 decline. From then until 1929, they fell on average the average of 1% per year. The cyclical expansion from 1927 to 1929 is one of the very few in our record during which prices were a shade lower at the three months centered on the peak than at the three months centered on the initial trough. The stock of money, too failed to rise and even fell slightly during most of the expansion—a phenomenon not matched in any prior or subsequent cyclical expansion. Far from being an inflationary decade, the twenties were the reverse. And the Reserve System, far from being an engine of inflation, very likely kept the money stock from rising as much as it would have if gold movements had been allowed to exert their full influence. (Page 298)

After the stock market collapse and the untimely death in 1928 of Benjamin Strong, Governor of the Federal Reserve Bank of New York, the "wringer" economists, along with Andrew Mellon, Hoover's "great" Secretary of the Treasury, became dominant in monetary affairs and put the economy "through the wringer" to squeeze out a nonexistent inflation. In the words of Friedman and Schwartz:

Many professional economists as well as others viewed the depression as a desirable and necessary economic development required to eliminate inefficiency and weakness, took for granted that the appropriate cure was belt tightening by both private individuals and the government, and interpreted monetary changes as an incidental result rather than a contributory cause. (Page 409)

As a result, the Federal Reserve System shifted from active, vigorous, self-confident policies in the 1920s to passive, defensive, hesitant policies from 1929 to 1933.

Thus, the conservative "wringers" aggravated a decline that should have been ended in 1930, in the opinion of Friedman, Schwartz and Carl Snyder, statistician and economist for the Federal Reserve Bank of New York. Then the left-wing structuralists get into the act and fostered restructuring the economy with tax increases in 1932 and 1934, along with a batch of regulatory interventionism that included restrictions as to depreciation write-offs.

To finance public works programs initiated in 1933 and 1934, the Treasury Department changed its position and in early 1934 issued Treasury Decision 4422, requiring taxpayers to prove the appropriateness of the useful lives of assets they used. According to Commerce Clearing House, taxpayers had to use unrealistically long lives because it was nearly impossible to prove a useful life with accuracy.

In retrospect, it can be asserted that fine tuning through fiscal and monetary means at that time would have been more productive and that a continuance of an unrestricted depreciation policy would also have been more productive. And as usual, regulation begets more regulation, and interventionists, never accepting any blame for any deleterious consequences, kept on dreaming up more excuses for more intervention.

One important conclusion emerges from the above considerations:

The rhetoric about loopholes and accelerated depreciation impedes economic progress and delays the arrival of a genuine workingman's capitalism.

XI

THE "SLUMPFLATION" OF 1974-75

The uniqueness of the 1974-75 inflation, dubbed "slumpflation" by the London *Economist,* is characterized by the inability of demand deflation to curb cost inflation. Slumpflation means the combination of slump, or deep recession bordering on depression and inflation. In 1970-71, we experienced what appeared somewhat extraordinary at that time, an inflation called "stagflation," or stagnation or minirecession combined with inflation. That was bad enough in itself; but worse still, it now degenerated into slumpflation.

What are the causes?

Stagflation and slumpflation can be attributed to long-continued, astronomical government deficits, unjustified wage increases and expansion of money supplies. Government deficits have a bearing on inflation in two ways. In the first place, government deficits are a factor in demand inflation—necessary in recessions but uncondonable during prosperity as it increases the supply of money chasing a limited amount of goods. Secondly, government deficits contribute to cost-push inflation by causing higher taxes and high interest rates. Wage-rate increases in excess of productivity gains are the prime cause of cost-push inflation.

Another question that follows logically: What are the causes of irresponsible government deficits in boom times and unwarranted wage increases?

We can ascribe these two developments to politics—the "politics" of politics and the politics of unionism—and their corollary accompaniments of arrant rhetoric and propaganda. Because they cannot substantiate their wild charges with facts, the demagogic politicians and union leaders, and their abettors in academia and the media, concoct falsehoods and distortions against profits and the market economy. Hence, our revolution of rising expectations; the intensification of expectations; the crisis in entitlements; and finally, the psychological momentum of expectations and entitlements.

Inflation in all its forms, beginning in a benign degree just recently and developing now into more virulent and destructive forms, is essentially a political problem. It was spawned, exists and persists because the most influential power blocs in our society have vested interests in policies that are inflationary. Most politicians, seeking or holding office, feel that they must not allow their opponents to out-promise them. Likewise, the union leader, to maintain or increase his empire, creates the adversary relationship and yells for "more."

"If you want to blame someone for this horrible inflation, it traces back to Johnson's 1965 decision to accelerate the war without raising taxes." Thus spoke Paul Samuelson in an interview reported in the *Fort Lauderdale News* of March 16, 1975. This should be identified as a demand-pull type of inflation. We would like to call attention to the origin of an unwarranted and unnecessary cost-push inflation when the Machinists' Union in the airlines strike demanded and received a settlement in excess of the wage guidelines that were initiated by Kennedy and maintained to that time by Johnson. The President of the Machinists' Union boasted, "We broke the guidelines." That initiated a chain of "me-too-ism" from which we are still suffering. That set off a wage-price spiral which is still continuing. "Me-too-ism" inflation developed a "whetted-taste" type of inflation in which union members got a taste of raises exceeding productivity gains and it became politically impossible for union leaders to ask for anything less. The spirit of moderation was subverted. Let's not forget Johnson's Great Society that committed this nation to costly social innovations that have legislated into our Federal budget outlays that are automatically renewed. This has led to a series of virtually uncontrollable deficits, increasing government participation in the money markets, thus contributing to the rise in interest rates.

And all of this took place in a decade when misconceptions about profits and profit margins and the limits of income distribution assumed the nature of historical facts through sheer, endless repetition. Is it any wonder that the rising tides of aspirations, expectations, entitlements and psychological momentum thereof kept swelling over onward? In reality, the world is suffering from a hyperinflation of half-baked welfare-state ideology in which soaking the rich is expected to pay for all intelligentsist nostrums and panaceas.

Then from 1970 to 1974 the economy was subjected to an unprecedented convergence of inflations, some new and some old, into wholly new and unique phenomena called "stagflation" and "slumpflation."

The different kinds of inflations emerging simultaneously to a degree never experienced before in history were the following:

1. Demand-pull; fiscal; deficit spending
2. Wage cost-push
3. Monetary
4. Exchange rate
5. Euro-dollar
6. Worldwide cyclical
7. Shortages induced through inadequate profits
8. Shortages induced through environmental controls
9. Shortages induced through price controls
10. Climate-induced
11. Ideologically induced
12. OPEC-induced
13. Taxation cost-push
14. Expectational
15. Politically induced

The "Slumpflation" of 1974-75

A few cautionary remarks are in order. This is not meant to be complete and all-inclusive. It should be apparent that these do not exist in tight compartments as there is a degree of overlapping.

1. DEMAND-PULL
2. COST-PUSH

The first two types of inflation will be treated more fully in the following two chapters. Here we will present a brief description of the other thirteen types of inflation.

3. MONETARY INFLATION

This inflation occurs when money supply is increased by the Federal Reserve Banks and the Federal Reserve Board at a rate that exceeds the growth of Gross National Product. According to University of Chicago economist Milton Friedman and other "monetarists," changes in money supply are a major, if not dominant influence on business trends.

There is one important conclusion to be derived from the role of money supply as it affects business trends. It may be true that changes in money supply are an important determinant in business activity. As the rate of money growth rises, business follows with an increase in activity. As the rate of growth in money supply decreases, a declining trend in business will result. However, the response of prices is not that neat. While an increase in the rate of growth in money supply will to some degree cause rising prices, a decrease in rate of growth in money supply does not necessarily result in a decrease in prices, as attested by stagflation of 1970-71 and slumpflation of 1973-75. Here the role of wage-cost-push inflation impedes price reductions and only increases unemployment. This is another effect of the irresponsible propaganda that emphasizes the uniqueness of the current recession.

The monetarists imply that a steady growth in money supply would not permit an acceleration and exaction of wage increases in excess of productivity gains. In our opinion, this is untenable. If wage rates increases are not amenable to monetary controls on the downside, it is hard to see why they should be more tractable on the upside.

4. Exchange Rate Inflation

This type of inflation occurs when the value of the dollar in terms of other currencies is decreased. For example, prior to the first devaluation of the dollar in December, 1971, a dollar was worth four marks, or a mark cost an American 25 cents. As of this writing in May, 1975, a mark cost 41 to 43 cents, or you would get about 2.4 marks for each dollar. The first devaluation reduced the value of the dollar, by 11% in terms of currencies of our major trading countries, weighed by their importance in U.S. trade as computed by the Morgan Guaranty Trust Company. The second devaluation of 6% occurred in February, 1973. As a result, import prices increased by a whopping 17%.

Since the dollar had been chronically overvalued for decades, it had been thought that devaluation would be desirable since it would make the U.S. more competitive in world trade because our prices to foreign buyers would be decreased by the amount of devaluation. Well, this had its wonderful as well as not so wonderful aspects. It was wonderful to have exports increase, but they increased to such an extent that many scarce items went overseas, creating shortages here and future price increases. This provides a lesson to would-be planners and price controllers. The interrelationships of prices and markets are so sensitive, intricate and complex, that no bureaucracy can hope or be able to cope with myriad phases of activities and consequences.

5. Euro-Dollar Inflation

Before going any further, it may be wise to define that Euro-dollars are dollar-denominated deposits in banks operating outside the United States. It would be more accurate to speak of Euro-currencies. It has been estimated that Euro-currencies grew from a net of $21 billion, of which 83% were dollars, to a net of $190 billion in November, 1974, of which 75% were dollars.

How did they get there? Since about 1957 they got there because we were running huge deficits in the balance of payments through foreign aid, investments abroad, acquisition by foreign central banks of dollars to build up official reserves and through purchases of dollars by central banks to maintain fixed exchange rates.

From the end of 1966 to 1974, the U.S. money supply grew about 60%, while the Euro-dollar growth was 740%. Monetarists ascribe the world commodity inflation to this dramatic increase. Some Europeans, notably the French, have maintained that we exported our inflation abroad. If so, they were willing accessories. They did not object to our foreign aid but eagerly accepted it. Also they purchased the dollar so as to maintain its overvalued status. Thereby, they maintained their unfair advantage in foreign trade.

6. Worldwide Cyclical Inflation

The worldwide monetary inflation was further compounded by the fact that all major industrialized countries experienced a simultaneous expansion in their economies to a degree never seen before. Hence, the aggravation of the commodity price inflation. A worldwide economic boom was superimposed on the boom in the United States.

7. Inflation Induced by Shortages Due to Inadequate Profits

There was a shortage of basic materials because the expansion in capacity needed to produce these materials was inadequate as a result of the abnormally low level of profits since 1966 in vital industries, such as aluminum, steel, chemicals among others.

8. Inflation Induced by Shortages Due to Environmental Controls

Expansion in capacity needed to produce basic materials was further eroded by numerous impediments to new investment on ecological grounds. There is no quarrel with the objectives of ecologists and environmentalists. Their cost-benefits evaluations, if they made any, were completely incompatible with sober reality. It is apparent that they were carried away by emotionalism, wishful thinking and in some instances by sheer vindictiveness. Some of the excessively stringent objectives have no sound scientific basis. They erred also on two other grounds—in their severe time schedules and in their timing. There is some suspicion that some of the elitists, envious of the better economic performance of the capitalist economies as compared with the socialist economies, exploited the situation to hamstring the bourgeois systems.

9. Inflation Induced by Shortages Due to Price Controls

In principle, just about everything is wrong, nothing is constructive but counterproductive, with price controls. They impede the functioning of the signaling system of free and competitive markets. This system is not perfect as there are time-lags and impediments to perfect and instant response. Imperfect human beings have a part in this system. It is most irritating to hear left-wing critics denigrate the performance of our markets but ignore the more colossal failures of socialist price systems. Let's get back to price controls in our economy. By distorting the vital signals normally conveyed by the free pricing system, controls misallocate resources, create shortages and impede capital investment. Sensitive price relationships that have attained wide business acceptance are distorted by human judgments that are substituted for the neutrality and anonymity of the competitive marketplace. Preposterously complex regulations make the system inoperative and, when controls are lifted, the subsequent price explosion is invariably worse than it would have been if no controls were instituted.

Our experience with food prices in the last five years is a striking example of the futility and counterproductivity of price controls as practised by the U.S. Department of Agriculture. In the face of a prodigious worldwide demand for food in 1972 and 1973, the basic policy of the Department was still to keep supply down and keep prices at the old level. If free markets were allowed to operate, prices would be allowed to go higher temporarily until the elastic supply response would become operative and relieve the shortages sooner than under bureaucratic planning.

10. Climatologically Induced Inflation

The weather factor as a cause of inflation was well portrayed in the following excerpt from an article entitled "The New Questions About the U.S. Economy," by Carol J. Loomis in *Fortune* of January, 1974:

> There was certainly bad luck in the fact that U.S. slaughter of both cattle and hogs fell late in 1972 to cyclical lows; the two cycles coincided for the first time in twenty years. So depressed, in fact, was the production of pork that total U.S. production of meat in 1972 ran 2 percent below the 1971 level. Our total production of food other than meat fell even more—with weather conditions getting most of the blame.
> Meanwhile, a lot of bad weather in other countries was also helping to reduce world grain production, which fell by about 3 percent in 1972; this was by far the biggest decline in a decade. Russian crop failures extended not only to grains but to potatoes, sugar, and sunflowers (which are a source of protein meal). Other sources of meal got hit too: in India and Senegal the peanut crop was poor, and off Peru there was that bad news about the Humboldt Current and anchovies. All these shortfalls exerted pressure on U.S. grain and soybean supplies, which for a variety of reasons were not up to the situation.

11. Ideologically Induced Inflation

It has been outlined by Kristol in the article cited in the preceding chapter that there are three main reasons for the current food shortage and resultant high food prices: (1) Russia, (2) China, and (3) India. To requote Kristol, "More specifically, it is the condition of agriculture and agricultural productivity in these nations that is at the root of the matter—a condition that has only a little to do with geography or demography, much to do with economics, and everything to do with politics."

Since the revolution 60 years ago, Russians have lost economic ground and personal freedom. They must depend on the free world to feed their own people as they cannot feed themselves. In Russia, about 33% of the population are involved in agriculture and yet cannot produce what 7% of our population can produce in supplying food and fibers. And yet the sham intellectuals have the temerity to propose bureaucratic planning and collectivization.

12. OPEC-Induced Inflation

When the OPEC oil cartel increased the blackmail prices far above marginal costs of production, they inflicted unwarranted hardships on developing and industrialized nations. The OPEC oil producers augmented inflation in several ways. The excessive rise in oil prices resulted in increases in gasoline, heating oil and fertilizer costs. They created undue balance of payments problems and caused havoc in the sensitive financial markets. The magnitude of their blackmail is illustrated in the accompanying chart, which appeared in the London *Economist* of May 11, 1974.

What's in a margin?

In the long run the free market price of a commodity should be equal to the marginal cost of production. As the chart shows, prices for all major commodities are now well above this level, and will eventually have to come down.

- Estimated marginal costs of production = 100%
- Free market price

Commodity	Marginal cost	Free market price
RUBBER	20p a kilo	35p a kilo
TIN	£1750 a ton	£4000 a ton
SUGAR CANE	£90 a ton	£230 a ton
ZINC	£300 a ton	£870 a ton
COPPER	£450 a ton	£1350 a ton
COCOA	£300 a ton	£1000 a ton
OIL (Opec)	20 cents a barrel	800 cents a barrel

First, a definition is in order. Economists define the marginal costs of production as the extra or incremental cost of producing an extra unit of output. We find empirical proof of this in the history of profit margins, which never stay out of line for any extended period.

Please note in the above chart that OPEC oil prices are 3900% above marginal costs!!! And yet we get this bit of ludicrous profundity from Arthur Schlesinger in the *Wall Street Journal* of October 30, 1974, in his article "How About Taking Inflation Seriously?"

> . . . "Our present troubles, for example have been aggravated by worldwide food and raw material shortages, by the determination of the oil-producing countries to *rip off the West as the West ripped them off* for so many years. (Italics supplied by writer of this book)

This article by Schlesinger is a classic example of economic ignorance or bias or both. For an entertaining pastime, a reading of the article is recommended as well as responses that were evoked and printed in the *Wall Street Journal* of November 25, 1974, among them several letters from economists, including one from Milton Friedman.

In view of the outrageous extortion perpetrated by OPEC countries, the effrontery of the Shah of Iran is difficult to condone when he recently suggested that oil prices will have to be raised as compensation for inflation. Is His Excellency implying hardship? Arrant rubbish!!! It should be borne in mind that, in the intervening year, some raw material prices have declined 30 to 50% toward their marginal costs. It will take some time but, as the *Economist* prophesies, a glut in oil is coming with lower prices, and we will be asked to provide relief for the impoverished Arabs and their friends.

13. TAXATION COST-PUSH INFLATION

Taxes serve to decrease purchasing power in two ways. They decrease take-home pay of the individual and are added to costs by businesses and thereby increase prices. Governments exist to provide useful services. However, the growth of government has outpaced the increase in GNP by such a wide margin that it lends credence to the belief that government bureaucracies have assumed the proportions of a paper-shuffling paradise. The crisis in New York City finances is highlighted by the facts that fiscal irresponsibility and kowtowing to municipal unions will balloon New York City debt to about $14 billion by next year, necessitating interest payments alone of about $2 billion, equal to the whole city budget of 15 years ago.

Calculations by this writer from data found in *Facts and Figures of the Tax Foundation* indicate that total public debt increased 2378% from 1929 to 1973; total corporate debt, 1094%; and, GNP, 1156%.

We will get into more detail on government operations in the next chapter.

14. EXPECTATIONAL INFLATION

Having experienced inflation for some time, individuals, businessmen and countries aggravate inflation by anticipatory buying. Witness the auto-buying binge of 1972-73, the overstocking of inventories by businessmen and the huge purchases of raw materials by the Japanese.

15. POLITICALLY INDUCED INFLATION

An example of this was provided by the unnecessarily high expansionary policies pursued in 1972 *to get Nixon elected.*

In summary, it can be stated that many of the inflationary phenomena were of the type that can be classed as once-for-all type of inflationary adjustments. In some cases, the inflations will breed their own deflation. However, three stand out in the realm of being subject to conscious political control. They are fiscal, wage-cost-push and monetary inflations. Having considered monetary inflation in this and the prior chapter, we will address ourselves to fiscal and cost-push inflation in the next two chapters.

XII

INFLATIONARY ASPECTS OF GOVERNMENT SPENDING

Government spending is big and getting bigger at an alarming pace. Before considering the inflationary implications, we will present a long-term look or perspective. As observed from year to year, or even from decade to decade, the size of the growth and the steady persistence of the growth are not fully appreciated. But examined in perspective over a longer stretch of time, the alarmingly increasing magnitude becomes obvious. Its persistent increments, perpetrated and fostered by the unconscionable rhetoric of leftist intellectuals, affects every taxpayer, big and little.

W. Allen Wallis, Chairman of the Tax Foundation, makes this disturbing commentary in the opening paragraph of his foreword in the previously cited 1975 issue of the Foundation's *Facts and Figures on Government Finance:*

> Early in 1975 spending by all levels of government will reach the annual rate of $550 billion—a half *trillion* dollars, twice the amount spent as recently as 1967, and 25 times the amount in 1940.

A look at one of the tables compiled by the Foundation in the aforementioned book shows that it took 186 years for the Federal budget to reach the $100 billion milestone; it took only nine more years to reach the $200 billion mark in 1971; and, only four more years to crack the $300 billion barrier in 1975. And yet the irresponsible politicians and demogogic do-gooders, whose extravagance has contributed to slumpflation, are now eager to pander to the economically illiterate with more government spending. The demagogic politician, whose greed for votes at any price, and the irresponsible union leader, whose greed for power in his empire, have brought New York City to its financial mess, are now eager to saddle the big uncle in Washington to relieve them of their onus.

These are the same members of anti-business propagandists who attack profits without appreciating the cost discipline of profits. Even though profits are small in relation to sales and gross national product, they exert a powerful impact in their cost discipline. In their efforts to maximize profits, businesses concentrate on costs where

Inflationary Aspects of Government Spending

they have some control. Thus, profits and costs are the driving forces that maximize the utilization of technology and more efficient methods to bring costs down as well as real prices. The sad part is that bureaucratic operations are not subject to the forces of market competition, and therefore there is no way to test their relative efficiency or acceptability. It is very disconcerting that the intelligentsia and liberal and radical economists are advocating more government and more governmental takeover of business functions. This would be retrogressive as more economic functions would escape the discipline of competitive forces. We would classify this in no uncertain terms as devoid of and counterproductive of redeeming social values.

The striking rise in government expenditures can be illustrated in one way by computing the total of federal, state and local expenditures on a per capita basis. This is shown in a table culled from the Tax Foundation's *Facts and Figures*.

Table XII-1
GOVERNMENT EXPENDITURES PER CAPITA, 1902-1974

1902	$ 21
1950	468
1964	1,034
1973	2,069
1974	2,210

Please note that the thousand dollar per capita figure was first pierced in 1964, and only 10 years later the $2,000 per capita mark was attained in 1974.

The following table was compiled by the writer of this book to show trends in government spending as compared with personal consumption spending:

Table XII-2

	Government Spending	Index	Personal Consumption Spending	Index	Ratio
1929	$ 10 bil.	100.0	$ 77 bil.	100.00	1.0
1940	18	180.0	70	90.9	1.98
1950	60	600.0	191	248.1	2.4
1960	136	1360.0	325	422.1	3.2
1970	312	3120.0	617	801.3	3.9
1974	461	4610.0	877	1252.9	3.7

The indexes with 1929 as the base for 100.0 and the ratios of the indexes show the dramatic rise in government spending. By 1970, government spending was rising four times faster than personal spending, as indicated by the ratio of 3.9.

If this trend goes on, the average consumer, who is the producer, will have less to spend on himself as the non-producer gets more of the pie. The rabble-rousers of the left had better take heed, because the average worker and the middle-class worker will get tired of the screwing they are getting from the elite leftists and become all the more receptive and amenable to the rabble-rousers of the right.

In 1961, a strange phenomenon occurred when the number of government workers exceeded, for the first time, the number of retail workers, 8.6 million to 8.3 million. By 1974 the gap was enlarged 14.3 million workers to 12.8 million. It should be construed as a day of infamy for the arrant rhetoric of what is called "The New Class" by Irving Kristol when government payrolls will soon exceed manufacturing payrolls for the first time in our industrial history unless the growth in government payrolls is brought to a screeching halt. It will be no easy and simple task to obtain our objective of diminishing government growth and payrolls.

Inflationary Aspects of Government Spending

It will be a formidable task merely to limit their aggrandizement because the "new class" has a vested interest in transferring the power of shaping our civilization from the capitalist free market system to the government where the "new class elitists" will exercise major control. Hence, their espousal of consumerism, environmentalism, liberal education, ecology, economic planning and governmental intervention in business to engender and foster a huge bureaucracy without realizing that government regulation begets more government; that bureaucratic failures, undisciplined by competitive market forces, only breed additional layers of bureaucracy; and that political demagogues duck responsibility for their mistakes by proposing more government intervention for their failures.

This "new class" and its machinations were ably and perceptively described in an article entitled "Business and The New Class" by Irving Kristol in the *Wall Street Journal* of May 19, 1975. The article in part follows with our appropriate comments.

> I should like to pursue the truly interesting question of why so many intelligent people manage to entertain so many absurd ideas about economics in general and business in particular. In truth, one can properly put that question in a much stronger form: Why do so many intelligent people seem determined to hold those ideas and to resist any correction of them? Such determination there must be, because mere error and ignorance are not of themselves so obdurate. When they are, it is usually because they also are an integral part of an ideology which serves some deeper passion or interest.

It is our conviction that envy, naivete and arrant intellectual dishonesty underlie the dissemination and acceptance of anti-profits propaganda and the consequent entertainment of absurd economic ideas. It appears that members of our academia are resentful that business positions are more lucrative than teaching, hence their receptiveness to misinformation about the size and nature of profits.

It is also hard to conceive that a professor of economics should propagate false information about profits and corporate pricing. Either he slept through vital courses in economics, accounting and statistics or he is willfully spreading erroneous and false information about these matters. While studying, he may have done his homework (library work) in a slipshod manner; or, while teaching, he failed to keep abreast of important studies by such organizations as the National Bureau of Economic Research, American Enterprise Institute, Russell Sage Foundation, Tax Foundation, etc., or he dishonestly ignored their findings when they did not dovetail with his preconceived leftist ideas. Instead, he may have preferred to spread the claptrap of Marcuse, *Ramparts*, avant-garde novelists, etc.

> And the more attentively one studies the problem, the clearer it becomes that what is commonly called a "bias" or an "animus" against business is really a byproduct of a larger purposiveness. There are people "out there" who find it convenient to believe the worst about business because they have certain adverse intentions toward the business community to begin with. They dislike business for what it is, not for what they mistakenly think it is. These people constitute what one may simply call, for lack of a better name, "the new class."
>
> This "new class" is not easily defined but may be vaguely described. It consists of a goodly proportion of those college-educated people whose skills and vocations proliferate in a "post-industrial society" (to use Daniel Bell's convenient term). We are talking about scientists, teachers and educational adminis-

Inflationary Aspects of Government Spending

trators, journalists and others in the communications industries, psychologists, social workers, those lawyers and doctors who make their careers in the expanding public sector, city planners, the staffs of the larger foundations, the upper levels of the government bureaucracy, etc., etc. It is, by now, a quite numerous class; it is an indispensable class for our kind of society; it is a disproportionately powerful class; it is also an ambitious and frustrated class.

To this "new class," we would add overzealous and vindictive consumerists and environmentalists; irresponsible union leaders and union member activists; naive religious leaders; Communist and Socialist rabble-rousers and activists; and, the demagogic and irresponsible politicians, whose lusts for votes and power surely cannot be characterized by redeeming social values. They rail against the "lust for profits" without analyzing the facts about profits where profits are so small in magnitude yet so powerful through their cost discipline in providing the utmost for mankind in food, clothing, housing and the amenities of life. In fact, their lust for power is counterproductive in these areas and totally devoid of redeeming social values as they actually screw the people they pretend to help.

Kevin Phillips calls this class "the mediacracy," in his new book of that title. Though the book has many shrewd observations, the term he chooses seems to me to be unfortunate. It helps prolong what might be called the "Agnew illusion"—i.e., that much of our troubles derives from the fact that a small and self-selected group, whose opinions are unrepresentative of the American people, have usurped control of our media and use their strategic positions to launch an assault on our traditions and institutions. Such a populist perspective is misleading and ultimately self-defeating. Members of the new class *do not "control" the media, they are the media*—just as they are our educational system, our public health and welfare systems, and much else.

Even if the president of CBS or the publisher of *Time* were to decide tomorrow that George Wallace would be the ideal President, it would have practically no effect on what is broadcast or published. These executives have as much control over "their" bureaucracies as the Secretary of HEW has over his, or as the average college president has over his faculty.

In the above allusion by Kristol to publishing, readers should be alerted to the fact that journalists and cartoonists reflect the bias of unions to which they belong. This is irresponsible advocacy journalism that "fits the news to print." The news in many instances, in fact too numerous, via TV and newspapers is distorted, slanted and presented willfully out of perspective.

What does this "new class" want and why should it be so hostile to the business community? Well, one should understand that the members of this class are "idealistic," in the 1960s sense of that term—i.e., they are not much interested in money, but are keenly interested in power. Power for what? Well, the power to shape our civilization—a power which, in a capitalist system, is supposed to reside in the free market. The "new class" wants to see much of this power redistributed to government, where they will then have a major say in how it is exercised.

From the very beginnings of capitalism, there has always existed a small group of men and women who disapproved of the pervasive influence of the free market on the civilization in which we live. One used to call this group "the intellectuals," and they are the ancestors of our own "new class," very few of whom are intellectuals but all of whom inherit the attitudes toward capitalism that have flourished among intellectuals for more than a century-and-a-half. This attitude may accurately be called "elitist"—though people who are convinced they incarnate "the public interest," as distinct from all the private interests of a free society, are not likely to think of themselves in such a way. It is basically suspicious of, and hostile to, the market precisely because the market is so vulgarly democratic—one dollar, one vote. A civilization shaped by market transactions is a civilization responsive to aspirations of common people. The "new class"—intelligent, educated, energetic—has little respect for such a commonplace civilization. It wishes to see its "ideals" more effectual than the market is likely to permit them to be. And so it tries always to supersede economics by politics—an activity in which it is most competent, since it has the talents and the implicit authority to shape public opinion on all larger issues.

Please note Kristol's allusion to the "new class's" hostility to the free market of capitalism. Hence, it has a vested interest in anti-profit and anti-bourgeois propaganda. It should cause no wonderment that they are eager to spread misinformation and thus contribute to rising expectations, rising entitlements and the inevitable psychological momentum for "more" from Washington under the illusion the rich people and corporations can finance the extravagances they have uncorked. Some of the "new class elitists" may not be so naive about Lenin's advice that capitalism can be wrecked from within through taxation and inflation.

So there is a sense in which capitalism may yet turn out to be its own gravedigger, since it is capitalism that creates this "new class"—through economic growth, affluence, mass higher education, the proliferation of new technologies of communication, and in a hundred other ways. Moreover, it must be said that the "idealism" of this "new class," though in all respects self-serving, is not for that reason insincere. It really is true that a civilization shaped predominately by a free market—by the preferences and appetites of ordinary men and women—has a "quality of life" that is likely to be regarded as less than wholly admirable by the better-educated class. To be sure, these classes could try to improve things by elevating and refining the preferences of all those ordinary people: That, supposedly, is the liberal and democratic way. But it is so much easier to mobilize the active layers of public opinion behind such issues as environmentalism, ecology, consumer protection, and economic planning, to give the government bureaucracy the power to regulate and coerce, and eventually to "politicize" the economic decision-making process. And this is, of course, exactly what has been happening.

Kristol very aptly summarized the crux of the matter in his reference above to the "new class" self-chosen leaders' "politicizing the economic decision-making process. They have taken out of perspective environmentalism, ecology, consumer protection, and economic planning and subverted desirable objectives as an excuse to add new layers to an overbloated bureaucracy. As a consequence, government payrolls are increased and they gain new servile adherents. As an example, witness the financial messes in New York City and Washington.

We should be alert as to what "politicizing" economic decision really means. It means government bureaucratic intrusion in many affairs of business. It means regulation, and don't forget that regulation begets more regulation; more people on government payrolls; more transfer payments and lower profits, thus less money for future jobs; lower profits, thus a diminishing exploitation of science and technology for the creation of new industries and jobs; more government trips to the money markets, causing more monetization of deficits, thus more inflation and higher interest rates and less money for industry and housing; ad infinitum.

The amounts that governments take from their citizens are grossly and shamefully unrecognized. As an example, take statements made about the relative stability of federal expenditures as compared with Gross National Product. This is erroneous because people don't pay their taxes out

Inflationary Aspects of Government Spending

of Gross National Product. This is important because about three-fifths of federal revenues come from personal and corporation income taxes, with more than two-fifths coming from personal income taxes. Efforts have also been made to relate expenditures to National Income. In this writer's opinion, the most meaningful comparison is between the total of all expenditures, federal, state, and local, and Disposable Personal Income, which consists of personal income less tax and non-tax payments to governments.

The following table was constructed from Department of Commerce figures:

Table XII-3
All Government Expenditures as % of:

	1929	1973-74
GNP	10	33
National Income	11	43
Disposable Income	12	51

Please note the contrast in the 1973-74 figures with those for 1929, especially the percentage of all government expenditures in reference to Disposable Income.

It is important to ask here, "What is the reason for this explosive growth of government?"

The basic reason is that we are in midst of an explosion in transfer payments.

While Disposable Personal Incomes were increasing 268% from 1959 to 1973, transfer payments were jumping upward at a 454% rate. Here is another startling statistic to behold. While transfer payments comprised only 1% of Disposable Personal Income in 1929, the 1973 figure was 12.5%. It is not our intention to bore you with statistics but just contemplate this startling development. In 1949 and 1959, transfer payments exceeded corporate tax liabilities by a shade; but by 1969 transfer payments were 52.5% higher and 126% higher in 1973.

The writer of this book in numerous instances has questioned the sincerity of many self-styled liberals and protectors of the poor as they have unleashed a huge propaganda against profits and the capitalist system, created the crisis in rising expectations and rising entitlements with one of the undesirable side effects being the huge explosion in transfer payments. This writer has found corroborative evidence in the perspicacious scrutiny and writings of Kristol. Further evidence of the insincerity of social workers and some union leaders was provided in a book by Daniel P. Moynihan, formerly United States Ambassador to the United Nations. His bluntness, frankness, and sincerity contrast vividly with the mealy-mouthedness of some members of the "new class." His book, *The Politics of a Guaranteed Income*, was reviewed by Jude Wanniski in the *Wall Street Journal* of March 5, 1973. The review in part follows:

THE INSIDE STORY OF THE DEATH OF THE FAMILY AID
by Jude Wanniski

Only an egotist or a dullard would write a 579-page book detailing the failure of Congress to pass a bill—and expect very many people to read it. At first glance, it may seem that Daniel Patrick Moynihan must be one or the other. But then the Family Assistance Plan wasn't just another bill. And it can be said with certainty that Pat Moynihan is no dullard.

Nor does he aim to merely chronicle the tribulations of FAP. The book, instead, is a deliciously bitter indictment of that class of Americans, in politics and the professions, whose careers rest on their assurances that they are the benefactors of the poor and the downtrodden. It is Mr. Moynihan's thesis that Richard Nixon's plan to assist the poor by putting cash in their hands directly (the "income strategy") died at the hands of those who are now enriched—politically, professionally, financially—by providing indirect aid to the poor (the "services strategy").

Why this opposition? Mr. Moynihan has an easy enough answer for the NWRO. "At the time of the President's address, AFDC (Aid to Families With Dependent Children) covered only 35% of the poor children in the nation: FAP would cover them all. NWRO represented children already covered, and could spare little concern for those not." A harsh judgment, richly deserved. Much of the NWRO hysteria over FAP was entirely based on the fiction that the FAP work requirements would "repeal the 14th Amendment," whereas in fact the FAP requirements were somewhat less rigid than current law.

The welfare pros and the antipoverty workers, including those directly financed by the Office of Economic Opportunity, "did all in their power to insure that a guaranteed income was not enacted."

Of course, the welfare pros correctly perceive that if the government gives the poor cash instead of services, their welfare services would no longer be in demand. "With astonishing consistency," says Mr. Moynihan, "middle-class professionals—when asked to devise ways of improving the conditions of lower-class groups would come up with schemes of which the first effect would be to improve the condition of the middle-class professionals." Sort of a liberal version of the "trickle-down" theory, which the author likens to "feeding the sparrows by feeding the horses."

While most of the liberals who opposed FAP cloaked their self-interest in fictions and pieties, some were blatant and straightforward. Jerry Wurf, head of the American Federation of State, County, and Municipal Employes, which represents 30,000 welfare workers, testified against FAP: "This legislation threatens to eliminate the jobs of our people." Federal jobs would replace state jobs, the comfortable status quo would be altered.

Mr. Moynihan observes the bitter irony that the poor "never showed any sign of comprehending the opportunity being offered them, nor of resenting those who in their name rejected the offer." For the short explanation of the episode is that Richard Nixon proposed to give $6 billion to the poor and the Democratic Congress refused.

Prominence to the foregoing review is given for two reasons. The first is to demonstrate as effectively as possible the arrant insincerity and dishonesty of a great segment of the "new class," the professional social careerists whose main concern is to maintain or even increase the size of their empires. The second is to stress the undesirable side effects with profound social implications of the demise of FAP, which was to supplant most welfare programs, especially Aid to Families with Dependent Children.

ADC has grown from less than $1 billion in 1959 to over $7.2 billion by 1973. But ironically it has done irreparable harm to our social structure. In his book *Real America,* Wattenberg makes this startling disclosure (page 62): "The percentage of families in poverty that had *female heads* increased sharply from 23% in 1959 to 43% in 1972."

Now, what are the social implications? This means ADC provided incentive for fathers, wed or unwed, to move away. This means that over two-fifths of families at poverty level are without a father to discipline and supervise children at ages when characters are formed. These children get their life's orientation in streets and alleys. The numbers of potential criminals, thereby, are increased disproportionately. It is imperative that ADC be abolished and replaced by FAP as soon as possible. In this writer's opinion ADC, coupled with the irresponsible attacks on profits, have combined to give the criminal the rationale to mug, rape, kill, push dope, cheat on welfare and food stamps, etc. The "new class elitists" in effect put the gun into the criminals' hands and helped pull the trigger. This is a strong indictment. It will have to be disproved before the writer would change his mind.

Inflationary Aspects of Government Spending

Another disturbing element about federal outlays are the amounts that are relatively uncontrollable under present law. The following table was constructed from the Tax Foundation's *Facts and Figures* and shows the percentage that uncontrollable items comprise of all budget outlays.

Table XII-4

1967	59.3%
1973	70.1%
1974	71.8%
1975	73.5%

Relentlessly, ever upward! Is it out of place to consider that the financial mess New York City is in can befall the nation? The demagogues are doing better from within this country than Lenin ever dreamed and yet they cry for "more."

Is it any wonder that many unskilled jobs are hard to fill when supposedly over 9% are unemployed at this time and when we contemplate the fact that total social welfare expenditures increased from $52 billion in 1960 to $215 billion in 1973, a whopping increase of over 313%. We have arrived at a condition where welfare now beats not only working but also unemployment benefits. It should be observed that incentives are increased to leave the producing sector of the economy and to join the non-producers. But what is more disturbing is that social workers actively and aggressively urge people to leave jobs in industry in order to go on welfare.

It is not our intent to burden the reader with a mass of statistics. This is done with a purpose to bring fiscal developments into proper focus and perspective. Concentration on only recent developments can mask deleterious long-range developments that can create a false sense of securtiy. As an example, we will repeat the observation that we made about erroneous conclusions that arise from naivete about economic data. We are referring to the assertion that has been made about the illusory stability of government expenditures in relation to GNP. The flaw in this reasoning is that even learned professors have taken a cause of inflation, government expenditures, and the end-result, an inflationary bloated GNP in current dollars, and come to an astounding conclusion: "Look, the ratio is the same before and after—hence government expenditures do not cause inflation."

Reference is often made in news commentaries with the cliché, "the news behind the news." Well, here we will give the reader some more exciting and informative data consistent with our objective of giving the reader "the statistics behind the statistics."

We have referred to the fallacy of relating data bloated by inflation to a cause of inflation as in comparing GNP in current dollars to money supply of government expenditures. A more realistic picture is obtained by relating money-supply-generating factors and government expenditures to Industrial Production, instead of GNP in current or even constant dollars. This is more consistent with the definition of inflation as too much money chasing a limited amount of goods. After all people don't buy GNP but they purchase goods that are produced. The following table was constructed to reveal an important element of demand-pull inflation.

Please observe that we have referred to total Federal

Table XII-5

Percentage Increases

	Industrial Production	Per Year	Government Expenditures	Per Year	FRB Credit	Per Year	Consumer Prices	Per Year
1950-60	47	4.7	114	11.4	32	3.2	22	2.2
1960-70	62	6.2	121	12.1	130	13.0	32	3.2
1970-73	18	6.0	30	10.0	28	9.3	28	9.3

Bank Credit outstanding because increases in bank credit are the basis for money supply growth and also reflect monetization of federal debt—this is the real engine of demand-pull inflation. Total FRB credit indicates the Federal Reserve Board intent and ability of accommodating to the growth of federal expenditures.

It is important to observe that government spending and FRB credit were outpacing the growth in the supply of goods produced. This picture contrasts vividly with the political and economic fantasies of sham liberals who attempt to lull the populace into accepting their illusions that government's spending growth should cause no concern as long as GNP in current dollars keeps pace.

We will interject one caveat here relative to the per year percentage increases that we derived by simply dividing by the number of years. This may not meet with the approval of statistical purists. However, since all data are likewise treated, this does not invalidate the comparison.

It should be noted that the last column lagged behind industrial production increases but then finally exploded and surpassed it.

The obvious conclusion is that government spendings are an important cause of demand-pull inflation. In addition, the growth of the public sector is encroaching upon the private sector—the non-producing segment is growing faster than the producing segment. The undue enlargement of the public portion is having a pernicious impact in the money markets, further hampering the functions of producers in private industry.

As the big picture unfolds, we are getting the harvest of the whirlwind of the frenzy of the Lindsay era in New

Inflationary Aspects of Government Spending

York City and the fantasies of Johnson's Great Society. We see huge and inexorably growing service and regulatory bureaucracies taking funds away from industries. The nonproducers are milking the producers besides interfering with the producers' functions of creating jobs for an ever-growing population. Irving Kristol warns that ". . . the new service bureaucracies and regulatory bureaucracies that were created in Washington have by now developed their own constituencies, both outside Congress and in, and it is going to be exceedingly difficult to diminish their size or curb their powers."

What is to be done and what can be done? That is the overriding question. Major problems require major measures. In the words of Kristol, it would be absurd and suicidal to abolish the welfare state. Many functions are necessary and desirable. However, bureaucracies are unwieldy and inefficient because there is no cost discipline—that redeeming social function that is an accessory part of the profit system. The welfare state should be reshaped, delimited and above all debureaucratized as suggested by Kristol.

Among bold measures we advocate a freeze on all government employment, and at least attrition of government employees through death and retirement if not some immediate outright paring. We also urge immediate enactment of FAP, which would include housing allowances in lieu of public housing. All job-training programs should be diverted to private industry.

Get ready for the blockbuster.

Abolish all corporate income taxes!!!

This may appear extreme, but let us consider the consequences. Again look at the table constructed in the foregoing paragraphs and observe that transfer payments are almost equal to corporate income before taxes. The corporate tax bite of $50 billion would do more good than the $113 spent on transfer payments. Industry that is starved for funds and modern plant capacity would immediately put those funds to work building new plants, creating new industries and new jobs. More money would be available for research thus enhancing our scientific and technological base. In this writer's opinion, the country would inherit a chronic shortage of labor. Is this what the bureaucrats are afraid of? They would lose people to service and appeal to for the sake of perpetuating their empires. It is possible that they do not relish losing their jobs and being forced to work in private industry under a cost-and-performance discipline.

It is pertinent to ask here why should the economy be subjected to $50-$100 billion deficits in the Federal budget for the sake of giving funds to bureaucrats, whereas private industry could better utilize human resources and technological resources. Thus, the non-producing sector would decline while the producing segment would grow and flourish, improving our social fabric enormously.

While immediate and total abolishment of all corporate income taxes would be too drastic, at least a phase-out should be considered, along with a tie-in that would limit tax exemption to corporations that do not raise prices other than pass-through cost increases.

Such a revolutionary program would reverse the trend of excessive and counterproductive demands that the elitists have been exacting from our productive capacity. Social demands would be fulfilled by a rise in productive capacity and jobs, not by the printing presses. Production produces the income to clear the market of goods without any inflationary impact. On the other hand, social demands, exceeding productive capacity and generated by rhetoric against profits and by rising expectations and entitlements and fulfilled by the printing presses, are inflationary. There is no doubt which method merits the stamp of approval of social redeemability. One route will lead to an ever-growing bureaucratization and collectivization of industry and jobs; the other route will point to a workers' capitalism.

XIII

WAGE RATES, INFLATION AND UNEMPLOYMENT

How can we expect workers to get true facts about economic affairs when college students are fed economic bunk? As an example, we present the following bit of economic humbug from a learned professor.

"The greedy labor unions didn't start inflation," according to Robert Lekachman, Distinguished Professor of Economics at Herbert M. Lehman College of the City University of New York, in an article entitled "Five Steps to Economic Happiness," in the June 8, 1975, issue of the *New York*

Times. This is an example of academic irresponsibility which is affecting our entire social fabric.

Such spokesmen make statements absolving unions of causing or starting inflation without any statistical verification. They both blame big business, as Leonard Woodcock referred to "oligopolistic corporations . . . among main forces continuing inflation," and Lekachman implying as much when he advocated proposals to "regulate concentrated industries."

What are the statistical facts?

In the words of Alfred E. Smith, "Let's look at the record."

The author of this book has constructed a table to present the true facts concerning U.S. manufacturing industries, one of the main targets of the "new class" liberal economists and union leaders. The indexes, compiled by U.S. Bureau of Labor Statistics, were converted from the 1967 base of 100.0 to a 1950 base as 100.0. The last column on profit margins was added from Federal Trade Commission and SEC data.

Relative to the data in the table other than profit margins, the following definitions are given by the U.S. Bureau of Labor Statistics in its issues of the *Monthly Labor Review:*

> Output is the constant dollar market value of final goods and services produced in a given period. Indexes of output per manhour, or productivity, measure changes in the volume of goods and services produced per unit of labor. Compensation per manhour includes wages and salaries of employees plus employers' contributions for social insurance and private benefit plans. The data also include an estimate of wages, salaries, and supplementary payments for the self-employed, except for nonfinancial corporations, in which there are no self-employed.

Wage Rates, Inflation and Unemployment

Table XIII-1
INDEXES OF COSTS IN MANUFACTURING
AND RELATED DATA
1950=100.0

	Output per Man-Hour	Compensation per Man-Hour	Unit Labor Costs	Unit Non-Labor Costs	Implicit Price Deflator	After-Tax Profit Margin
1950	100.0	100.0	100.0	100.0	100.0	7.1%
1960	121.8	171.1	140.5	112.6	131.1	4.4
1970	161.5	270.4	167.4	117.1	150.5	4.0
1971	170.3	288.4	169.3	127.5	155.1	4.2
1972	178.8	304.4	170.1	130.3	156.6	4.3
1973	182.1	325.8	178.9	125.6	160.8	4.7
1974	174.8	358.0	204.6	115.0	174.4	5.5
1975	173.7	395.3	227.4			

SOURCE: *Monthly Labor Review*, April 1976, Table 31 (revised).

Unit labor costs measure the labor compensation cost required to produce one unit of output and are derived by dividing compensation per man-hour by output per man-hour. Unit nonlabor payments include profits, depreciation, interest, and indirect taxes per unit of output. They are computed by subtracting compensation of all persons from the current dollar gross national product and dividing by output. In these tables, unit nonlabor costs contain all the components of unit nonlabor payments except unit profits.

The implicit price deflator is derived by dividing the current dollar estimate of gross product by the constant dollar estimate, making the deflator, in effect, a price index for gross product of the sector reported.

The figures shown above irrefutably debunk the assertions of Woodcock and Lekachman. The most important item is the one for unit labor costs, because it reveals that wage-rate increases have outpaced output per man-hour, thus leading to price increases. This is shown by the close condition between unit labor costs and the price index for manufacturers, the implicit price deflator. Manufacturers' prices have lagged behind unit labor costs. The after-tax profit margin data shows that profit margins were not a factor in price inflation. As a matter of fact, the figures show that profit margins had decreased, indicating that manufacturers had absorbed some of the inflationary cost increases. Here we have statistical proof that wage increases in excess of productivity increases are a major cause of cost-push inflation.

Woodcock also wrote of the "need of workers . . . to avoid distortion of income distribution to their disadvantage."

In his own words, Woodcock's absurdity is all the more bizarre when we consider the perspectives in the table on National Income by Distributive Shares as presented in Chapter One in Table I-4.

A close scrutiny of the table in Chapter One, besides illustrating the falsehoods of Woodcock and all his camp followers of the "new class" and the sham intellectuals, will reveal some startling developments. This illustrates the value of historical perspective. The rises in wages and salaries have exceeded by a substantial margin the rises in after-tax corporate profits. The percentage allocations reveal the true picture.

Special attention is called to the unprecedented surge in supplements to wages and salaries. In data not shown above, in 1973 employers contributed $48.4 billion for social insurance and $39.2 billion to pension and welfare funds for a total of $87.6, which exceeds after-tax corporate profits.

The foregoing not only debunks the anti-business rhetoric

of Woodcock, Lekachman and the rest, but also provides proof of the ingenuity of the entrepreneur, the engineer, the technician, scientist and business manager. Pressured by unwarranted demands from union leaders and the regulatory and service bureaucracies, they exploited science and technology to maintain industrial progress. However, a critical junction was reached in the late sixties and early seventies when the innovators and producers were denied funds to increase capacity to provide jobs and to further exploit technology. They were denied funds by the rapacity of greedy unions and government bureaucrats who combined to unleash a rhetoric that unduly increased aspirations, expectations and entitlements, with unprecedented transfers of funds from producers to non-producers. Thereby, they were largely instrumental in uncorking demand-pull inflation of government spending and cost-push inflation of wage-rate raises exceeding productivity. Monetary inflation was an accessory to accommodating both in the upward phase. But when monetary brakes were applied, they could not halt the inflation but created unemployment—leading to the new phenomenon called "slumpflation."

Again consider the following two gems of economic claptrap:

> *Woodcock:* . . . "oligopolistic corporations . . . are among main forces continuing the present inflation . . ."
> *Lekachman:* . . . "Inflation is explained by . . . (5) the tendency of large corporations (as in autos) to raise prices while demand shrank."

This is consistent with the propaganda of the "new class" that manufacturers control prices, and resort to price gouging and profiteering. In our numerous refutations, we have cited data to pove that the cost discipline inherent in the profit system is a tremendous force of redeeming social values working toward the betterment of mankind in providing food, clothing, shelter and the amenities of life at a reasonable price. Our contentions are further buttressed by a table, which we have captioned "A Tribute to Establishment Know-How."

The table presents pertinent economic indexes with 1950 as a base of 100 and also a 1960 as a base of 100. The indexes were converted by a writer to these bases from data appearing in the U.S. Department of Labor publications such as *Handbook of Labor Statistics, Employment and Earnings,* and *Wholesale Prices and Price Indexes.*

As stated before, the American manufacturers should be accorded bouquets not brickbats for their splendid performance. While their profits were squeezed to less than five cents on the dollar, they turned out goods at very reasonable prices while paying out in wages and supplements more than ever before.

Take autos as an example. The automakers on average paid in increased wages 194.8% more in 1973 than in 1950, but increased prices only 49.8%. In a most remarkable span from 1959 to 1969, auto prices remained stable while hourly earnings were up 47.3%.

The table shows where the real oligopolies really are. They are in union power. Freed from anti-trust legislation, unions are irresponsibly exercising their extortionary powers. For a prime example, just look at the figures in construc-

Wage Rates, Inflation and Unemployment

Table XIII-2
A TRIBUTE TO ESTABLISHMENT KNOW-HOW

	1950	1973	1960	1973
Durable Goods				
Hourly Earnings	100.0	284.2	100.0	177.8
Consumer Prices	100.0	184.5	100.0	150.0
Durable Goods Prices	100.0	137.9	100.0	126.1
Household Durable				
Goods Prices	100.0	118.6	100.0	116.6
Household Appliance				
Prices	100.0	100.8	100.0	100.9
Home Electronic				
Equipment Prices	100.0	73.6	100.0	78.0
Construction				
Hourly Earnings	100.0	347.8	100.0	210.0
Cost of Home				
Ownership			100.0	170.0
Hourly Earnings				
Transportation Equipment	100.0	294.8	100.0	185.0
Motor Vehicle				
Prices	100.0	149.8	100.0	114.2
Physicians' Fees	100.0	250.4	100.0	179.5
Dentists' Fees	100.0	213.5	100.0	166.1
Gas and Electricity	100.0	155.7	100.0	128.2
		1959	1969	
Motor Vehicle Prices		100.0	100.0	
Hourly Earnings				
Transportation Equipment		100.0	147.3	

tion. Construction hourly earnings have by far outpaced all other wages and price indexes. The table clearly shows that the manufacturers are the real benefactors of the working man by giving him a well-paying job—in most cases with union prodding—and providing the workers with goods at reasonable prices. The table also shows who is screwing whom. The construction unions are not only screwing their members out of jobs through their extortionate wage rate increases, but also screwing the other workers and especially the poor out of buying housing at a decent price.

The table also buttresses our proposal to give the manufacturer a freer hand to exploit technology and create new jobs by abolishing the corporate income taxes for qualifying corporations.

These facts of economic life are at a variance with the froth coming from the intelligentsia and the "new class." The American manufacturer can better utilize funds than the bureaucrats and should also be freed of overregulation by the bureaucrats. Adam Smith's "invisible hand" should be accorded a sympathetic atmosphere rather than unwarranted hostility.

It is not our intent to denigrate some of the meritorious achievements of the New Deal and the Great Society. However, we do object to the belief that the Big Uncle in Washington can solve all of our problems. We do object to the income redistributive philosophy that has been carried too far, spawning the crisis in rising expectations, the revolution in ever-growing entitlements and the psychological momentum for "more" from industry and government without regard to consequences. The crucial difference to bear in mind is that business recycles profits into jobs while bureaucracies recycle funds into paper-shuffling empires, where bureaucracies are not subject to the forces of market competition, and, therefore, there is no way to test their relative efficiency or acceptability.

In numerous instances in this treatise, we have alluded to the irresponsible and misleading propagandism of our

Wage Rates, Inflation and Unemployment

intelligentsist academics who must be charged with the mischievous brainwashing of our student body into false and distorted images of profits, prices and capitalism.

On this point, we present some divergent views. Roger A. Freeman, Senior Fellow of the Hoover Institution, wrote that we should look at the prevailing direction of the division of income between labor and ownership. Mr. Freeman shows that employee compensation has accounted for an increasing portion of the national income. Indeed, in the first half of 1971, it rose to 75.8 percent, from 69.8 percent in 1965. Meanwhile, the proportion of pre-tax profits declined from 13.8 percent to 9.6 percent, while that of after-tax profits fell from 8.2 percent to 5.2 percent. Mr. Freeman argues that any freeze of profits should be made on their average share of the national or corporate income during the last five years, while at the same time freezing labor's share on the same basis. This, says Mr. Freeman, would result in a rollback for labor and an increase for profits. Mr. Freeman indicates that this would mean setting profits at higher than the current level, providing a great lesson for those who claimed that President Nixon's policy favored corporations to the detriment of the working man.

On October 14, 1971, however, another *Times* letter to the editor, jointly signed by Richard DuBoff, Associate Professor of Economics at Bryn Mawr, and Edward Herman, Professor of Finance at the Wharton School of Finance, takes issue with Mr. Freeman. The Messrs. DuBoff and Herman feel that Freeman's figures do not tell the whole story—he compares the percentages of national income claimed by employee compensation to corporate profits from 1965 through 1970. But, argue DuBoff and Herman, using gross aggregates for such a comparison is questionable, because "employee compensation" includes such items as wages, salaries and military pay, but fails to cover wages of the self-employed—farmers or small-business men. DuBoff and Herman feel that more valid figures would be the internal statistics of the corporate sector. These figures, they assert, clearly show that 1960-70, average, after-tax corporate profits rose 72 percent, and after-tax profits plus depreciation or "cash flow" rose 88 percent, while at the same time average weekly gross earnings for manufacturing workers increased by 51 percent.

Further, say the professors, Freeman's data, covering only 1965-70 as it does, is biased, because 1970 was, relatively, the worst year for corporate profits since 1958 and the lowest in absolute levels since 1964. On the other hand, 1965-66 was a time of peak profits. The years from 1967 to 1970, they say, were only a catching-up period for wages and salaries, an attempt to close the gap that had opened up earlier. They state parenthetically that, even with the catching-up increases, real take-home pay for manufacturing workers has remained essentially stagnant, and, although they agree with Freeman that inflation-propelled wage hikes did push up unit labor manufacturing costs after 1965, these increases had no effect on the long-term profit positions built up by the corporations during the pre-1965 period when the unit labor costs had been falling.

In both letters, references relative to international comparisons in unit labor costs were deleted because they were considered irrelevant to the theses in this chapter and because there is no agreement as to when a state of equilib-

Wage Rates, Inflation and Unemployment

rium is considered to exist in the matter of unit labor costs.

In no uncertain terms, DuBoff and Herman have expressed their views. We will now present their claims as separate items with appropriate rebuttals.

DuBoff and Herman Claim: *These figures, they assert, clearly show that 1960-70, average, after-tax corporate profits rose 72 percent, and after-tax profits plus depreciation of "cash flow" rose 88 percent, while at the same time average weekly gross earnings for manufacturing workers increased by 51 percent.*

Rebuttal: The writers of the letter err in two respects. First, they are comparing two items which are not comparable—an aggregate and a rate. An aggregate can easily outpace a rate. They took aggregate profits and compared them with average weekly earnings.

What are the true facts when we compare congruous figures? We will again refer to our tabulation of distributive shares and set them to 1959 as a base of 100. We get the following results:

Table XIII-3

	Wages and Salaries	Supplements to Wages and Salaries	Corporate After-Tax Profits
1959	100.0	100.0	100.0
1969	197.7	266.6	155.0

The percentage increases are as follows: 97.7% for wages and salaries; 166.7% for supplements thereto; and,

55% for profits. Quite different from the figures in the letter. In fact, profit margins, the only statistically fair test of corporate profit performance, actually deteriorated in that decade, as evidenced by the figures in the first table in this chapter.

Second. Many teachers of economics and finance have resorted to the spurious practice, concocted by *American Federationist,* the official publication of the AFL-CIO, of attempting to use cash flow as a measure of corporate profitability. In this respect, Dexter M. Keezer wrote:

> I disagree completely with the *American Federationist,* official magazine of the AFL-CIO, which recently argued, "The cash flow, which is reported profits plus depreciation allowances, is the accurate measurement of a company's returns, since it is the amount of money left over after payment of all costs and taxes. (June, 1962). If that becomes the accepted conception of profits or business returns, it will be a most effective way of getting rid of the business system. Depreciation is a cost."*

It is an indication of the mental bankruptcy of the AFL-CIO economists and their ilk to take the cost of recovering moneys that were spent for physical assets and add them to profits for measuring profitability. This surely can be taken as proof of their inability to offer statistical proof or alleged excessive corporate profits.

DuBoff and Herman Claim: *The years from 1967 to 1970, they say were only a catching-up period for wages and salaries, an attempt to close the gap that had opened up earlier. They state parenthetically that, even with the*

---

*Dexter M. Keezer, *Profits in a Modern Economy—Selected Papers from a Conference on Understanding Profits.* (Minneapolis: University of Minnesota, 1967,) p. 35.

Wage Rates, Inflation and Unemployment

catching-up increases, real take-home pay for manufacturing workers has remained essentially stagnant.

Rebuttal: As proof of our views, we present Table XIII-4, based on material from the *Handbook of Labor Statistics, 1974,* of real compensation per man-hour for all persons in manufacturing.

Table XIII-4
Real Compensation per Man-Hour

1967-100.0

1947	55.4
1966	98.0
1973	112.7

DuBoff and Herman Claim: *They agree with Freeman that inflation-propelled wage hikes did push up unit labor manufacturing costs after 1965, but these increases had no effect on the long-term profit positions built up by the corporations during the pre-1965 period when the unit labor costs had been falling.*

Rebuttal: A referral to the table in Chapter One indicates that profit margins have been eroding. If profit margins were corrected for loss in purchasing power, real profit margins have declined significantly. The losses would be shown to have decreased more if allowance were made in the increased cost of replacing assets. (The true picture in long-term perspective for unit labor costs was shown in Table XIII-1 of this chapter.)

Here we have the results of the diabolically contrived propaganda against profits. Is it any wonder that college students, high school teachers and adults are brainwashed into accepting a false picture when college professors of economics and finance and labor economists peddle distorted and untrue versions of corporate profitability? They are to a large degree responsible for our problems of rising expectations, excessive entitlements and unrestrained psychological momentum for "more." These tactics of "new class" irresponsibility and mischief are important factors in abetting the cost-push inflation of big unions and demand-pull inflation of the governmental regulatory and service bureaucracies.

And what do the "new class" elitists propose to cure the mess that they have concocted? More government and more government interference in the affairs of business!

Robert Lekachman writes, "Move toward sensible, democratic planning. . . ."

Leonard Woodcock also advocates planning because, "Experience has taught us that the unseen magic of the so-called free market does not work."

Another illustration of arrant buncombe! He, among others, puts handcuffs on the "invisible hand" of free enterprise, besides burdening it with a ball and chain, and then points out, "Look, it doesn't work."

The advocates of national planning appear to be misguided by the notion that the right kind of government bureaucracy can change human nature. They also are completely oblivious of cost-benefit ratios. These elitists of the left should consider that the new large middle class is entitled to give free enterprise a reasonable chance to function. The crucial choice is between leaving more funds with business and free enterprise—the producing group—or keep on transferring funds to the welfare state bureaucracy—the non-producing group. The choice is between rewarding efficiency or subsidizing the inefficiency of a paper shuffling paradise. The choice is between productive jobs or boondoggling. The choice is between profit and cost disciplines or egregious waste with no cost restraints. We are stressing these choices to emphasize the redeeming social worthiness of abolishing all corporate taxes with the view of generating funds for job creation.

Contrary to leftist and radical nonsense, the primary product of capitalism is not profits but competition. Profits are merely a means of keeping score—especially on costs, thus reducing real prices and making more goods available for more people.

The arguments and data cited above debunk the myths concocted by the intelligentsist "new class" about profits and the profit system. In the same vein, there is a great deal of fuzzy thinking and loose talk about unemployment, especially "full employment unemployment."

A timely and thought-provoking article in this respect appeared in the *Wall Street Journal* of May 9, 1975. The article in full follows:

A Measuring Stick for Employment
by Geoffrey H. Moore

During 1974 the unemployment rate averaged 5.6%, a relatively high figure by historical standards. At the same time, the percentage of the population of working age that had jobs averaged 57%, exceeding any preceding year since World War II and probably before that. According to the unemployment rate, the economy was a considerable distance away from full employment. According to the employment ratio, it was more fully employed than ever before. Which is the more appropriate guide to the hypothetical condition of full employment?

Although no categorical answer can be given, a substantial case can be made for the employment ratio on the grounds of its objectivity, its statistical reliability, and its close relation to wage and price inflation. While the economy currently is far short of full employment as a result of the recession, and inflation also is receding for the same reason, it is a good time to take a look at this issue, well before it confronts us once again.

With respect to objectivity, the concept of employment is firmer than the concept of unemployment. Having a job and being paid for it is, for the most part, an observable experience. True, there are some fuzzy situations—as when a person is on strike, or has accepted a job but hasn't yet started to work, or is on vacation without pay, or is working only a few hours a week. But most of these situations can be objectively identified and don't affect the great bulk of those who are employed.

The concept of unemployment is quite different. For those who have had a job and have just been laid off, the situation may be obvious. Nevertheless, unless the worker is doing something to seek work, he will not be counted as unemployed according to the definition used for many years in the United States. Moreover, those who are unemployed because they have been laid off usually constitute less than half of the unemployed. The rest have either quit their jobs voluntarily or have not recently (or ever) had a job. Now they are seeking one.

Seeking a Job

Seeking a job is not as clear-cut a condition as having a job. One can seek work now and then, or systematically. One can seek a job, yet turn down one or more offers. One can set realistic or unrealistic standards for pay, hours, type of work or location. Or one can give up seeking a job because none is to be found, yet be quite ready to take one if the opportunity comes along. Indeed, not a few persons become employed without having been unemployed in the strict sense of the term.

In short, for a sizable number of the jobless, whether one is unemployed or not is to some degree a matter of opinion. In the monthly household survey conducted by the U.S. Census Bureau from which estimates of total employment and unemployment are derived, questions are answered by the respondent—often the housewife who happens to be at home and who answers for the entire family. Hence there is bound to be some variability in opinion from one household to another, or from the same household at different times. A serious effort is made to reduce this variability, but much of it is inherent in the concept itself.

This is one reason for paying close attention to unemployment rates for those whose unemployment status is not likely to be in doubt—married men or heads of household, those who have lost their jobs or those who are seeking full-time work. It is also a reason for focusing on the employment figures, since variability of opinion is likely to be much less important regarding whether the individual is employed.

With respect to statistical reliability, the employment figures also have an edge. Because the number of unemployed is much smaller than the number who are employed, the former is subject to a much larger sampling error than the latter. The sampling variability of the unemployment count is somewhat less than 2%; for the employment count it is about one-fourth of 1%. Moreover, seasonal variations are easier to eliminate in employment than in unemployment so the results are less subject to revision.

When the comparison pertains to the unemployment rate, which is the number of unemployed divided by the civilian labor force (employed plus unemployed), and the employment ratio, which is the number employed divided by the noninstitutional population 16 years old and over, the conceptual and statistical differences also favor the employment ratio. The labor force, since it includes the unemployed, is subject to many of the same problems that pertain to the identification of who is unemployed. The population figure, of course, is free of these definitional difficulties. Similarly, the labor force figure is subject to sampling error while the population figure is not. Other types of estimating errors, which do affect the population figure, equally affect the labor force, because the latter is estimated on the basis of proportions derived from the sample and applied to the population estimate.

These considerations point to the desirability of giving careful attention to the employment figures as well as the unemployment figures in assessing the economic situation. This would not be true if employment and unemployment were simply reverse sides of the same coin. But unemployment does not always rise when employment declines, or vice versa. Job loss is not the only source of unemployment. Decisions to enter the labor market, i.e., to seek work and therefore become unemployed, can be made quite independently of changes in employment, for example, by those who have never had a job before. Moreover, increases in the number of persons with jobs can induce others to seek work because they view the opportunities more favorably. Hence an increase in employment can add to unemployment, and a reduction in employment can eliminate some unemployment.

For all these reasons, therefore, it is important to determine whether the percentage of the population employed is useful as a measure of the degree to which the economy is fully employed and in particular to see how closely related it is to the rate of inflation. As it turns out, the employment ratio is quite closely related to the rate of change in the consumer price index during the same year. High employment ratios have been associated with high rates of inflation. The relationship seems to be somewhat curvilinear. There has been relatively little inflation when the percentage employed has been in the range 53.5% to 55.5%, but higher employment ratios have been associated with increasingly sharp advances in the rate of inflation.

Moreover, the relation is reversible. Peak years in the business cycle bring forth higher employment ratios and higher inflation rates while trough years do the opposite. However, a reduction in the employment ratio during a recession is associated with a smaller reduction in inflation than an equal increase in the employment ratio during an expansion phase of the cycle. Perhaps this is an additional bit of evidence that it is harder to get rid of inflation than to generate it.

The Historical Relations

During the current recession the employment ratio declined from its all-time high, 57.5%, in October 1973 to 54.9% in March 1975. The April figure was up a bit, to 55%. Although the reduction in employment has been sharp, the percentage employed in March and April was higher than in any previous recession year, save 1970. As the historical relation would lead one to expect, the rate of increase in consumer prices has declined also. The latest figure, for March, showed an increase at an annual rate of less than 4%, down sharply from the double digit rates of last year.

In general, rates of wage and price inflation have been far more closely correlated with the employment ratio than with the unemployment rate. The relation between inflation and unemployment is a very loose one, despite all the discussion about the trade-off. In particular, 1974 was off in a class by itself, with considerable unemployment and a great deal of inflation. What was largely overlooked was the record high employment ratio.

How is it possible, as in 1974, that a large percentage of the working age population is employed and at the same time a large percentage is unemployed? A high employment percentage demonstrates that opportunities to find work exist and that efforts to find work are likely to be successful. It is not surprising then, that more people are induced to look for work. By definition, they become unemployed. Under such circumstances a high unemployment rate is not an indication of difficulty in finding work, but rather the opposite. Nor is it an indication of softness in the labor market and that smaller wage increases would be acceptable—quite the opposite.

Of course it is true that much of the time a high employment ratio and a low unemployment rate go together, and vice versa. During the current recession, the employment ratio has declined and the unemployment rate has risen. But here again it is well to keep both measures in mind. The unemployment rate is high now partly because the employment ratio was extraordinarily high in 1973 and 1974. Many of those who were employed then but not employed now are naturally seeking to be reemployed; if they had not been employed in 1973-74 some of them might not be seeking employment now.

Moreover, when a recovery develops and the employment ratio rises again to a higher level, the overhang of unemployment created by the unusual employment experience of 1973-74 may still remain for some time. A condition of "full employment" in terms of the rate of inflation may again be accompanied by less than "full employment" in terms of the unemployment rate. Alternatively, a recovery, at least initially, might reduce unemployment as some drop out of the labor force but be insufficiently vigorous to raise the employment ratio, which is what happened during the first two years of recovery after the 1961 recession. Would such a recovery, with a lower unemployment rate but a stable employment ratio, be moving the economy to full employment, or not?

Revising a '20s Theory

It should not be supposed that the close relation between price and wage changes and the employment ratio reflects only the effect of high employment on wages and therefore on prices. It may also reflect the effect of rapid price increases on incentives to hire and the effect of rapid wage increases on incentives to become employed. Indeed, when Irving Fisher wrote about this relationship in the 1920s, he thought the influence of price inflation on employment was dominant. Nowadays, as a result of the attention given to the "Phillips curve," the causal relation, if any, is thought to run mainly the other way. Probably it runs in both directions. Moreover, employment, prices and wages are also affected jointly by other factors.

At this point it seems reasonable to conclude only that the employment ratio should not be ignored in measuring the tightness of the labor market and the position of the economy with respect to the goal of full employment without inflation.

Mr. Moore is Vice President, Research, of the National Bureau of Economic Research Inc. and Senior Research Fellow of the Hoover Institution at Stanford University. He was formerly U.S. Commissioner of Labor Statistics.

In line with Mr. Moore's suggestion, the writer constructed Table XIII-5.

The non-institutional population is the population of working age, 16 years old and older. Column three of Table XIII-5 provides us with the employment rate that is held to be so significant by Geoffrey H. Moore in his article in the *Wall Street Journal* (May 9, 1975).

Attention should be focused on several of Moore's assertions that carry significant connotations.

> *Moore:* There has been relatively little inflation when the percentage employed has been in the range 53.5% to 55.5%.
>
> In general, rates of wage and price inflation have been far more closely correlated with the employment ratio than with the unemployment rate. The relation between inflation and unemployment is a very loose one despite all the discussion about the trade-off. In particular, 1974 was off in a class by itself, with considerable unemployment and a great deal of inflation. What was largely overlooked was the record high employment ratio.

Table XIII-5
EMPLOYMENT STATUS OF NON-INSTITUTIONAL POPULATION
(numbers in thousands)

	(1) Total Non-Institutional Population	(2) Total Employed	(3) Percent of Population (2) ÷ (1)	(4) Percent Unemployed	(5) Non-Agricultural Employees	Percent (5) ÷ (1)
1950	106,645	58,918	55.2	5.3	51,758	48.5
1951	107,721	59,961	55.7	3.3	53,235	49.4
1952	108,823	60,250	55.4	3.0	53,749	49.4
1953	110,601	61,179	55.3	2.9	54,919	49.7
1954	111,671	60,109	53.8	5.5	53,904	48.3
1955	112,732	62,170	55.2	4.4	55,722	49.4
1956	113,811	63,799	56.0	4.1	57,514	50.5
1957	115,065	64,071	55.7	4.3	58,123	50.5
1958	116,363	63,036	54.2	6.8	57,450	49.4
1959	117,881	64,630	54.8	5.5	59,065	50.1
1960	119,759	65,778	54.9	5.5	60,318	50.4
1961	121,343	65,746	54.2	6.7	60,546	49.4
1962	122,981	66,702	54.2	5.5	61,759	50.2
1963	125,154	67,762	54.1	5.7	63,076	50.4
1964	127,224	69,305	54.5	5.2	64,782	50.9
1965	129,236	71,088	55.6	4.5	66,726	51.6
1966	131,180	72,895	55.6	3.8	68,915	52.5

Table XIII-5 (Continued)
EMPLOYMENT STATUS OF NON-INSTITUTIONAL POPULATION
(numbers in thousands)

	(1) Total Non-Institutional Population	(2) Total Employed	(3) Percent of Population (2) ÷ (1)	(4) Percent Unemployed	(5) Non-Agricultural Employees	(5) ÷ (1) Percent
1967	133,319	74,372	55.9	3.8	70,527	52.9
1968	135,562	75,920	56.0	3.6	72,103	53.2
1969	137,841	77,902	56.5	3.5	74,296	53.9
1970	140,182	78,627	56.1	4.9	75,165	53.6
1971	142,596	79,120	55.5	5.9	75,732	53.1
1972	145,775	81,702	56.9	5.6	78,230	53.7
1973	148,263	84,409	56.9	4.9	80,957	54.6
1974	150,827	85,936	57.0	5.6	82,443	54.7
1974:						
October			57.3	6.0		
1975:						
March			54.9	8.7		
April			55.0	8.9		
May			55.1	9.2		
July			55.4	8.4		

Wage Rates, Inflation and Unemployment 267

With the above comments in mind, let us scrutinize the table. For all of 1974, we had an unemployment rate of 5.6%. In prior years, unemployment rates of about 5.5% were associated with employment ratios of less than 55%. There appears to be a rising bias and plausibly could be explained by Moore's belief that high employment induces more people to seek employment.

It is significant to observe that by July, 1975, the employment rate was the 1950-74 average while the unemployment rate was at 8.4%, contrasted with the 1950-74 average of 4.8%.

It would be prudent to observe that in May, 1975, when unemployment was at its peak rate of 9.2%—4.4% above the 1950-74 average—, the employment rate was at 55.1%—a picayune 0.3% percentage points below the 1950-74 average.

It should be obvious that the condition of the labor market did not warrant throwing money at the unemployment problem.

With jobs begging for workers, all that is needed is a change in motivation and attitudes, both of which are in a deplorable condition because of the rhetoric against profits and the free enterprise system. Employment would further be reduced in the two basic industries of autos and construction by applying a no-nonsense approach. More reasonable environmental and safety standards would go a long way to revive the auto industry. More reasonable wage rates and lower government deficits would reduce the price of homes and lower interest rates, thereby reviving construction. With both of these major and basic industries in uptrends, the rest of the economy would fall in step.

This brings up the question of what is "full employment unemployment." The figures and conclusions of Moore appear to confirm the belief that the definition of full employment is changing.

It appears that it would not be gratuitous to conclude that, at 9%, unemployment is really about 5%. That means that 95 to 96 out of every hundred are gainfully employed.

Hence, the question arises: Is it justifiable to vote additional government expenditures to throw more government money at problems caused by inflation when excessive governmental expenditures were an important factor in causing inflation in the first place? Another question: Are redeeming social objectives served by penalizing the producers to aid non-producers? It is our observation that it would be more socially redeeming to allow industry to create meaningful jobs. Rather than increased government expenditures, the following four-fold program would better relieve the destitute and the unemployed:

1. Institute FAP.
2. Abolish corporate income taxes.
3. Establish the National Technical Center.
4. Establish youth employment scholarships by subsidizing employers who would provide on-the-job training for teenagers to undo the damage minimum wage laws have inflicted on teenagers.

We have also added column six because it gives us another employment rate we consider important. This eliminates agricultural employment and gives proof of the ability of industry to assimilate people leaving agricultural work. This is also added proof of the efficiency of capitalist farming over collectivized farming. A smaller number of agricultural workers are providing our country and the world with more food and fiber than ever before.

And yet we get ludicrous proposals from the elitists, as evidenced by the following editorial in the *Wall Street Journal* of January 27, 1975:

> *Considering Alternatives*
>
> A group called the Democratic Socialist Organizing Committee is circulating a statement signed by six Nobel laureates urging that "exploration of alternatives to the Western economic systems be placed on the agenda at once." The statement says, in part: "The threat of hunger in the world is not so much the result of natural limitations upon Western (which is to say American) agricultural resources but derives rather from political limitations serving the interests of agribusiness." The signers of this declaration include a physicist, two prize-winners in medicine and three economists, counting Gunnar Myrdal.
>
> In light of the fact that American agribusiness has been exporting 67% of its wheat crop and more than half of its soybeans and derivatives while India, with its rich but untapped agricultural potential is still barely able to feed itself, we wonder if these gentlemen would also sign a statement calling on India to explore alternatives to its quasi-socialist system of central planning.

Here again, we will requote George Orwell's well-known dictum, "You have to belong to the intelligentsia to believe things like that: no ordinary man could be such a fool."

Unemployment data have been disputed for years by economists but nothing generates more heat than figures bandied around teen-age unemployment, especially black teen-age unemployment. Wattenberg in his *Real America* delved into the data with his customary and exemplary thoroughness and came up with these findings on black employment (pages 129-130 and 131):

> For about two decades the reality of the black-white employment situation was summed up this way: Black unemployment rates have been twice as high as white rates. That is still the unhappy case.
>
> But there has been a massive shift in who the black unemployed are. Thus, a cross-tabulation of black married men reveals a far sharper drop than for the population as a whole, as this comparison of two early years of the Sixties with two early years of the Seventies shows:
>
> Table XIII-6 (Table No. Added)
> UNEMPLOYMENT RATE AND RATIO, BLACK TO WHITE
> FOR MARRIED MEN, 20 YEARS OLD AND OVER,
> WITH SPOUSE PRESENT, 1962 TO 1972
>
> | 1 | Negro and Other Races | White | Ratio |
> |---|---|---|---|
> | 1962 | 7.9% | 3.1% | 2.5 to 1 |
> | 1971 | 5.0% | 3.0% | 1.7 to 1 |
> | 1972 | 4.5% | 2.6% | 1.7 to 1 |
>
> The drop in the ratio from 1962 to 1972 is 53% (from 2.5 to 1 to 1.7 to 1—with 1 to 1 representing parity).
>
> Again, then, one can observe a steady and powerful movement into the middle class. Black family men are—like white family men—"at work," that is, at least 95 out of a hundred even during recessionary times.
>
> At the same time, however, teen-age unemployment has gone up. Among black teen-agers (sixteen to nineteen), unemployment rates in 1960 were 24%—apparently strikingly high. In 1970, the rate had climbed to 29%—substantially higher, and by 1972 it was 34%. In each case the rate for white teen-agers was between 13% and 15%.
>
> But there is something to be said about black teen-age unemployment that is not generally understood. These numbers, from 1972, tell the story:
>
> • In all there were 2.2 million teen-agers sixteen to nineteen.

Wage Rates, Inflation and Unemployment

- Of these, 1.43 million were "not in the labor force," about two-thirds. (About 1.2 million of these are students; most of the balance are housewives.) They were neither "at work" nor "looking for work." They are not tabulated in unemployment statistics. They are doing what most teen-agers in America do—going to school or tending house.
- That leaves about 770,000. These are the black teen-agers "in the labor force"—either "at work" or "looking for work." About two-thirds—about 510,000—are at work.
- That leaves about 260,000 who are actually unemployed, i.e., "looking for work." (The fraction of 260,000 over the denominator of the 2.2 million total teen-agers, the resultant percentage would be about 12%, which is a far cry from the 34% "unemployment" figure.)
- But even of the 260,000, unemployed black teen-agers, about 45%—116,000—are in school and about 83% of these are looking for part-time work.
- That leaves about 144,000 black teen-agers—males and females—who are out of work, out of school and looking for work, a condition that would somewhat more closely approach the popular perception of what "teen-age unemployment" actually represents.
- The out-of-school out-of-work component represents 6.6% of the total number of black teen-agers!

That is a far cry from the stereotype of hordes of young blacks hanging around street corners staring vacant-eyed toward a dead-end future, remembering a dead-end past. About 70% of black teen-agers are in school. About another 25% are at work or at home as housewives. The rest—about 6%—may well be perceived as hard-core teen-age unemployed.

Why then the stereotype of massive black teen-age unemployment? Part of the fault lies in the statistical reportage system. The "unemployment rate" is defined as the percentage of those "in the labor force" who are "looking for work." But among young people almost two-thirds are "not in the labor force," although they are usefully occupied, typically as either students or housewives. "Unemployed" also involves students seeking part-time work, surely an important consideration, sometimes a critical consideration for a family, sometimes a necessity to be able to stay in school, but also surely not generally in tune with the notion of desolated young men hanging around on street corners with no future before them. They are students. They are going someplace.

The second reason for the stereotype is the high visibility—and the dangerous potential—of such young, unemployed, black males as there are. Of particular significance in this connection is the ominous—and terrifying—rise in the crime rate generally and specifically the very high rate of young black criminals, particularly in urban areas.

On balance: Teen-age unemployment rates are up, adult male rates down, particularly so among married males. The teen-agers are mostly in school. The adults are mostly supporting families. The net result would seem to be a social and economic plus despite the continuing "two to one" ratio of black to white unemployment rates.

While we are on the subject of unemployment, it would be appropriate to ask the following question:

To what extent does unemployment reflect raw poverty?

This question was asked and answered in good perspective by the *Detroit News* in an editorial on August 2, 1975, which follows:

THE SATURDAY EDITORIAL
Unemployment is a Cushioned Shock

To what extent does unemployment reflect actual hard times?

Amid recession, it's never popular to talk about mitigating factors. To suggest that things aren't as bad as they might be makes one sound callous and unfeeling. Further, such a suggestion challenges a theme which political prophets of doom find most useful.

W. Allen Wallis, a widely respected economist and statistician, now chancellor of the University of Rochester, observed in a recent lecture at the University of Chicago that "unemployment figures cannot be read directly as figures on economic hardship."

Taking a sample month, Wallis found that less than half the

unemployed had actually lost jobs. "The majority were new entrants, voluntary quits, or seasonally unemployed. Also, less than half had dependents. Furthermore, the average duration of unemployment was under two months."

Moreover, he notes, many of the jobless suffer little reduction in disposable income. Unemployment benefits go a long way toward plugging the gap and in some cases may actually give the worker more after-tax income than he had when employed.

Another expert, Martin Feldstein, professor of economics at Harvard, bolsters that point with a Massachusetts example: a $500-a-month worker with two children and with a wife who earns $350 a month.

If jobless for two months, the man loses $1,000 in earnings. However he saves $268 on federal and state income tax and Social Security tax. He saves on transportation and other costs of working. These savings plus unemployment compensation and benefits for dependents bring his income to within $15 a week of what he got while working.

If the wife were the one out of work for two months, the family's income would drop by less than $60. She gets 25 cents an hour less than she got while at work.

These facts do not make high unemployment a desirable state of affairs. Nor do they lessen the pain of the genuine cases of hardship, which become more numerous when the rate of unemployment rises. They do suggest, however, that unemployment does not automatically translate into raw poverty.

An understanding of that point casts in better perspective the sometimes hysterical efforts of politicians to pass massive public programs to alleviate the suffering of the starving masses.

The hysterical panic-button-pushing by politicians may get some cheap votes from the economically illiterate but is actually counterproductive in social redeemability. Just witness the number of jobs that are going begging because of the disincentives provided by our welfare bureaucracies. This is just one of the consequences of the arrant claptrap that fosters anti-profit rhetoric and the surging growth in expectations and entitlements.

The rhetoric has created an unwholesome attitude toward work. The "new class" elitists have apparently succeeded in creating an atmosphere in which they have brainwashed a sizable segment into believing that they are entitled to "positions" at all times or to incomes commensurate with "positions." Hence, pickiness and the lack of desire to take a job that's considered to be menial and subservient. Lenient welfare and food stamp requirements are accessories to a growth in these attitudes.

The objectives of full employment and price stability will be the subject of the next chapter.

XIV

ECONOMIC GROWTH AT FULL EMPLOYMENT WITHOUT INFLATION

The objectives of steady economic growth at relatively full employment with minimal inflation are attainable by means of the following measures:

1. Wage guidelines with guaranteed full employment through a National Technical Center.
2. Income tax exemptions for corporations adhering to guidelines regarding prices, research and job creation.
3. Establishment of FAP.
4. Reduction of government expenditures.

5. Control of regulatory bureaucracies.
6. Maintenance of money supply growth at a steady pace.
7. Control of Euro-currency markets.
8. Floating exchange rates.
9. Condominium ownership for the poor.

Don't be surprised or alarmed at the rejection of these proposals by the intelligentsia and the "new class." They will resist because this package will be considered as a threat to their empires and bureaucracies. Some of the suggestions may appear bold, ambitious and visionary and may certainly be held as such by detractors from the elite left, who arrogate to themselves the right to shape society. However, we have provided and will furnish more logical and statistical substantiation for these measures. The underlying theme is recognition of what makes the invisible hand work-economic incentive. It is the failure to recognize the psychology of economic incentives that largely lies at the bottom of Communist and socialist bungling in the economic area. As proof, witness the ludicrous and fruitless efforts of socialist planners in trying to supplant profits as a guiding beacon in their economic societies. They further compound their problems by installing a huge bureaucracy to make countless decisions better executed from the interplay of free choices in a competitive market.

We will now consider in more detail each of the items enumerated above.

Wage Guidelines

Before delineating the wage guidelines, it would be appropriate and timely to explain the reasons for wage guide-

Economic Growth at Full Employment

lines. It has been stated frequently by economists and others that full employment without inflation is unattainable. They speak of a trade-off. We were told that we could have price stability only if we subjected a certain segment of our population to unemployment. On the other hand, we are also told that we could have full employment with some inflation —a creeping variety. In their siren song, we were gulled into believing that we could tolerate some inflation in the interests of achieving full employment. Well, it turned out that a little bit of inflation was like getting a little bit pregnant. As a result of such advice, we managed for the first time in our industrial history to harvest the worst of both possible worlds, a high degree of unemployment and inflation—the stagflation of 1973-1974 and the slumpflation of 1974-1975.

How did we get into this economic quagmire? We got into this predicament because of an unusual convergence of inflationary phenomena, as explained before. Many are self-corrective, barring bureaucratic interference. However, three types of inflationary causes stand out. Two of them, monetary and fiscal, cause demand-pull inflation, while the third, wage-rate increases in excess of productivity gains, causes cost-push inflation, which is our concern in this section of this chapter.

Unions and Inflation

The principal cause of cost-push inflation is unbridled union power. We have shown in the prior chapter that unit labor costs have increased, leading to price increases while squeezing profit margins and inhibiting manufacturers from making new investments. We indicated that increases in plant capacity were inadequate not only to meet demand, augmenting inflation, but also inadequate to create jobs for a growing working population.

The union in inflationary developments was well depicted by John Davenport in an article in the *Wall Street Journal* of April 22, 1975. One excerpt follows:

> It is elementary that unions, comprising something less than 25% of the working force, cannot possibly fulfill their promise of bettering the lot of all workers, for real wages began to rise long before unions became powerful and are basically the result of increased business investment and advancing technology. What unions can and do do is to raise the money wages of some workers in the more remunerative trades at the expense of workers in the less remunerative trades. This distortion in wage rates, plus minimum wage laws which prevent some of the poorest members of our community from working at all, has a powerful "unemployment effect," setting the stage for still more government fiscal and credit expansion, according to Keynesian prescriptions. As the late Jacob Viner predicted years ago, the result is "a race between labor demands and the printing presses."

In our observation, Viner was not exposed to the "new class" of the more recent vintage and neglected to mention the political demands arising out of the explosive growth in expectations and entitlements.

Economic balderdash that affronts intelligence was recently exhibited by the *New York Times* in a derisive editorial entitled "Back to Adam Smith," in its issue of June 20, 1975.

We object strenuously to the *Times* allusion to "the misuse of concentrated economic power" to business. In previous chapters on corporate profits and corporate prices, we have debunked the myths concerning profits, prices and

Economic Growth at Full Employment

alleged corporate economic power. The *New York Times* did the working and middle classes a disservice by failing to ascribe "the misuse of concentrated economic power" to virtual union monopolies.

What should be done to defuse union monopoly power? Some are advocating the application of anti-trust laws to unions. As Davenport explains:

> In the case of organized labor we have forfeited such protection and in addition have given unions other unique exemptions and privileges: exclusive bargaining rights where a union commands a bare majority of workers in a plant or factory; legalization of compulsory union contracts, and the toleration of mass picketing, intimidation and violence. Morally reprehensible in themselves, these privileges and practices have far-reaching economic consequences, though they are different from what all union leaders and many businessmen suppose.

It is our sincere observation that this would be socially divisive and counterproductive. Unions have been a constructive factor in economic growth, and viable unions will always be necessary to maintain gains that have accrued to the workers. However, we do object to union irresponsibility and to union proclivity to ignore the economic facts of life that govern the viability of corporations and the nation. Union exactions of wage-rate increases exceeding productivity gains are unjustified and should not be countenanced. Union encouragement of featherbedding should not be condoned. Union distortions and misrepresentations of profit figures should not be tolerated.

It is our observation that wage rates should not be subjected to free market competition, as it would be an act of social irresponsibility to subject wage rates to the vicissitudes of the economic cycle. Union wage rates should be considered as regulated utility rates—however, with more flexibility than accorded utility rates. It has been demonstrated that unions have abused their monopoly power. For many years, managers and engineers were able to compensate for these excesses. However, we are now at a critical juncture when they can no longer cope with these excesses. The result has been an erosion of profit margins and cash flow. Because of inadequate retained profits and depreciation reserves, business is not able to generate internally funds for capital goods replacement, let alone expand capital. This is well depicted in data cited in Tax Foundation's *Facts and Figures* and based on figures compiled by the Board of Governors of the Federal Reserve Board.

Table XIV-1
SOURCES AND USES OF CORPORATE FUNDS
(Billions)

	1949	1959	1965	1970	1973
Internal sources	$19.11	$35.0	$56.6	$59.4	$84.6
External sources	.5	20.1	34.8	44.2	91.6

The change in trend is very striking, more so in the 1970-73 period, when funds from external sources exceeded funds from internal sources for the first time in recent history at least. It is more disconcerting to note that a disproportionate amount of new external funds in 1973 arose from short-term loans. It is a sad commentary to observe that papers of the stature of the *New York Times* should join the bush-league intellectuals misrepresenting economic facts.

To curb excessive union power, Davenport advocates that "unions become what they started out to be, namely purely voluntary associations on a par with any other private association."

We disagree. Unionists argue, and rightly so, that it is unfair for union members to provide the protective umbrella of union benefits to workers who do not belong to unions. However, unionists will have to admit that unions cannot be trusted with monopoly power, because it has been shown that they will exploit to the hilt the exercise of that power. As proof, it has been shown that wage-rate increases have exceeded productivity gains, raising unit labor costs, the true criterion of cost increases. Further proof is provided by the irrational demands of construction unions, whose exactions have priced homes beyond the reach not only of the poor but even of the lower middle classes.

To constrain labor, but not penalize it, the following guidelines are suggested:

Wage-rate increases to be limited to 3% per year plus a cost of living adjustment, which would be allowed in full when the cost of living grows 5% or less; one percentage point would be deducted when the cost of living increases 5 to 10%, and another percentage point would be deducted when the cost of living increases over 10%.

The main objective here is to provide incentives so that there is no gain from inflation to the few unions with inordinate economic power that was used irresponsibly. The result would be that real wages would grow at a 3% rate with inflation at less than 5%; 2% with inflation at 5 to 10%; and only 1% with inflation at 10% or more.

What would be the long-term effect on real wages? A growth at a compounded rate of 3% would mean a doubling in real growth in less than 24 years, a quadrupling in 48 years in real purchasing power, that is, purchasing power adjusted for the change in cost of living.

More on this and the guaranteed full employment after we touch on the second item in our suggested program, that regarding the exemption of corporate profits from taxes.

Abolish Corporate Taxes?

Consistent with one of our prime objectives of providing incentives within the context of our philosophy of social redeemability, we propose exempting certain corporations from income taxes within guidelines relative to prices, research activities and job creation. Corporations that maintained prices and created new jobs would be fully exempt from taxes. Corporations that reduced prices more than employment likewise could qualify for tax exemption. Profit margins increases would be allowed on a gradual basis, so that they would be allowed to increase to an average of the last 10 years. Any excessive jump in profit margins would accrue to workers as a special bonus.

It should be obvious that there are logical reasons behind these proposals. The tax exemption would provide funds to corporations to increase research and development and to provide funds for new more efficient equipment and to provide labor with the incentive that their productivity efforts would make their jobs more secure, expand markets for their products and lay the foundation for uninterrupted economic growth to the benefit of their families, their company and the country. This would accelerate the emergence of a workers' capitalism.

The unions and corporations would be free to bargain for wage increases exceeding their wage guidelines, provided prices would not be increased.

It would be prudent to disallow tax exemptions to corporations that would accumulate idle cash or utilize idle cash for merger or conglomerate activities or speculating in foreign exchange markets.

It is our intent to reward the real producers in corporate life and to give no solace to financial wheeler-dealers. We have an obsession about this because we want to channel as much money as possible to productive use for technological advancement and exploitation.

We now return to our first topic of wage guidelines, but now with respect to guaranteed full employment through the establishment of a National Technical Center.

The National Technical Center

There exists in this country a colossal waste of technical talent through unemployment and underemployment. Such a waste of talent resides in our recently graduated scientists and engineers who are seeking and have been seeking positions. There is and has been a prodigious waste at times of cyclical high unemployment.

To counteract this underutilization of technology and technologists, it is proposed here to establish a National Technical Center with branches in several strategic industrial and scientific centers.

Corporations, think tanks, universities, the Bureau of

Standards, Lewis Propulsion Laboratories, the Batelle Institute, and the like would be eligible for membership. It would be mandatory for corporations to become members in order to qualify for a tax-exempt status. Members would feed the Center and its branches with requests for special research, tests, and prototype products to be researched, designed, built and tested in coordination with their own staffs.

A computerized data bank would be operated by the National Research Center for the benefit of all making requests. Naturally, members would get a preferred rate.

The Center would be financed by unemployment insurance and membership fees paid by corporations after being established through the issuance of stock certificates, available only to members, who would elect a Board of Directors, who in turn would hire an operating staff.

The Research Center and branches would be administered by a minimal full-time staff. The bulk of the employees would be drawn from the unemployed, who would be paid about 75% of their basic pay for a normal forty-hour week when last employed. They could not work permanently, but would be required to return to their last employer when recalled. They would be free to get employment elsewhere if not recalled first by their former employers within a designated period of time.

Patents would accrue to the National Center or the Corporation as determined by the origin of the patentable ideas. In gray areas, it would be advisable to favor the corporation because this would result in the greatest benefit to the country in terms of prosperity and health.

It would be advisable to change the anti-trust laws to

Economic Growth at Full Employment 285

permit industries to form research pools. For example, the automobile companies would be allowed to form a research pool on new engines and pollution control. A research pool or pools could be organized to develop alternate energy resources. In order to make our country invulnerable to foreign pressures and gouging, mineral companies should be formed to discover substitute materials for bauxite, chromium, etc. Research groups should be sponsored for botanical and biological research.

The physical plant should be as complete as possible, with libraries, laboratories, machine shops and test facilities.

The eligible unemployed for temporary work at the research center would include physicists, chemists, engineers, mathematicians, technicians, machine and tool designers, toolmakers, machinists, etc.

At times of prosperity, there may be a dearth of participants. In such instances, the projects would be put into a bank for future action. During recessions, a surplus of participants may eventuate. In such instances duplicate teams could be formed to spur competition. Boondoggling would be fought strenuously.

The country would gain tremendously because this would increase our technological base and would exploit to the fullest extent possible our huge reserve of active and latent technological know-how. Minds and skills would not be wasted.

Our current crop of scientists, engineers, technicians and skilled workers would be encouraged in knowing that they would always be usefully employed.

Our young people in high schools, vocational schools, technical schools and universities would be relieved of uncertainties concerning gainful employment and could choose confidently a career and delve into it wholeheartedly. Corporations would be induced to hire these people or sponsor them into the Technical Centers in order to qualify for tax exemption.

The technological know-how exists for the reduction of poverty, crime, dope, and even racism. All we have to do is to avail ourselves of our huge latent and prospective technology instead of wasting knowledge, minds and skills and exacerbating social tensions.

Visionary! Absolutely not.

This certainly would beat unemployment and welfare.

Before continuing one should dwell momentarily on item 3, Establishment of FAP, and item 4, Reduction of government expenditures.

THE NEGATIVE INCOME TAX

The establishment of the Family Aid Plan would be instituted by means of the negative income tax. This, combined with the National Technical Center, would automatically take care of item 4, reduction of government expenditures. The Technical Center could also serve as a training and retraining facility.

One major development of these measures—tax exemptions, FAP, and the National Technical Centers—would be a diversion of funds from the governmental and welfare bureaucracies to private enterprise, from non-producers to producers. Hardly anything would be more salutary for economic and social welfare—a worthy objective of redeeming social values.

Economic Growth at Full Employment

Despite all the economic progress made in the last twenty-five years, one element of retrogression is painful to contemplate. We are speaking here of the disturbing rise in the percentage of families headed by a female. Wattenberg in his *Real America* cites three sets of figures.

Wattenberg writes that ". . . the percentage of families in poverty that had female heads increased sharply from 23% in 1959 to 43% in 1972" (page 62).

The other set of data provided by Wattenberg shows that the percent of female-headed families increased from 9% in 1950 to 10% in 1973 among the whites and from 18% to 33% among the blacks (page 137).

Further, Wattenberg asserts that ". . . in 1972, more than half (53%) of black female-headed families were living below the low income level. . . . only 16% of black male-headed families were poor" (page 137).

The disturbing trends and results are bad for several reasons. Millions of black children are reared without the benefit and influence of a father in the house to help educate the children and reinforce discipline at ages when the presence of a father is of paramount importance in social and economic impact. They are entrapped in an environment and neighborhood that abound in crime and are conducive to more crime.

It is our conviction that Aid to Families with Dependent Children (AFDC) provides incentives to increase female-headed families. It is also our further conviction that the increase in female-headed families, unemployment and the unwarranted propaganda against profits have been responsible for the inordinate growth in crime.

Can the process be reversed?

Yes. But not by rhetoric that overpromises instant cures, that foments a rise in expectation and entitlements, that casts aspersions on what can be most productive in alleviating deprivation of decent family life, education and secure income and jobs—namely, more profits for industry.

The process can be most effectively reversed by supplanting AFDC with FAP (Family Aid Plan) or the negative income tax, coupled with guaranteed employment and reduction and finally elimination of profit taxes for qualified corporations.

The immediate establishment of FAP would definitely decrease female-headed families. Person-power training must be given proper emphasis and direction. This means the transfer of job-training programs from the bureaucrats to industry. The National Technical Center should be made an integral part in job training. It should be used as a training and retraining facility. A system of youth employment scholarships should be set up under a program whereby industry would be subsidized to provide schooling and on-the-job training for teen-agers.

While we are on the subject of education for employment, we will add a few comments on education in general that may outrage some leaders in the educational complex.

In our humble, non-professional opinion on education, too much stress is accorded orienting high school students toward a college education. Academic subjects are overstressed, and vocational training is not only underemphasized but even neglected. In the college area, career programs have been neglected and restricted in the overemphasis on the humanities. The recent emergence of career

Economic Growth at Full Employment

training and vocational schooling can only be construed as salutary despite some bemoaning of liberal arts purists.

It is important to note that a sizable number of young people are "voting with their feet" and that they are choosing worthy goals of relevance and self-realization. They are living proof that educational intelligentsists have their priorities all screwed up. Instead of leading our adolescents to a skill or profession—that is, a job—they prefer to educate them first to the amenities of leisure and contemplation. The liberal arts colleges are in effect mills of pendantry and sophistry. Manhood and womanhood, so eagerly sought by adolescents, are delayed, with the consequent disorientation that is fertile ground for social theorizing that is at variance with the economic facts of life. Instead of teaching our young people how to earn a living, our educational complex elitists prefer to infuse them with what H. G. Wells calls "a pompous and unintelligent classical pretentiousness."

Nothing would be more conducive to social progress for the black high school dropout who "has had it" with academic subjects than worthwhile vocational training. Youth scholarships under an industry and National Technical Center guidance would provide a tremendous psychological and economic uplift to deprived blacks and whites. With "jingles in their pockets" and self-fulfilling jobs a certainty, the path to crime and dope would lose its attraction.

Vocational training has been too long the stepchild of our education system.

The colleges are beginning to move in the right direction. The change in trend from liberal arts courses to career programs was recently depicted in an article that appeared in the *Wall Street Journal* of February 18, 1975.

The efficacy of career training was well illustrated in the following news dispatch, quoted in part, in the *Detroit News* of April 13, 1975:

By Robert W. Irvin

Big Rapids, Michigan—Like to find a place where the family car is fixed without any labor charges even though it may be in the shop for a week or more?

That is the way it is in one place in this city of 12,000 located about 60 miles north of President Ford's home town of Grand Rapids.

It is at the automotive center of Ferris State College. This is where about 500 students take one of several courses dealing with automotive service and in the process fix cars for only the cost of parts.

The program at Ferris is broader than that offered by trade schools or community colleges. Indeed, it is one of perhaps only four major schools which offer major automotive technology programs (others are in North Dakota, Oklahoma and Texas).

And Ferris has the only program where a student can attend four years and receive a bachelor's degree.

These are popular courses at Ferris. One reason is that dealer mechanics today can earn $25,000 a year, although the pay in other places is often less than $10,000.

Nevertheless, there is an 18-month waiting list to get into the automotive service school.

But the wait apparently is worth it for at a time of record postwar unemployment Ferris officials said virtually all their students find work (not only in the auto but in the other programs the school offers as well).

"If these kids can do what they are supposed to do when they get out there are jobs available for them; we don't have very many students out looking for jobs," said Charles H. Rathjen, head of the automotive department at Ferris.

With cars and trucks more complex than ever these days, there is more need for technical training. "Twenty or 30 years ago most cars were relatively simple," he said. "But now it's hard to learn service pumping gas in a station and so more kids are getting formalized training."

A recent study by the U.S. Labor Department estimated that the country will need 200,000 more mechanics for vehicles and heavy equipment by the end of the decade. This is one reason why schools like Ferris are expanding their programs.

If the academic classically inclined purists would do their homework, they would find this illuminating commentary by H. G. Wells in his *The Outline of History* (Garden City, N.Y.: Garden City Books, Doubleday and Company, 1961, pages 761 and 762):

> We have told how in England the universities after the Reformation ceased to have a wide popular appeal, how they became the educational preserve of the nobility and gentry, and the strongholds of the established church. A pompous and unintelligent classical pretentiousness dominated them, and they dominated the schools of the middle and upper classes. The only knowledge recognized was an uncritical textual knowledge of a selection of Latin and Greek classics, and the test of a good style was its abundance of quotations, allusions, and stereotyped expressions.
>
> The early development of British science went on, therefore, in spite of the formal educational organization, and in the teeth of the bitter hostility of the teaching and clerical professions. French education, too, was dominated by the classical tradition of the Jesuits, and consequently it was not difficult for the Germans to organize a body of investigators, small indeed in relation to the possibilities of the case, but large in proportion to the little band of British and French inventors and experimentalists. And though this work of research and experiment was making Britain and France the most rich and powerful countries in the world, it was not making scientific and inventive men rich and powerful. There is a necessary unworldliness about a sincere scientific man; he is too preoccupied with his research to plan and scheme how to make money out of it.

The economic exploitation of his discoveries falls very easily and naturally, therefore, into the hands of a more acquisitive type; and so we find that the crops of rich men which every fresh phase of scientific and technical progress has produced in Great Britain, though they have not displayed quite the same passionate desire to insult and kill the goose that laid the national golden eggs as the scholastic and clerical professions, have been quite content to let that profitable creature starve. Inventors and discoverers came by nature, they thought, for cleverer people to profit by.

In this matter the Germans were a little wiser. The German "learned" did not display the same vehement hatred of the new learning. They permitted its development. The German business man and manufacturer, again, had not quite the same contempt for the man of science as had his British competitor. Knowledge, these Germans believed, might be a cultivated crop, responsive to fertilizers. They did concede, therefore, a certain amount of opportunity to the scientific mind; their public expenditure on scientific work was relatively greater, and this expenditure was abundantly rewarded.

By the latter half of the nineteenth century the German scientific worker had made German a necessary language for every science student who wished to keep abreast with the latest work in his department, and in certain branches, and particularly in chemistry, Germany acquired a very great superiority over her western neighbors. The scientific effort of the sixties and seventies in Germany began to tell after the eighties, and the Germans gained steadily upon Britain and France in technical and industrial prosperity.

As can be seen, we have a divergence of opinion between the idealists and the pragmatists. The idealists seek to make us philosophers first and then breadwinners; while the pragmatists would first concentrate on giving a person a salable skill, trade or profession.

Let us contemplate the consequences if we went whole hog in either direction. If we followed the advice of the idealists, we would have a surplus of philosophers, theorizers and visionaries with an abundance of young people seeking relevance and self-realization with no means of reaching their goal. They would be shiftless and rudderless and fertile fodder for the speciousness of leftists and radicals.

However, if we went the route of the pragmatists, we would build a huge technological base. Coupled with ample funds in industry, it is conceivable that we would suffer from a chronic shortage of person-power. The ranks of those receptive to the blandishments of the idealistic pseudo-liberals and radicals would diminish perceptibly.

With full employment achieved, some may be apprehensive that another inflationary spiral would be generated. This need not be necessarily so. The obejctive should be the attainment of full employment in a manner that is non-stimulative. The trick is to get full employment from internal production growth where production provides its own demand. In recent years, we have erred by attempting to employ the non-employables. As shown by Geoffrey Moore, we don't know at what level full employment unemployment occurs. It is possible that full employment unemployment was at a level higher than we realized.

In the futile attempt to employ the non-employables, an overstimulative policy was pursued, unleashing a demand-pull inflation that pulled upward in a ratchet-like effect the cost-push inflation. This is an additional reason why it is "harder to get rid of inflation than generate it," as concluded by Moore.

Under present conditions, we are faced with the necessity of guessing the level of full-employment unemployment.

However, full employment with reasonable price stability can be achieved with the measures outlined above, with some additional comments as presented in the program that follows:

1. Wage guidelines. Guaranteed full employment under National Technical Center and person-power training by industry and NTC.
2. Income tax exemptions for corporations adhering to guidelines regarding prices, research and job creation.
3. FAP with dismantling of welfare bureaucracy.
4. Reduction of government expenditures through elimination of bureaucratically operated job-training programs.
5. Control of regulatory bureaucracies. All regulations should be voted upon on a piece-by-piece basis only after regulators had issued a cost-benefit impact analysis. This proposal is brought up to hinder regulators from issuing counterproductive regulations and to prevent them from overstepping their bounds.
6. Maintenance of a money supply growth rate at a steady pace as outlined by Milton Friedman.
7. Control of Euro-currency markets. Corporation activities in foreign exchange markets should be limited to hedge operations. According to the London *Economist,* foreign exchange operations are an important budgetary item for many corporations. This should not be allowed. Transfers of funds unnecessarily exaggerate foreign exchange rates and are at times unstabilizing factors and hinder the Federal Reserve Board in its control funtcions.
8. Floating exchange rates should become a permanent feature. They prevent exporting of inflation and will also

permit countries to pursue independent monetary policies best suited to their domestic situations.

9. Condominium ownership for the poor. HUD should be abolished. Housing should be transferred to private industry. Private condominium developers should be on projects for low-cost housing for the poor. Ownership will develop incentives for proper maintenance. Condominium members would automatically keep in line those prone to neglect their properties.

The institution of the above proposals would provide the feasibility of attaining a semblance of full employment without the danger of generating a deleterious inflationary spiral. The lower two-fifths of our income segments would gain the most. The middle class majority would be greatly augmented.

In our plan to control inflation, it is obvious that we did not include price and profit controls. It is considered unnecessary to control them because it has been shown that competition has resulted in keeping them in downtrends on relative and real bases. However, we must consider the possibility that the "new class elitists" and union leaders may seize upon this as an excuse to discredit the foregoing proposals. After all, the recommendations would erode the reason for their existence.

To forestall their counteroffensive, it is further suggested that dividend increases be limited to the same amount as wage-rate increases. The surprising fact is that this would have no practical effect because dividends have woefully lagged behind wages for over seventy years.

However, it must be admitted that the inclusion of

dividends under the same restraints as for wages could have a tremendously constructive effect on the attitude of the worker toward productivity.

It would be advisable to allow exemption for wage and dividend restraints if prices were held stable or even declined. Here we would have a tremendous force working toward productivity and technological advancement.

Along with the absence of price and profit controls, under certain conditions we would advocate giving corporations free rein relative to depreciation schedules.

In such an environment, prices would be held stable or even decline and profits would be recycled into technological advancement and job creation. Price stability with full employment would be attained. Increased job opportunities would increase employment and increase allotments into pension funds, thereby accelerating the emergence of a workers' capitalism. In effect, accelerated depreciation would accelerate the fruition of the working man's capitalism.

It has been demonstrated that neither workers nor corporations profit from inflation. Real wages and profits have registered their biggest gains in times of price stability rather than during inflation. However, in times of inflation, wages gained more slowly and profits at times declined. Thus, it should be obvious that mutual interests of workers and corporations are served in constraining inflation. Contrary to Marxist and sham-liberal rhetoric, workers have more in common with their employers than is commonly realized and accepted. These factors will be accorded an extended treatment in the next chapter.

XV

COMMUNITY OF INTERESTS AND THE COMING WORKERS' CAPITALISM

Myths die hard, especially economic myths nurtured by the intelligentsia and directed against profits and the profit system of capitalism.

The myths of adversary relationship, class conflict, exploitation of labor and the bottomless pot of gold are favorites of the new class because they have a vested and self-serving interest. The adversary relationship is a favorite of union leaders along with the bottomless pot of gold. In their propaganda they portray the manufacturer as their adversary, unfairly ripping off with exorbitant prices while attempting to exact as much production as inhumanly as possible at the lowest wage rate possible. They picture the corporation as having secreted away in its treasury a bottomless pot of gold into which it can dip endlessly for wage raises and fringe benefits. The class conflict and exploitation theories are favorites of the Marxists. While railing against the rip-off artists of capitalism, the self-styled friends of the workingman depict themselves as his benefactors. Their subtle innuendos and outright blatant lies, distortions and misrepresentations are repeated so often that the unwary accept them as fact.

These sham intellectuals include demogogic politicians, irresponsible union leaders, professors, teachers, avant-garde writers, columnists, TV pundit commentators, satirists, religious leaders and activists of our service and regulatory bureaucracies. The more naive among them labor under the illusion that they can supplant the "unfair, outmoded system based on greed and exploitation" with a better life under a benevolent bureaucracy. The more perceptive among them are simply jumping on the bandwagon that they hope will lead them to prestige and power and the emoluments thereof. They rail at the greed for money but they ignore that the history of the world can be written in the greed for power and fame and the appeal to envy.

The incentive for profit has been a constructive force and properly channeled can bring middle class status to virtually all willing to make the effort, while greed for power and fame has been destructive, as attested by such examples as Robespierre, Napoleon, Kaiser Wilhelm, Lenin, Stalin, Hitler, Allende, and Sukarno. The final verdict is

Community of Interests

yet to be written for the Shah of Iran, Indira Gandhi and some of the emerging chiefs of state among the developing countries.

The leadership among the sham intellectuals, naive or shrewd, pose as the protectors of the working and poor classes against the imagined rapacity of the business tycoons. In reality, however, the working and middle classes have more in common with the managers and technologists of business than they have with their deceitful "protectors."

The common interests occur in the following areas:

1. Profits
2. Cost control
3. Prices
4. Productivity
5. Technology
6. Jobs
7. Future jobs
8. Pensions
9. Career and vocational education
10. Fiscal responsibility
11. Inflation control
12. Reasonable environmental objectives

As in previous enumerations, we must inject a cautionary note. In economics, you cannot isolate factors into tight compartments. The neglect of this fact has been the prime reason why planners and price controllers of socialist systems, or modified versions thereof, cannot succed in planning and price controls. Too many factors are interdependent. Throw in random events and you have the inevitable chaos. As a result, we may be talking about one of the items listed above and drift and overlap into others.

Profits Benefit Workers More Than Others

It has been demonstrated that profits are small in magnitude compared to the final product and wages, but are of prime importance because they furnish the means to maintain jobs and create new employment. The worker benefits more currently as well as in the future, with benefits also accruing to his future generations. Hence, regarding profits, he has more in common with his managers and stockholders than he has with those whose visionary schemes reduce profits through attitudes, featherbedding and governmental largess for excessive welfare state expenditures. We are not opposed to prudent spending but do not approve unreasonable excesses of throwing money at problems.

Cost Control Through Profits Brings Reasonable Prices

In numerous instances, it has been shown that the incentive for maximizing profits is not the economic cancer as imagined by its detractors and distorters. We will repeat that the incentive for profits furnishes the cost discipline and control that serves mankind so nobly. The process engineer is always searching for new methods and technology to reduce costs, thereby enlarging the market for his products. This element of cost control is one of the most overlooked and unappreciated in our economic life. In our judgment, hardly anything matches it in social and economic benefits. This is one of the most essential features of our competitive economy. This component explains why fewer hours of work are required to purchase manufactured goods as times goes on and it explains why capitalist societies outperform socialist societies.

The worker, no doubt, has a bigger stake in cost control through profit incentive than in the theorizing of pseudo-liberals who seek to replace profit with bureaucratic manipulation.

The Attitude on Productivity is Important

The anti-profit rhetoric has turned the tables around and indoctrinated workers with the false belief that hard work only increases the obscene huge profits of corporations, with no benefit to the worker. In reality, the opposite is true. In undermining the work ethic, the new class irresponsibility actually screws the worker out of lower prices. In many instances, resistance to technological innovations is encouraged. This is reminiscent of the railing of the blacksmith against the automobile and the candlestick maker against the electric light.

Profits Help Exploit Technology and Create Jobs

Profits lead to jobs. Profits exploit technology to create more jobs. Profits and technology are a prime necessity to create jobs for a growing working population. We should remove all obstacles to a growth in profits and our technological base. These are the reasons why, in the preceding chapter, we suggested creation of the National Science Center, guaranteed full employment for scientists, engineers and technicians, and the exemption of corporations from taxes within guidelines. We espoused vocational and career education for the same reasons. Instead of exporting our technology to Russia and China, we should send them Angela Davis, Herbert Marcuse, Shirley MacLaine and Jane Fonda, our left-wing professors and all their adherents from the liberal arts colleges. They distort and lie about profits and screw current and future generations out of jobs and careers.

Profits Mean Viable Pensions

Profits are of importance to pensions in two areas where the interests of workers, their managers and their employers coincide. In the first place, profits mean pension fund contributions. If a corporation is not viable, pension fund contributions will cease. After profits provide funds for pension fund allotments, this is only the beginning. Second, these funds must be invested, with security and growth. In other words, they must be invested in the stock of the corporation making the contribution or other corporations. The implications boggle the mind and provide proof that workers have as much of a vested interest in the profitability of their company and the companies in whose securities they have invested as their managers and employers.

The magnitude of pension fund money is revealed in an article, "The Corporate Pension Fund Burden Is Going to Get a Lot Heavier," by Charles D. Ellis in the *Fortune* issue of August, 1974. According to Ellis:

> The pension and profit-sharing funds of U.S. corporations make up the largest aggregation of private investment capital in

the history of the world. Their assets—something like $175 billion—amount to more than three times the total assets of U.S. mutual funds.

* * *

The enormous size of pension funds, moreover, is only half the story. The other basic fact about these funds is that their rate of growth is extraordinarily rapid. For quite a few years now, corporate employee-benefit funds have grown at an average compound rate of 14 percent a year.

Anything growing at a compound rate of 14 percent doubles in size in a little more than five years. If corporate pension and profit-sharing funds continue to grow at that rate—which seems virtually assured for some years to come—they will double to around $350 billion by 1980. At the same rate, they would double again to around $700 billion by 1985. That's more than the present total market value of all the stocks listed on the New York Stock Exchange.

* * *

One way to get an idea of what a realistic investment objective would be is to look briefly at the most popular unrealistic objective: to beat the market. Or more specifically, to earn a higher compound rate of return in equities than that of the S.&P. 500. Some 90 percent of the executives we surveyed agree with the view that "With the right money manager we should be able to beat the market," but they are simply not being realistic. It is impossible for 90 percent of these funds to beat the market, because the funds are the market.

The above article contains the elements for profound implications concerning the future of this country and particularly the worker in the three following areas:

1. Protection of pension funds against erosion from inflation.

2. The role of profits in the growth of pension funds.
3. The future development of a workers' capitalism.

1. THE PROTECTION OF PENSION FUNDS AGAINST INFLATION

With huge aggregations of these funds, problems arise as to investment means. An investment medium must be found that can absorb these funds. The medium chosen must provide security, income and protection against loss in purchasing power. It would be a gigantic hoax to set money aside and 10, 20, or 30 years later dispense the money in greatly reduced purchasing power.

It has been established that, even if inflation were brought under control to a reasonable degree, there exists an inflationary bias in our economy because service industries have outpaced manufacturing industries in growth. Because of technological factors, service industries cannot match the manufacturing segments in productivity advances. Bonds and mortgages must be ruled out as major investment media for pension and profit-sharing funds. Common stocks are the only media left to consider. Thus labor has a huge vested interest in the profitability of corporations as well as in price stability of the economy. Labor must realize its responsibilities and ponder the fact that there is no bottomless pot of gold that will rescue it from its indiscretions. Labor will have to consider good "micro-economics" and good "macro-economics" in both the short- and long-term perspectives. All this means is that labor has as much a vested interest as the corporate manager and technocrat in profits, cost control, productivity and prices. If

Community of Interests

labor is prudent, it will realize that the radicals and liberals in effect are screwing the worker of his desired goals, not the capitalist bastard.

2. Corporate Profits and Fund Growth

The last sentence that we quoted from Ellis' article should be given serious consideration by the working class. To repeat, Ellis wrote that "it is impossible for 90 percent of these funds to beat the market, because these funds are the market." Thus the worker has a big stake in the profitability and viability of his employer company as well as in the companies in which pension fund moneys are invested. Prudence will dictate against investing a disproportionate amount in any one company or industry. Diversification will assume a dominant role.

As the aggregations in pension allotments grow, more and more the interests of labor will coincide with that of management.

3. Toward a Workers' Capitalism

The potential of the emergence and function of a workers' capitalism is being overlooked by even the most perceptive analysts of our economic life.

Consider the following excerpt from Samuelson's *Economics* (page 74):

People's Capitalism

> The New York Stock Exchange for many years tried to sell the notion of "people's capitalism," in which everyone owns stock and therefore will vote to take account of the interests of property. Few would oppose the notion of a wider and more

equal distribution of wealth, but it is a bit of a confidence trick to entice union workers—or their wives—into owning a few shares of a mutual fund so that at the polls they will go easy on corporation tax rates—when, in fact, their own well-being is trivially affected by what happens to the few shares they own in comparison with even a 1 percent change in wage rates or pension benefits.

In any case, only about 35 million out of more than 200 million Americans own any appreciable amount of stocks, and that is a generous estimate. Indirectly, now that private and public pension funds are beginning to invest in equities (i.e., in common stocks), low-income people are beginning to get some protection of their savings against inflation, a privilege that up until recently was enjoyed mostly by the affluent.

While Samuelson is right in pointing out that direct personal stockholdings of union workers are trivial, he appears to have overlooked the huge aggrandizement in the total of the sums allocated to pension and profit-sharing funds. Herein lies a huge pool of stockholder voting rights held by union workers. Henceforth, this pool will continue to grow.

Also in the context of the future development of a workers' capitalism, contemplate the following excerpt also from Samuelson's monumental book (pages 112-113):

DIVORCE OF OWNERSHIP AND CONTROL IN THE LARGE CORPORATION

Let us examine the internal workings of one of these giant corporations. The most striking feature is the diversification of ownership among thousands and thousands of small stockholders. In the 1970s, more than 3 million different people have shares in AT&T. To be sure, half these people have less than 15 shares each; one-quarter of the shares are held in blocks of less than 100 shares; and no single owner has as much as 1 per cent of the total. The Stock Exchange has a goal of "people's capitalism," in which the masses have appreciable ownership of society's capital. While more than 35 million people do own some common stocks, still less than 1 in 10 gets an appreciable return from such ownership.

In a pathbreaking study,[9] Berle and Means pointed out that this wide diversification of stockholding has resulted in a separation of ownership and control. Recent studies show that in the typical giant corporation, all management together—officers and directors—holds only about 3 percent of the outstanding common stock. The largest single minority ownership groups typically hold only about a fifth of all voting stock. Such a small fraction has been deemed more than enough to maintain "working control."[10]

In their cited book, Berle and Means in 1932 pointed out that the "wide diversification of stockholding has resulted in a *separation of ownership and control.*" As economic forces are unfolding now a dramatic change is about to develop, with profound economic consequences in two, hitherto, unexpected areas:

1. Diversification will lead to pooling.
2. Separation of ownership and control will develop into unification of ownership and control.

---

[9] A. A. Berle, Jr., and Gardner C. Means, *The Modern Corporation and Private Property* (Commerce Clearing House, New York, 1932). See R. A. Gordon, *Business Leadership in the Large Corporation* (Brookings Institution, Washington, 1945), chap. II. R. J. Larner, in a 1966 *American Economic Review* study, has shown that the Berle-Means thesis on separation of ownership and control was even truer in the 1960s than in 1929; whereas 6 of the 200 largest corporations were privately owned (80 per cent or more of stock) in 1929, in 1963 there were none; and 84.5 per cent of the firms had no group of stockholders owning as much as 10 per cent!

[10] You can even pyramid control by owning one-fifth of a million-dollar company, which owns one-fifth of a 5-million-dollar company, and so forth. Such a pyramid of so-called "holding companies" can give control over billions to small ownership at the base.

VISIONARY! Not in the least.

When the ideas hit home, sooner or later, and possibly sooner than later, there will be no way found to prevent union workers from pooling their diversified stockholdings in pension and profit-sharing funds and thus emerging as owners and controllers of their employing corporations.

In essence and effect union labor will control its managers. It may be argued that union labor comprises only 25 percent of the labor force. However, most pension funds are in union-organized corporations and industries. Even more important the pension and profit-sharing funds of union-dominated companies can be unified, while the others will continue to be diversified and fragmented.

The possibility of this denouement poses grave responsibilities as well as great potential for the worker. Prudent management and sober application can bring an unparalleled prosperity for himself and future generations; while an attitude of arrogance and smug self-complacency could lead to an economic and social debacle. A healthy work ethic will redound to his benefit. If he has visions of a lackadaisical approach to work with perfunctory work habits, he will not exercise good judgment but court disaster. He will be grossly mistaken if he thinks every laborer will have a posh swivel chair and a desk for propping up his feet. Such an attitude was Allende's downfall, not the CIA as alleged by leftists' interpretations.

Getting back to current pension implications, it must be realized that the feasibility of a meaningful pension will entail work. This important facet was the object of an article, "That Ever Expanding Pension Balloon," by Gilbert

Burck, in *Fortune* of October, 1971. Portions of the article follow:

> Too many Americans of good will tend to assume that a country "as rich as ours" can somehow afford anything, including working less, without sacrificing anything. Specifically, they fall into that old trade-union trap, the assumption that every company and corporation has hidden in its treasury a bottomless pot of gold into which it can dip endlessly for wage raises or pensions. The fact is, of course, that companies and corporations are essentially intermediaries. Assuming that their pension plans are being managed well, they must cover their pension costs as they always have, either by reducing unit costs (i.e., by using less manpower per unit of output), or by keeping wage levels down, or by raising prices, or all three. Inevitably it is the people who pay for their benefits.
>
> Suppose the pension income of Americans, now retired was suddenly elevated to 50 percent of their final wage. The total cost would probably amount to $60 billion, or about 10 to 12 percent of the nation's current payroll. If pensions were raised to 75 percent of final pay, the payroll deduction for everybody would be 15 to 18 percent. Such a decline in spendable income, coming all at once, would be intolerable to most working Americans. Even if national productivity increased at 3 percent a year, which it has not been doing lately, several years would elapse before those at work recovered their former income level. Obviously the imbalance between the incomes of working and pensioned Americans must be redressed at a rate that working Americans, particularly the labor unions, will stand for. Once again, this is not to argue that the U.S. cannot afford high pension standards. It can. But they will have to come gradually.
>
> The chief offenders in reducing the nation's ability to pay for more generous pensions have been the labor unions themselves. In some cities, policemen, firemen, and garbage men have already won contracts that allow them to retire at half pay after twenty years, and they want full pay after forty years. Steel and auto workers have also won very liberal contracts. Many of these pensioners, of course, do not actually retire; they merely move to other jobs for a few years. Nevertheless, they represent a disturbing trend. Sidney Willis, manager of employee benefits for

General Electric, reckons that universal retirement at sixty instead of sixty-five could amount to putting the whole labor force on a 31.5-hour work week, and that universal retirement at fifty-five could amount to putting the whole labor force on a twenty-seven-hour week. Such a loss of manpower, he persuasively argues, cannot possibly be offset by any foreseeable productivity gains.

If early retirement becomes commonplace, the very living standard of the country could stagnate or even decline. As it is, the working population will find it harder and harder to pay for the pensions the reformers say the people crave. What the reformers should be striving for is more production per capita—higher productivity, less featherbedding, a slowdown in early retirement, and even longer hours.

It should be emphasized that more production per capita will be required not only to make the more meaningful pension plan feasible and viable but also because more profits will be needed for capital investment for the creation of new jobs for the ever-growing working population.

Union leaders will bear a grave responsibility as they contemplate goals and means. The goal could be, by natural, evolutionary development, a workers' capitalism under the aegis of a free political democracy and free market competition. The incentives are extant now and should be properly oriented in the future. With pensions portability and guaranteed full employment, inefficient plants should not be subsidized as is the practice in welfare state and socialist economies. The means employed to implement the workers' capitalism should be acceptance and implementation of the measures outlined in the preceding chapter on the achievement of economic growth at reasonably full employment with relative price stability.

In fact, the current arrant rhetoric of the intelligentsia

against profits and the free market is actually delaying the attainment of the workers' capitalism.

History may show that the labor leaders in this country have pursued a prudent course in eschewing an alliance with the radicals and the ultra-liberals. It is within their grasp that history will have a chance to prove that a workers' capitalism will outperform a workers' socialism, if such an eventuality were even feasible. There is the chance with great odds in its favor that under a workers' capitalism the invisible hand of free enterprise may achieve its highest development. That would be a fitting mockery to Marxist prediction of the demise of capitalism.

We have had in sequence industrial capitalism, financial capitalism and now managerial capitalism. At the present time, we are at the threshold of a workers' capitalism. If American labor were to conduct itself with prudence and patience, it would be in a position of providing a fitting mockery to the prognostications of Karl Marx.

Once labor reaches its pinnacle, it will have to guard against the lust for luxury that toppled the empires of Babylon, Persia, Greece, Rome, Spain and Britain.

Babylon's lust for luxury rendered it an easy victim for the Medes and the Persians. The Romans were so engrossed in free bread and circuses, eschewing hard work and patriotism, that, according to H. G. Wells, they recruited foreigners for their security forces. As a result, they were subjugated by the tougher Vandals.

A few pertinent and disturbing questions arise:

How wise is a nation that allows the lack of discipline on the part of labor to notch ever upward the ratchet of cost-push inflation?

How prudent is a nation that permits the lack of self-restraint by labor and environmental overkill to allow foreigners to capture world leadership in vital industries?

How wise is a nation that exports technology to nations who in return export revolution?

How intelligent is a nation that allows bureaucracies to throw billions at problems under a socialist philosophy that seeks to equalize all at the lowest denominator?

How wise is a nation that overzealously protects the criminal more than the victim?

No doubt there were Babylonians, Persians, Romans and Incas who warned of excesses and lack of self-discipline, but were rebuffed with a complacent, "It can't happen here."

But it did, with ample warnings that were ignored.

Getting back to the present juncture, it can be said that labor has a rendezvous with history. Whether labor will flub its chances, delay the denouement or succeed will depend on its exercise of wisdom, patience and self-discipline. Labor can hasten the objective of a lasting and viable workers' capitalism by adhering to the proposals made in the preceding chapter and by rejecting the leftist propaganda against profits and by reinstituting the work ethic. It should be obvious that labor has a common interest with managers and current owners in building a technological and economic base that it can automatically inherit.

In the next three chapters, we shall give our attention to the energy problem, which is of vital interest to everyone, especially the working and the middle classes.

XVI

ENERGY: GEOPOLITICS AND POLITICS

An adequate supply of energy is of paramount importance if we are to attain steady economic growth at reasonably full employment at a minimum of inflation. These objectives are as important to the workers if they are to fall heir to the ownership and management of our industrial corporations. We have shown that the workers and the middle classes have a vital stake in refuting the irresponsible "Big Lies" against profits and a capitalist market economy, because acquiescence will not only delay the achievement of a workers' capitalism but may even be the instrument of denying it. Just as labor and the middle classes have a vested interest in the presentations of facts about profits and capitalism, they also have a like interest in being on guard against fuzzy thinking and demagoguery about energy. In the next three chapters, our attention will be devoted to getting facts and figures in their true perspective, because arrant rhetoric is already taking its toll in delaying the implementation of an effective energy policy.

On October 17, 1973, a handful of oil-rich nations, mostly Arab, declared geopolitical warfare by shutting off a few spigots, sending economic shock waves that are still buffeting the economies of the United States, Western Europe and Japan. The sad part is that the development of an effective countervailing force is being hampered and delayed by cheap and self-serving demagoguery that calls for rolling back gasoline and oil prices. Profits are branded "obscene," giving the false impression that these profits are stashed away in the greedy tycoons' caches.

On January 1, 1974, the organization of Petroleum Exporting Countries, OPEC, ratified the geopolitical war with a vengeance by raising prices to an unjustified level. The Arabs and the Shah of Iran have had their appetites for billions whetted to such an extent that their greed for money and power will not wane until they are confronted with a countervailing force of equal or greater leverage.

It should be stressed that our tasks in nurturing economic growth, in combating unemployment and taming inflation have been rendered more difficult by the addition of another vexing problem of energy. All these problems are interlinked and interdependent and it behooves us to analyze all these problems honestly and objectively.

First of all, we must present some background on the energy problem. How did we get into this mess, or better, how did we allow ourselves to work our way into this predicament?

Our present energy problem is the result of many developments—some foreseen but others unforeseen. While a few were sounding warnings decades ago, those in authority, especially in the bureaucracies, were too complacent. While domestic sources were being neglected, or even hampered, we drifted into an ever-growing dependence on foreign oil. The Arabs actually did us a favor in bringing our problem to a head in 1973-75. The results would have been more catastrophic had they waited five or ten more years.

Underlying our problems are several foibles of human nature itself, complacency and the propensity to "let sleeping dogs lie" or lack of leadership. In his column in the *Wall Street Journal* of March 6, 1974, Vermont Royster provides this bit of journalistic reversion to the archives:

THINKING THINGS OVER BY VERMONT ROYSTER
Unheeded Voices

The top line of the headline read: "Power Crisis." Below, it said: "Shortage of Energy Threatens Industries . . . Gas, Coal, Oil All Tight."

The headline was over a front-page story in *The Wall Street Journal*. The date: June 2, 1970.

Yet there is both fascination and instruction in burrowing into the archives. You quickly discover that few national problems have come to us as well-advertised as this one or with as clear portents of its coming. And you are also reminded, sadly, of the fate of all Cassandras, those prophets of ill tidings. They can speak but nobody listens. Sometimes even the prophets don't listen to their own prophecies.

Moreover, this somewhat morbid research leads to another depressing thought. Namely, that the painful measures needed to deal with the problem weren't shrouded with secrecy either, but if no one was listening then hardly anybody is listening now. Thus most of the measures being taken to relieve the problem seem to be aggravating it.

* * *

In any event, the record shows plainly enough that this energy shortage cast its shadows before it, visible to all who cared to look.

In the pile of newspaper clippings going back two to three years ago you find a vice president of Allegheny Ludlum warning that "lack of energy is going to start inhibiting our economic growth and perhaps our standard of living," an electric utility executive worrying that energy consumption was out-galloping the supply, a Shell Oil executive gloomily noting that the 1972 summer shortage of gasoline was "a warning of more serious long-term problems."

Nor were the alarmists just from industry. In its 1971-72 report the Carnegie Institution of Washington was noting our "dangerous dependence on foreign sources of petroleum" which would give the oil-producing countries "more leverage than they now have." The institution also foresaw a consequent rise in oil costs: "Simple extrapolation of current trends suggests that the price of oil could quadruple by 1980."

Nor was the government blind to the problem. As far back as 1970 the staff director of the White House Office of Science and Technology was noting that "we have a crisis amid abundance," and by 1972 the Office of Emergency Preparedness was urging a drastic program of energy conservation. President Nixon took note of the problem in his 1972 State of the Union message and returned to the subject in later messages to Congress long before the Arab oil embargo.

With so many seeing so much, why was so little done about it? One reason, no doubt, is simply the human propensity to ignore a problem until it arrives; it would have been politically difficult in 1970 or 1972 to persuade the public to accept the necessary remedial steps. Another reason, though, is that those involved didn't heed their own warnings.

Thus while issuing all those warnings the oil companies kept right on with active sales campaigns, the electric power companies kept promoting the increased electric consumption their own figures showed they could not supply. The government did nothing to change the regulatory policies, the import policies that might have mitigated the problem. Though this latter was mostly congressional inertia, Mr. Nixon did not follow up his proposals with much vigor until the problem had become a crisis.

Indeed, we have the absurdity now of Congressmen wanting to roll back the price, when even if it were possible to do so that would only make the problem worse by perpetuating the cause of it.

No one disputes that this energy crunch is painful; it would be nicer not to have it. But there is nothing mysterious about it; whatever the public may think, it did not arrive unheralded by perceptive voices, many of them reported in the media. It was just that nobody was in a mood to listen.

There is equally nothing mysterious about what has to be done about it. We are going to have to stop being profligate with energy and pay more for it; we shan't be spared that by rationing, allocations, price rollbacks or whatever. But of course nobody wants to listen to that either.

It is sad and ironic to observe politicians failing to see the necessity of higher prices and compounding the problems by advocating counterproductive measures. First of all, they contributed to wild spending sprees, helping to create an inflation that forces up the prices of items essential to produce energy, from steel tubing to steel used in drilling bits and the labor required to do the drilling. Their bureaucratic partners kept the price of natural gas so low that prices could not keep pace with rising costs. Then they teamed up with environmentalists to delay pipeline construction, restricted the use of coal and delayed unnecessarily the construction of nuclear plants—and now they posture and pontificate that the shortage has ballooned into a crisis. What hypocrisy! "The hypocrisy of the situation is stunning."

There are no easy and facile answers to our energy problem. Least of all do we need demagogic appeals for low energy prices. Despite the irresponsible fulminations of politicians, higher energy prices are the only solution to restore adequate energy supplies from a domestic base. Economically, our best choice would be to await the forthcoming glut of oil that will engulf the world. This, however, entails reliance on international market forces. In any case, national security policy must take precedence over economic policy. Hence, domestic economic incentives are required to ensure an adequate supply of energy for years and decades to come, so as to obviate roadblocks to our economic progress.

An honest and objective analysis will reveal that the choice is between low prices and inadequate supplies currently and into the foreseeable future, with vulnerability to economic blackmail by OPEC, or high prices currently with assured adequate supply in a few years from domestic sources and freedom from the threat of OPEC pressures.

Politicians of the strain of Henry Jackson, Birch Bayh, Adlai Stevenson III, James Abourezk, and others, are guilty of perpetrating a cruel hoax on the populace by calling for price rollbacks, higher taxes on oil profits. Such proposals are asinine and counterproductive of everything except a handful of cheap votes.

We now have a twofold problem. Not only is our supply

Energy: Geopolitics and Politics

inadequate but demand is excessive and wasteful. Energy prices were too low, thus talk of conserving our energy resources fell on deaf ears. Besides there is the human proclivity to ignore a problem until it develops into a full-blown phenomenon. It should be obvious that higher energy prices are required to provide incentives and/or funds for the following:

1. The recovery of abandoned and currently available reserves.
2. Offshore drilling and exploration.
3. Conservation of current resources.
4. Creation and development of alternate resources.
5. Development of more efficient auto engines and other machines that utilize energy resources.

"There is Oil in Them Thar Holes!"

It has been estimated that under conventional technology and controlled prices only 30% of the oil in a given field is recovered. This is known as primary recovery. The technology for doubling the recovery rate is available now. The only missing ingredient is an attractive price, high enough to cover costs and an adequate profit. This emphasizes the need for higher prices. The oil industry is now working on tertiary recovery. A timely article in this respect was written by Sanford Rose and appeared in *Fortune* of April, 1974. Excerpts from the article, entitled "Our Vast, Hidden Oil Resources," follow:

> In the 1940's there was no thought of new energy technologies coming onstream. In fact, oil was the new technology.

In addition, the technology of oil recovery was still in its infancy in the early postwar period. Nearly all recovery was primary—that is, either the oil flowed to the surface under the pressure of the reservoir's natural drive or, if reservoir pressure was weak, the oil was lifted by pumps. Since the 1940's the oil industry has perfected methods of secondary recovery and is now working on tertiary recovery.

These methods of recovering oil involve a number of artificial techniques for rebuilding reservoir pressure once it has been weakened or exhausted. Secondary methods include simple water injection—that is, flooding the areas under the oil sands—hydraulic fracturing of the oil formation, gas injection, and (when the unrecovered oil is highly viscous) heat injection. Tertiary methods generally involve one or more of the above, closely followed by the injection of surfactants—e.g., chemical detergents.

Right now primary recovery is gathering only about 20 to 30 percent of the total oil in the ground. Secondary recovery can double that proportion. And tertiary methods can boost total recovery to 75 percent.

Flooding Becomes Attractive

It is true that even the cost of secondary recovery is still high and the cost of tertiary recovery is a lot higher. When oil sold for $2 to $3 a barrel, operators found it economical to waterflood only some fields. But when the price gets to $7 or $8 a barrel, waterflooding becomes an attractive proposition for most oilmen.

After a field has been waterflooded, output will not rise immediately. It takes anywhere from six to eighteen months for the water to rebuild the original pressure. But after that time, production could increase quite substantially.

Henry Steele, a professor of economics at the University of Houston, has calculated that if prices settle at around $8 or $9 a barrel, a lot more production would come on. It would become profitable to use a great deal of secondary and even some tertiary recovery methods.

Turning on the Gas

In contemplating the possibility of expanded oil production, we should not forget that it would come with a major fringe

Energy: Geopolitics and Politics 321

benefit: production of natural gas would also increase. Gas is usually found along with oil, either entirely dissolved in the oil or in the form of a "cap" located above it.

But there is no doubt at all that the potential for a rapid rise in output is there. All that is required is that we know how to take advantage of it. Energy companies must become convinced that it makes sense to produce now rather than to wait. If we revise those state and federal policies that encourage the companies to think otherwise, huge increases in energy supplies will follow within the next few years.

An obvious conclusion from the above study is that adamant advocacy for maintaining "old oil" at $5.25 a barrel, as insisted by Senator Henry Jackson, is unwarranted and counterproductive. The Senator has been unwilling to budge from his notion that the United States can make itself independent of foreign oil producers by holding down the price of domestic oil.

What Senators Jackson and Hubert Humphrey and others, suffering from economic myopia, fail to comprehend is that we are suffering the long-term economic consequences of asinine proposals. They are in effect putting a limit on economic growth. This will restrict capital formation and job creation and delay or possibly thwart what should be the inevitable workers' and middle class capitalism. The Senators fail to see, or resort to demagoguery for self-serving votegetting, that we cannot afford the luxury of subjecting our economic growth to the whims of sheiks and shahs, greedy for power and fame.

The higher energy prices should be considered as a form of insurance to guarantee unhampered economic growth. It also should not be overlooked that higher energy prices would provide an important pollution dividend. Higher prices would render economical desulfurization of oil and strip-mining reclamation.

It cannot be overstressed that higher energy prices are desirable and necessary to fully exploit what we have currently available in energy resources so as to buy time and provide funds for unleashing our latent and potential technology that will develop new sophisticated energy resources. We should avail ourselves to the fullest extent possible of our current resources in what is called the critical "middle period" from a few years hence to about 1985. In this matter, an informative focus and perspective are provided in the following quotes in the previously cited article in *Fortune* by Sanford Rose:

> Over the years, U.S. oil producers have discovered about 430 billion barrels of oil in the U.S. Approximately 100 billion barrels have been extracted thus far, leaving 330 billion still in the ground.
>
> Some of this oil is in abandoned fields; some of it—including all the proved reserves—is in currently active fields. The new higher prices for oil make it profitable to attempt recovery of perhaps half that remaining 330 billion barrels. In other words, potentially recoverable reserves now represent over fifty years' supply at present rates of production.

It would be sheer economic stupidity not to exploit these resources through secondary and tertiary recovery while simultaneously researching and developing the scientifically sophisticated alternates such as fusion, hydrogen, coal gasification and liquification, solar energy, wind power, wave power, oil from shale, oil from tar sands, etc. Thus, higher prices for about ten years will guarantee adequate energy for the middle period and provide the stimulus for the development of new alternate energy resources in abundance and eventually much lower prices.

What will these higher oil prices at the well mean to the consumer?

This is a fair and important question that will serve to provide a good perspective for the benefit of all. The startling answer is that it will cost the consumer less than anticipated and less than conjured up by the irresponsible politician. It will not be as onerous as customarily depicted.

The economics of old oil, new oil and decontrols was admirably presented in a *Wall Street Journal* editorial of July 11, 1975, "President Ford's Oil Opportunity." Relevant portions follow:

> In fact, the price of gasoline is more likely to fall than to rise after decontrol. The scenario rests on the observation that with decontrol the price of "old" domestic crude would leap from $5.25 a barrel to $13, the world price plus the $2 tariff—and on the hallucination that retail prices would behave more or less in proportion.
>
> To begin with, since controlled oil is only 40% of the total, the current average price of crude is about $10. Beyond that, the price of crude is a relatively minor component of the retail cost of gasoline; a $1-a-barrel increase in crude costs means a 2.5-cents-a-gallon increase in gasoline prices. So, if the total increase is passed on, lifting the average price of crude to $13 would mean an increase of 7.5 cents at the gasoline pump (or 2.5 cents if the President simultaneously lifted the tariff). We doubt that this increase would set off riots even in Senator Jackson's offices and it is the most pessimistic possible prediction. An increase of 7.5 cents is the upper limit, the maximum.
>
> Actually, anyone who believes elementary economics ought to predict that decontrol would leave the price of gasoline totally unchanged. Elementary economics teaches that prices are set at the margin. What matters is not the average cost but the cost of the last additional barrel necessary for supply to equal demand.

Of course, the marginal barrel of oil is now imported at a cost of $13. Decontrol would not change this marginal cost, and therefore would not change the price of gasoline.

As a background, it should be noted that gasoline in Europe has retailed at more than a dollar a gallon, equivalent to the U.S. gallon, for years. That is the one prime reason Europe designed more economically operating engines in terms of gasoline consumption. In final analysis, the pocketbook does the talking.

According to a UPI dispatch appearing in the *New York Times* of July 11, 1975,

> Senator Hubert H. Humphrey, Democrat of Minnesota, who was chairing the hearing, said the price the country pays for oil could easily rise by $70 billion this fall, with a devastating impact on the economy. That alone would revive the recession and inflation, he said.

We question the Senator's charge that decontrol would add $70 billion to consumer gasoline, fuel oil and oil bills. Either he was misquoted or he or his staff are guilty of some sloppy research. The writer watched a television presentation of part of the hearings and what he saw and heard was very distressing. Government energy "czar" Frank Zarb's answers to Humphrey were anemic and lacked perspective. If Zarb, Commerce Secretary Morton or economics advisor Greenspan made more convincing arguments, they were not shown in the press or on TV.

The TV presentation ended with the Senator resorting to his customary posturing and pontificating when he concluded that "the higher prices would be a black eye to the consumer and a bonanza to the oil producers." Viewed in

Energy: Geopolitics and Politics

long-range perspective, this is unadulterated rubbish. For the present, the higher prices would help decrease unnecessary and wasteful consumption; for the near future, six months to two years, we would get more ample supplies; and, for the middle years, we would be guaranteed rising supplies and then a glut in the years after 1985. The Senator should forget the 1976 votes and concentrate on workers' incomes five years ahead and beyond. His remarks about "the bonanza to the oil producers" will be treated in considerable detail later. For the present, it will suffice to say that, as far as energy is concerned, nothing could be more constructive than just such a bonanza. Let's pray and hope that we get it. The Senator and his buddies should observe that low energy prices will perpetuate our inadequate supplies and make us more vulnerable to the whims and fancies of the sheiks and shahs.

"What the U.S. should Be Doing About O.P.E.C." was the caption and subject of an editorial in *Fortune* of December, 1974. The concluding portions of the editorial are set forth below:

> According to a number of engineers and independent oil operators consulted by *Fortune,* a price of $11 a barrel—which is approximately the current O.P.E.C. price—would make it profitable to attempt recovery of about half of the 330 billion barrels of oil that remain in the ground in already discovered fields. In other words, producible U.S. reserves probably total something like 165 billion barrels, about five times the A.P.I.'s 35-billion figure for proven reserves.
>
> By far the most important obstacle to a great expansion of U.S. oil output is the inertia of governments, state and federal. Most oil production in the U.S. remains under the control of state authorities, which generally confine output in an oil field to the MER—the "maximum efficient rate," defined as the highest rate

of production that can be sustained without significant loss of ultimate oil and gas recovery. As an engineering concept, MER leaves much to be desired. In many cases, moreover, MER's have not been set according to an engineering standard.

Oil is a migratory resource. Increased production from any well reduces the amount of oil that can be produced from other wells in the same reservoir. Since most reservoirs are worked by more than one operator, the small producers are always afraid that the large producers, with access to more and better equipment, will steal their oil. So when a large operator petitions for an increase in production, smaller operators are likely to oppose it. Various producers, moreover, may hold different opinions about the future behavior of oil prices. Those who anticipate lower prices will want to maximize current output, while those who expect prices to rise will want to hold down on output.

Faced with such disputes, the Texas Railroad Commission, the most important of the state regulatory bodies, usually arranges a compromise production quota, often mislabeled MER. For example, Exxon has estimated that the giant East Texas oil field can safely produce up to 400,000 barrels a day; but the MER is set at 240,000 barrels a day, and operators are currently allowed to produce only 86 percent of that.

A Conspicuous Holdout

As a major step toward getting a lot more oil pumped, the federal government should enact a law requiring "unitization," as it is called, of all U.S. oil fields. Under unitization, each oil reservoir is operated as a single entity, with the various producers sharing costs and profits. At the state level, compulsory unitization has been tried with great success in Louisiana, Oklahoma, and several other oil-producing states. Texas is a conspicuous holdout.

Once a field has been unitized, the smaller producers need no longer fear that their oil will be siphoned off by competitors. All operators have an incentive to demand immediate upward revisions in MER, if they believe that increased output is in their interest.

There can be no doubt that with unitization and an end to price controls, U.S. oil output can be greatly expanded within the next few years. The reserves are clearly there, and the neces-

Energy: Geopolitics and Politics

sary equipment to lift, store, and transport the oil can be obtained. What is lacking is the will to adopt the appropriate policies. The sooner American leaders summon up the will, the better for the U.S. and the other oil-importing countries of the world—and for the prospects of Western civilization.

In essence, it boils down to the fact that irresponsible claptrap from politicians and their concomitant unwarranted roadblocks with the aid of bureaucrats are denying the nation much-needed energy supplies. The arrant propaganda against profits is also delaying the implementation of Project Independence, which would reduce our dependence on unpredictable foreign oil.

BLACK GOLD PROFITS

Let's have a look at the record of profits and other relevant matters in the petroleum and associated industries. Petroleum industry profits have been branded unconscionable, exorbitant, obscene or just plain excessive. By definition, *excessive* means more than necessary. The politicians don't spell out their criterion and don't provide documentary evidence, lest they lose the vote-getting appeal of labeling profits a bonanza to Big Oil. Where is their proof that profits were more than adequate from the standpoint of the financial needs of the oil industry? But more important we should see what industry is doing with those profits and observe whether oil profits are accruing to the benefit of the general public or the oil industry stockholder.

Table XVI-1 has been reconstructed from data furnished by the First National City Bank.

We are presenting this table to show in historical perspective the returns of the petroleum industry on equity and

Table XVI-1

	After-Tax Profits as % of Equity		After Tax-Profits as % of Sales	
	All Manufacturers	Petroleum Refining	All Manufacturers	Petroleum Refining
1960	10.6	10.3	5.5	9.1
1965	13.9	11.9	6.4	9.5
1970	10.1	11.0	4.5	7.3
1971	10.8	11.2	4.7	6.9
1972	12.1	10.8	5.1	6.5
1973	14.9	15.6	5.7	8.1
1974	15.2	19.6	5.2	7.1
1975	12.3	14.1	4.4	5.1

Source: Economics Department, First National City Bank of New York.

on the sales dollar. The other industries are also shown for the sake of comparison. We have commented on the profit margins on sales because they show that profits have not been excessive and that it is a hoax and a delusion to hope and believe that profit margins can absorb cost increases.

An understanding of the significance of the return on equity is essential because business has not been able to generate enough in profits and cash flows for necessary capital investment and must enter the capital markets to float bond issues. Hence, to get favorable interest rates, it is mandatory that they show an adequate return on equity.

In making historical comparisons, caution should be observed in relating both series of 1972 and 1973 to 1960 and 1970 because both 1960 and 1970 were recession years, when profits declined more than other economic data. A reading of the table for the petroleum industry indicates

Energy: Geopolitics and Politics

that returns on equity are a shade below the level for all manufacturers. In 1972, the level fell below the figure for all manufacturers and even below the oil industry's data for recent years. The return on sales in recent years has been lower than the historical average. These figures refute the myth of an oligopolistic market.

However, the figures cited do not reveal the true picture when allowance is made for the loss in purchasing power. To adjust for loss in purchasing power, we used the implicit price deflator for non-residential structures and producers' goods—the items petroleum refiners purchase for replacement and expansion of capacity. The results in terms of constant (1960) dollars are as follows:

Table XVI-2

	Return on Equity	Margin on Sales
1960	10.1%	9.9%
1973	8.2%	5.4%

Now let us look at the price record. Table XVI-3 is compiled from the *Handbook of Labor Statistics*, showing the manufacturing price index in petroleum refining, with 1967 as a base of 100.0.

Table XVI-3

1957	106.9	1963	95.7	1969	98.9
1958	99.2	1964	91.5	1970	100.1
1959	98.5	1965	94.4	1971	105.7
1960	98.3	1966	97.9	1972	107.5
1961	98.5	1967	100.0	1973	145.1
1962	97.1	1968	97.9		

Please note that, in 1972, the wholesale price level of refined products was about equal to the price in 1957, fifteen years earlier. This compares with a rise of over 42% in all wholesale prices; and over 50% in all consumer prices. This relative stability in the face of lower or stable returns on investment and sales is all the more remarkable when cognizance is given the facts that in this same period gross weekly earnings in construction increased over 140%; in all manufacturing, over 103%, and truckers' hourly wage rates increased over 130%. Truly, this is hardly a picture of an oligopolistic price gouger or profiteer. This is another example of one of our themes—that the production engineer is always at work reducing costs, in absolute or relative terms.

Now we shall turn our attention to investigate the activities of the five major U.S. oil producers, refiners and marketers. We present Table XVI-4, constructed from tables furnished by the *Value Line Investment Survey*, published by Arnold Bernhard & Company, Inc., New York, New York.

The tables shown are replete with some surprising developments—all to the ultimate benefit of the U.S. automobile owner and energy user. If the pompous and self-righteous liberals and politicians will care to observe, they will find that net income margins have been and are very reasonable. The percentages earned on total capital and net worth have improved. But before the bamboozling babblers get apopletic fits, they should be honest to admit that, in real terms (returns adjusted for loss in purchasing power), the rise is minimal.

It should be of interest to everyone, including the demagogues, to inquire what the corporations did with their profits. It is important to ask—Did the profits go to the stockholders or were they recycled into the economy to ex-

Table XVI-4

	1964	1965	1966	1967	1968	1969	1970	1971	1972	1973	1974	1975
Exxon												
Net Margin	% 9.7	9.0	9.0	9.3	9.1	8.3	7.9	8.1	7.5	9.5	7.5	5.6
% on Equity	12.6	11.9	12.2	13.0	13.3	12.3	12.0	13.1	12.5	17.8	20.0	14.7
% Dividends to Net Income	62	66	65	60	62	65	63	56	56	39	36	45
Capital Spending per Share	4.85	4.51	5.59	7.52	9.04	7.86	8.02	8.08	8.85	9.98	13.01	15.91
Texaco												
Net Margin	%16.2	16.9	16.0	14.7	15.3	13.1	13.0	12.0	10.2	11.3	6.8	3.3
% on Equity	15.2	15.5	15.9	15.3	15.4	13.1	13.1	13.4	12.4	16.2	17.6	9.5
% Dividends to Net Income	51	52	48	48	47	55	53	48	51	36	36	65
Capital Spending per Share	2.07	2.36	2.53	3.12	3.76	2.68	2.93	3.85	4.09	4.56	6.84	5.11
Mobil												
Net Margin	% 6.5	6.5	6.8	6.7	6.9	6.9	6.7	6.6	6.3	7.5	5.5	3.9
% on Equity	8.9	9.2	9.7	10.0	10.5	10.6	10.6	11.2	11.2	14.9	16.3	11.8
% Dividends to Net Income	48	48	47	49	48	50	50	48	47	34	31	43
Capital Spending per Share	3.76	4.55	5.78	5.72	5.95	6.73	7.45	8.97	10.12	11.64	14.23	11.81

Table XVI-4 (Continued)

STANDARD (California)

Net Margin	%15.1	16.0	15.7	12.8	12.4	11.9	10.9	9.9	9.4	10.9	5.6	4.6
% on Equity	11.3	11.9	12.1	10.8	10.7	10.3	9.8	10.4	10.5	14.5	15.0	11.9
% Dividends to Net Income	45	45	45	48	48	52	52	48	45	31	34	44
Capital Spending per Share	2.93	3.30	2.60	3.10	3.11	3.58	3.81	4.26	3.52	4.35	6.74	6.04

GULF

Net Margin	%12.5	12.6	13.4	13.8	13.7	12.3	10.2	9.4	7.2	9.5	6.5	4.9
% on Equity	11.0	11.2	12.4	13.1	13.2	12.1	10.4	10.2	8.3	14.4	16.8	10.8
% Dividends to Net Income	45	45	43	45	46	51	57	56	70	37	29	47
Capital Spending per Share	2.79	2.87	3.45	4.17	5.24	4.59	4.52	4.37	3.26	4.03	7.22	6.31

pand plant facilities and to search and drill for more oil and gas? If the puffed-up ignorantly prating leftists would care to inquire, they will be shocked to learn that the stockholder is getting a smaller share and more funds have been spent for plant and drilling and exploration.

As an example, take Exxon. From 1964 through 1970, Exxon distributed over 60% of net income as dividends. In 1971 and 1972, the ratio dropped below 50%; and in 1973 and 1974, below 40%.

The reader should now direct his attention to the data on capital spending per share. All companies have made significant increases in this category. The lines below on per share expenditures for drilling and exploration indicate substantial increases for four major producers, the only exception being Texaco.

It cannot be overstressed that the oil producers should be allowed to make good profits for recycling into more energy, but also because they must show healthy income statements and balance sheets so that they can keep on borrowing funds for research, drilling and exploration. All companies have increased their funded debt. To expand their facilities and spend more sums in the future to increase our domestic base and develop alternate resources, they will have to borrow not billions but trillions of dollars. Demagogues may deceive themselves and economic ignorami by taking sadistic glee in what they believe will be a screwing they will give the oil producers by price rollbacks and profit reductions. However, ultimately they will end up screwing those they pretend to benefit by depriving them of vital energy sources and hamstringing economic growth that is essential for jobs and inflation control.

Senator Humphrey objects to decontrol of oil prices on the basis that this would be a "bonanza" to the oil companies. What he fails or is unwilling to perceive is that it would be a bigger and more significant "bonanza" to the average worker in the near, middle and distant future.

The oil companies should be allowed to operate with less abuse from the demagogues and with greater funds and under higher prices, because they must be given the incentive to develop and use secondary and tertiary recovery methods and because they must drill deeper. From 1973 to 1974, the number of oil wells completed increased from 9,902 to 12,718 or over 28%. However, this is woefully inadequate, as indicated in the following table compiled from the U.S. Bureau of Mines' *Minerals Handbook:*

Table XVI-5
OIL WELLS
SUCCESSFULLY COMPLETED

1950	24,000
1955	32,000
1960	22,000
1965	19,000
1969	14,000
1970	13,000
1971	12,000
1972	11,000

The oil companies must be given the incentive not only to dig deeper for onshore supplies but also be given the incentive and rights to offshore drilling. Bureaucratic inertia and environmentalist interference have delayed the necessary development of offshore resources; not one acre of the Eastern Seaboard has been leased for exploration. The fear of spill has been exaggerated. Over the past quarter century, oil searchers drilled nearly 20,000 wells in American waters and only four accidents resulted, with no evidence that the environment was permanently damaged. This is not to condone spills. Even one spill is one too many. A combination of higher prices and stiffer penalties would serve to decrease spills.

There are risks inherent in failing to tap all potential areas for future supplies. All avenues should be pursued and it serves no good purpose to belittle any potential, however insignificant it may appear. This appears to have been a characteristic of the *New York Times* in its editorial pages as evidenced in the following retort of Frank Ikard that appeared in the *New York Times* of March 13, 1975:

OFFSHORE OIL FACTS

To the Editor:

Your Feb. 17 editorial "Oil From the Shelf" reflects your continued preference for procrastination in all things relating to oil and the industry's efforts to increase U.S. petroleum supplies.

Four years ago (Jan. 26, 1971) you brushed aside the 37-volume environmental-impact statement on the Alaskan pipeline by saying that "this should not pave the way for an immediate approval of the pipeline." On September 30, 1971, you stated that no one is claiming that Alaska oil is vital "to this country's welfare this year, next year or even the next decade."

Had the pipeline been built on schedule, the economic impact of the Arab oil embargo would have been far less.

Now your obsession with obstruction has shifted to the Outer Continental Shelf. You say: "The offshore program has no bearing on the immediate economic crisis and . . . scarcely rates a priority that would justify headlong action." Elsewhere you state that oil from the Atlantic would not begin to flow until at least six years from now, and that it would account for no more than 8 percent of the nation's daily consumption (or about one and a half million barrels a day).

Your readers may be interested in some facts ignored by your editorial:

First, the Atlantic offshore area may contain, in addition to billions of barrels of crude oil, as much as 110 trillion cubic feet of natural gas. (While the natural-gas potential can obviously not help the "immediate economic crisis," it can both lessen the chances of layoffs on East Coast factories and create new jobs in the years ahead.)

Second, the six-year lead time your editorial mentioned corresponds exactly to the length of the moratorium on further drilling in the Santa Barbara area. The years of delay there only added to the problems caused by the Arab oil embargo.

Third, the daily volume of oil that you mentioned may be found in the Atlantic is almost equivalent to the drop in imports that occurred during the height of the Arab embargo. That amount may be "modest," but it was enough to bring about long lines at service stations last year.

It's time for positive actions to solve those problems. Specifically, it's time to begin to get Atlantic seabed oil and natural gas off the shelf.

FRANK N. IKARD
President, American Petroleum Institute
Washington, February 27, 1975

Further, in amplifying on the subject of risks, we have the option of an intolerable risk of inadequate supplies resulting from energy prices that are too low or a tolerable risk that may eventuate from surplus of energy culminating from high prices. In its editorial advertisement in the *New York Times* of April 3, 1974, Mobil put forth this pertinent question:

Doesn't it make sense for our country to provide some insurance in the form of additional energy supplies—in case those who think we can easily control demand turn out to be wrong?

Mobil lucidly and perceptively answered with the following commentary:

Energy: Geopolitics and Politics

> If we fail to provide sufficient additional energy supplies to meet demand, the inevitable result will be continued energy scarcity, higher energy prices, unemployment, increased reliance on foreign oil, in precisely the way we have recently experienced —and, in addition, pervasive government controls to cope with the many problems. In all of this, the greatest impact may well be on the poor, who will probably be hurt in two closely related ways: They may be unable to pay higher energy costs, and they will generally be the first to suffer from severe unemployment.
>
> Mobil thinks the better alternative would be to increase supplies while at the same time working to hold consumption down. If we prove to be wrong and if it turns out to be easier to reduce energy use than now seems possible, the nation will find itself with surplus energy at lower prices—clearly a more tolerable risk. We think most Americans would opt for this alternative.

Thus, it should be obvious that it would be imprudent and counterproductive for the politicians and industry critics to risk a shortage of energy supplies and increase our vulnerability to OPEC geopolitical pressures and extravagances.

Senator Humphrey is commendably concerned about the impact of higher oil prices on the economy. He justifiably fears that the recession may be revived. However, he should realize that there is no painless and facile option. Dependence on OPEC crude has been increasing rapidly and will continue to do so once the economy turns up, unless dramatic steps are immediately undertaken. Humphrey, Jackson, Stevenson and others should become aware of the fact that increased dependence means an increased vulnerability to another embargo. In effect, they are increasing our exposure to an unnecessary risk. They also should face up to the fact that increased dependence may provide OPEC with the encouragement to raise prices further still.

It is quite possible that higher domestic prices will put a limit on OPEC prices and trigger the trend toward lower prices. The crux of the irony is that keeping domestic energy prices fairly high provides the only chance of producing enough domestic oil to undermine the OPEC stranglehold on the world market and bring some reduction in world prices and lessen the dependence on the cartel.

The oil companies don't win friends and thus fail to influence people when they give rise to reports that they attempt to drive out of business the independent gasoline distributors by allegedly curtailing refinery output and eliminating the surplus that independents buy and market at discount prices.

Furthermore, the oil companies have exposed themselves to allegations that they have pressured service stations to stay open longer hours in order to sell more gasoline.

These activities of the oil producers have been imprudent, unjustified and unwarranted. Furthermore, they have been counterproductive. However, it must be admitted that they are best equipped to provide us with ample fuel supplies in the near future and ultimately at lower prices. They must be tolerated like an intractable child. Congressmen and consumerists, eager to punish them, should realize that the gasoline consumer will bear the ultimate and the greater punishment. Mobil Oil was unwise to use surplus funds to buy control of Marcor. It would be more appropriate for Mobil to confine all its activities to energy.

While we are on the subject of energy, we should not overlook the utility companies. They have not been spared by the anti-profit bias of politicians, consumerists and sham liberals, let alone the radicals. This unholy alliance of per-

Energy: Geopolitics and Politics

nicious prevaricators, in their blatherings, has depicted utilities as greedy price gougers. So, again let's look at the record.

Table XVI-6, compiled from U.S. Federal Power Commission reports, shows the progress of electricity bills.

Table XVI-6
AVERAGE RESIDENTIAL MONTHLY BILL FOR ELECTRICITY
(Average Bill—Dollars)

	100 Kilowatt-Hours	200 Kilowatt-Hours	500 Kilowatt-Hours	Price of Coal (1940=100.0)
1940	$4.06	$7.37	$10.55	100.0
1950	3.76	6.98	10.11	198.8
1955	3.82	7.18	10.30	196.4
1960	4.04	7.44	10.62	228.2
1965	4.02	7.38	10.41	222.9
1970	4.09	7.51	10.51	358.0
1971	4.25	7.84	11.13	433.9
1972	4.51	8.35	11.90	462.5
1973	4.65	8.67	12.56	520.5

Sources: U. S. Bureau of Labor Statistics.
U. S. Federal Power Commission.

A column was added for an index number for the price of coal. We changed the index base to 1940 as 100.0.

Here we have statistical proof that explodes another myth concocted by the moral and intellectual degenerates of hypocritical liberalism. Here is an example of superior performance in the face of handicaps. Please observe that, from 1940 to 1970, a period of 30 years, electricity bills exhibited an astonishing stability, while coal prices increased 258%.

While the average bill of all three categories rose about 17% from 1970 to 1973, coal prices increased 45%.

In the face of this stupendous performance, what kind of claptrap do we get from the self-styled friend of the laborer and consumer? We are dished out deceitful rhetoric that denies funds to utilities for expansion. They will cut back on "green-outs" and risk "brown-outs" and "black-outs." With friends like these does the average man need an enemy?

Because the energy problem is so critical, we will devote the next chapter to a critical analysis of a book hailed by liberals as outstanding.

XVII

SLIPPERY RHETORIC ON OIL

The subject of this chapter is a book, *Energy: The New Era,* by S. David Freeman. The book was sponsored by The Twentieth Century Fund and published in 1974 by Walker and Company, New York.

The book was extolled lavishly, as exemplified by the following:

> This is a desperately needed book . . . a penetrating analysis of the whole complex issue by one of the nation's few broad-gauged experts.
> —STEWART L. UDALL

David Freeman's book is outstanding! The homework and background are there. . . .
—Harrison E. Salisbury

Both quotes appeared on the back of the jacket.

A lucid examination of current energy problems . . .
—*Booklist,* September 15, 1974

With degrees in law and civil engineering, service with the TVA, FPC and Office of Science and Technology, Freeman is undoubtedly an expert on the energy crisis. . . . and reaches the obvious conclusion that we must live with a system of "intelligent austerity" that will make "fundamental changes in our economy and our values." "A message the people and the administration apparently do not want to hear."
—*Publishers' Weekly,* May 1974

Freeman, director of the Energy Policy Project of the Ford Foundation, and former head (1967-1971) of the President's energy policy staff, has written an extensive and impressive primer on the energy problems that have been confronting the industrial societies of the West long before the events of winter 1973-1974. Unlike many of the sensational, quickie, or excessively polemical energy books Freeman's volume is sober in tone and judgment and careful in its handling of the facts. Freeman convincingly and persuasively demonstrates that there is no single "heart" to the energy problem: energy dilemmas relating to use, conservation, supply, pricing, environmental consequences, and the like are inevitably linked together in a systematic fashion. We have consumed too much energy, too cheaply, too thoughtlessly, for too long, and now the day of reckoning has arrived. Freeman's work offers the informed layman a basic outline on the problem and a perspective on policies for the future.
—Henry J. Steck, Department of Political Science, SUNY at Cortland, *Library Journal,* September 15, 1974

The book-reviewing segments of the news media are powerful instruments for molding public opinion, and it is of fundamental importance to analyze to see if their commentaries are fair, objective and unbiased. It is regrettable to find that the opposite is true. It is the object of this chapter to expose their prejudices of sham liberalism. A true liberal may disagree with you but he will not resort to oblique intimations or omissions of relevant facts.

The adversary relationship we have discussed before, but we must allude to it again. It has been pointed out that the adversary factor is a result of an unjustified propaganda against profits unsupported by statistical data. Elitists in journalism and education and powerful unionists are largely responsible for his "adversary mess" by the repetitions of misleading lies and half-truths.

On the subject of prices, how can the public get a clear picture of price factors when perspectives on the relationship of wages, profits, taxes, costs and prices are ignored by biased critics of profits and capitalism?

Michael C. Jensen, in a review of Freeman's book in the *New York Times*, leaves the impression that revenues (income or profits) and prices outpace wage rates. As we have demonstrated for all manufacturing industries and for the oil producers, the opposite is true.

In his statements on "fat and arrogant oil industry" and "profit-hungry industry," Mr. Jensen implies an amassment of profits at the expense of the public. On the contrary, industry in general as well as oil has passed on cost reductions for the benefit of the consumer, while "hungrily" and "avariciously" taking in only a nominal amount of profit on sales.

Following is a listing of prices the gasoline dealers paid the oil producer, exclusive of taxes, according to the U.S. Bureau of Mines:

Table XVII-1
1950	15.18 cents
1965	15.38 cents
1972	17.72 cents

If you were to roll back the 1972 price to the 1965 or the 1950 price, you would more than wipe out the oil producers' profit. This is hardly a picture of a "fat" and "profit-hungry" industry. However, proper perspectives and foci are not in the repertoire of anti-business propagandists. On the contrary, their arsenal against profits and the free market brims with insinuations and innuendos, if not half-truths and outright lies. As a consequence, their supposed beneficiaries, the working and poor people, bear the brunt of the screwing.

So much for the favorable book reviews that we could garner. A critical review will be presented toward the end of the chapter.

In our review of Freeman's book, we will first turn to our pet peeves—irresponsible treatment of profits and prices. Again we will quote without introductory remarks and quote as much as possible in context and follow with our comments.

> *Freeman:* The money at issue is enormous. Each additional penny on the price of gasoline transfers a billion dollars a year from consumers' pocketbooks to the oil companies' treasuries. Obviously clean energy costs more than dirty, and higher costs of labor and materials must be reflected in higher prices for energy. Citizens may be persuaded to accept price increases reflecting increased costs, but increases reflecting increased profits are hard to take. (Page 9)

Rebuttal: Although profit margins increased by one penny from 1972 to 1973, they improved from a record low level of recent years and did not approach the levels of the 1950s and 1960s. Freeman cited no statistical proof. He just gave credence to a popular myth fabricated by the intelligentsia.

> *Freeman:* . . . there are still many people who believe that a purely market oriented solution is the best way to overcome the energy crisis. The problem is that a free market economy pays more attention to short-term benefits than to the long-term social and economic costs that are at the heart of the energy crisis. The market place doesn't pay much attention to the future because investments that don't pay out for many years are seldom profitable to a private company and therefore aren't made. (Page 11)

Rebuttal: This bit of sophistry is but a specious excuse for bureaucratic research and development. As will be shown later, industry must share some blame for the energy mess, but the bureaucrats and Congressmen must be saddled with the major blame. The bureaucrats and politicians ignored the Paley Report of the early 1950s, penalized capital formations, obstructed the laying of pipelines, held up offshore drilling, discouraged opening of new gas heads, restricted the uses of coal, delayed the construction of nuclear plants—and now act outraged that a shortage escalated into a crisis. These no-good do-gooders shackled the free market, then point to its shortcomings, and come up with a grandiose solution—more bureaucratic bungling. This is not to say that the free market won't make mistakes. However, the mistakes are corrected sooner than those perpetrated by a bureaucracy than can bungle into perpetuity.

Freeman: Concerning prices, there is a serious doubt whether the fuel industry is sufficiently competitive to assure consumers of prices reflecting only a reasonable profit. (Page 11)

Rebuttal: Rubbish! Need more be said?

Freeman: It is now clear that adequate supplies of clean energy will require a massive federally financed research and development effort. . . . (Page 12)

Rebuttal: It takes a special brand of mentality to deny funds to an efficient industry and entrust those funds to bureaucrats. Freeman contradicts himself on page 23.

Freeman: The energy industry in America developed swiftly because it was innovative and dynamic.

Non-rebuttal: Hallelujah! Why not give massive funds to industry to solve our problems by tax exemptions if they stick to energy?

Freeman: . . . By the year 2000 the structure of our economy may have changed fundamentally. By then we may be a service economy, with a proportionately smaller industrial sector than we have now. . . . (Page 36)

No rebuttal or non-rebuttal here but a **TUT? TUT?** According to Emma S. Woytinsky in *Profile of U.S. Economy*, published by Frederick A. Praeger, New York, 1967, we have been in a service economy since the early 1950s, when employment in the service industries went above employment in the goods-producing industries (page 112). Woytinsky included agriculture, mining, manufacturing and construction in the goods-producing industries; and trade, finance, service, government, transportation and public utilities in service industries.

Freeman: As Barry Commoner points out, the increased consumption of energy doesn't necessarily mean that we live markedly better. (Page 37)

Rebuttal: Freeman and Commoner ignore or don't know what is shown in Table XVII-2

Table XVII-2

83% of U.S. families owned an automobile in 1971 (*Statistical Abstract*, page 559).
99.8% of American homes have radios.
94% of American homes have vacuum cleaners.
84% of American homes have electric food mixers.
40% of American homes have blenders.
91% of American homes have automatic coffee makers.
Source: Wattenberg, *The Real America*, page 103.
77% of American homes have black and white TV.
43.3% of American homes have color TV.
71.3% of American homes have washing machines.
44.5% of American homes have clothes dryers.
83.3% of American homes have refrigerators.
32.2% of American homes have freezers.
18.8% of American homes have dishwashers.
31.8% of American homes have air conditioners.
Source: Statistical Abstract, page 397.

It should be noted that availability of appliance is higher than ownership.

Freeman: . . . But it would be foolish not to recognize the market's imperfections which have to be removed before the price system can begin to help ease energy consumption. (Page 37)

Rebuttal: We disagree and agree—how's that for doubletalk? But lest Mr. Freeman be carried away, we should say that we agree but not in the sense held by Freeman. Get the bureaucrats off the backs of the energy industry and the market's imperfections will be reduced.

> *Freeman:* . . . Thus far we have exploited perhaps not more than 10 percent of the oil and gas beneath the waters off the United States shores. (Page 52)

Rebuttal: Nowhere in the book does Freeman ascribe the failure to exploit these huge resources to the bureaucrats, politicians and environmentalists.

> *Freeman:* . . . Yet price controls are an important part of federal policy to control inflation and prevent windfall profits to energy producers. (Page 80)

Rebuttal: Here is an example of bureaucratic lawyer and civil engineer exhibiting ignorance of economic facts and financial data. He even contradicts himself. Just observe these remarks from earlier pages in his book:

> *Freeman:* . . . yet higher prices are a powerful tool for cutting out the waste in energy consumption and encouraging greater production of new sources of supply. (Page 10)
> . . . If the foreign policy problems arising from increasing imports are deemed of overriding importance, then we must take strong measures to reduce energy consumption, including higher prices and some environmental degradation, in order to obtain the needed supply from domestic resources. (Page 12)

Rebuttal (continuation): If Freeman were an objective observer of price controls, he would find that bureaucrats invariably err in holding prices too low, thus counterproductively not only restricting resource development but also aggravating the inflation that they purportedly set out to restrain. Free markets may not do it perfectly and in-

Slippery Rhetoric on Oil 349

stantly; nevertheless, they will do it sooner and better than statist controls.

Also, we question Freeman's remarks about windfall profits. The data that we cited for the oil industry and individual oil companies show a declining trend in profit margins on sales. Take Exxon as an example; its net income margins in 1974 and in 1972 were the lowest in 10 years. The other four companies revealed record low margins in the past 11 years. Returns on equity increased substantially. In essence, what happened was that increased volume of sales at lower profit sales margins increased equity returns. If the detractors of capitalism would unshackle themselves from Marxist dogmas and consult Adam Smith and Alfred Marshall, this is how capitalism is supposed to work.

The remark about "windfall profits" lacks the "penetrating analysis" attributed to the book by Udall. In the first place, profits have not been excessive; and, second, there appears to be an obsession that the oil producers may benefit from higher prices and profits. We indicated previously in our chapter on profits that profits mean future jobs. Here, it is important to realize that profits mean not only future jobs but future higher domestic energy resources, independence from foreign blackmail and the acceleration of a workers' capitalism with stable economic growth and prices with reasonable full employment.

> *Freeman:* . . . Private industry must obtain government permission before it can exploit fuels on government lands. . . . In the off-shore areas government has behaved like a sensible monopolist. It has sold the fuel it owns at a slow pace. . . . The pace pleases the environmentalists and government budget makers, who are a powerful combination. (Page 81)

Rebuttal with a question: Isn't it preposterous to restrict the development of domestic fuel resources to appease environmental and bureaucratic mischief and allow the shahs and sheiks to aggravate an inflation and recession to a large degree spawned by bureaucratic and intelligentsist economic rhetoric and malfeasance?

> *Freeman:* . . . Consumers tend to believe that energy companies are making enough profit and don't need large price increases to spur more rapid exploration. The environmentalists tend to feel that limits on production are essential to prevent destruction of the ecology. In a democratic political system, these values are bound to make themselves felt. (Page 84)

Rebuttal: In plain words, Freeman appears to look favorably on these values which, in our opinion, are veritable "dis-values" in the current popular construction. The first is the result of a misguided or misleading unwarranted attack on profits, and the second is either deliberate leftist mischief or naivete about sensible goals and timetables as to ecological objectives. Efforts to condone or appease these "values" are sheer stupidity.

On page 84, Freeman finds values in consumer objection to higher prices and almost immediately, on page 85, he writes that "the root of the energy problem is that in recent years there has been no limit on growth in demand," forgetting that on page 10 he wrote:

> . . . Yet higher prices are a powerful tool for cutting out the waste in energy consumption and encouraging greater production of new sources of supply—obviously, higher energy prices will encourage better insulated houses, cars with improved mileage and more efficient use of energy in industry.

> *Freeman:* Energy supply is indeed a complicated, interdis-

ciplinary problem, yet most discussions treat it in an amazingly simplistic manner. Intelligent economists say flatly that the shortage of natural gas can be cured if price controls are removed and that higher prices will bring a surplus of oil to market in a few short years. They are blind to the environmental limits imposed on drilling offshore as well as the environmental and political opposition to development in the U.S. and around the world. (Pages 85-86)

Rebuttal: If Freeman and his much beloved environmentalists were not so "simplistic" and "blind," they would recognize that higher prices would not only spur exploration and development but also cover the higher costs inherent in sensible ecological costs associated with offshore drilling and strip-mining.

> *Freeman:* . . . current technology and prices permit recovery of only about 30 percent in a "given field."
> . . . Oil in a reservoir does not occur in a free flowing pool. It is found in porous rocks or trapped under high pressure in dense rock. An increase in the percentage recovered, therefore, cannot automatically occur. It requires additional expenditures for secondary and tertiary recovery techniques that entail a higher production cost per barrel, and subsequently would require a higher price or subsidy for the extra oil discovered. (Page 88)

Comment: It is difficult to reconcile the facts that Freeman on the one hand reveals that he is so knowledgeable about fuel geology and that he appears so simplistic and blind about the fuel economics that make him carry aversions about prices and profits to absurd degrees. There's oil in them thar holes, so why not get it out in the short and middle periods while we develop more sophisticated resources for the long term?

We have demonstrated that profits have not been excessive and that they have been directed more to reinvestment rather than to dividends for stockholders, so why the unwarranted aversion and hostility to profits? It is conceivable that this would erode the ability of the intelligentsia and their lackeys to exploit their appeals to envy, prejudices, greed and ignorance. These sordid appeals explain to a large degree the explosive growth of the "gimme" attitude in expectations and entitlements. It is also conceivable to conclude that if profits were construed as a powerful force for progress benefiting the worker more than the stockholder, the left elitist would lose the rationale for his appeals to envy and prejudice and ignorance. Does he feel the reason for his existence would be undermined?

It is essential for the producers, the workers and the middle classes to take heed and realize that profits in general in industry and the oil industry in particular are of vital concern to assure jobs and ample energy resources in the future.

While the statists and elitists completely misread the perspectives on prices, profits and petroleum and repeat by rote the fashionable liberal views of woolly neo-Marxism, let's take a look at another significant development egregiously underreported by the media.

In a remote inside page of the financial section, the Sunday *New York Times* of July 13, 1975, reported a plan known as "unitization," by which all property interests in an oil reservoir are operated jointly for highest production at lower cost. Instead of operating each well separately, with no regard for the status of the reservoir as a whole, each tract is allocated a percentage of total daily production during the life of the reserve. For the Yates field in West

Slippery Rhetoric on Oil

Texas, the nation's second largest reserve, it is estimated that this plan will double daily production and increase the ultimate recovery by approximately 200 million barrels.

While the sham liberals and their fawning bootlickers were obstructing the growth in energy supplies, the oil companies without any fanfare were going about doing the opposite—taking measures to get "oil from them thar holes."

After this diversion, let's get back to Freeman.

> *Freeman:* The pace of drilling is of course now increasing in response to price increases. Even so it seems unlikely that the industry will launch the kind of dramatic increase in drilling that would appreciably expand domestic oil production.

Rebuttal: His prejudgment is wholly gratuitous and reflects ignorance of the elasticity of supply. Remove uncertainties and controls and business will respond with new sources, more efficient use of old sources and new refining capacity.

> *Freeman:* . . . But the new values of our society are slowing down the energy producers and growth rates will reflect that conflict. . . . (Page 112)

Rebuttal: It is asinine and ludicrous for anyone to accept the values fabricated by Marxists and their truckling and naive cohorts. A case can be made for the suspicion that Marxists and phony liberals are conspiring to thwart the economic growth of capitalist countries that far outperformed the collectivized economies.

> *Freeman:* Our relations with the Soviet Union provide a good example of the way that prospective imports and natural gas and oil can contribute to world peace. Trade is the symbol of U.S.-

Soviet efforts to bury the Cold War. The U.S.S.R. needs our grain, capital and technology, and we need their oil, so that trade may be the solvent of national differences. . . . (Pages 114-115)

. . . Arab oil is subject to interruption without notice. . . .

Rebuttal: The Russians were never known to pass up a chance to exploit a political or economic event. In fact, Soviet oil would be as interruptible as Arab oil.

Freeman: . . . the oil companies are still managing to do quite well at the expense of the American consumer. (Page 123)

Rebuttal: More anti-business hogwash devoid of statistical proof. He neglects data that we cited proving conclusively that gasoline prices were a bargain until OPEC blackmail. Profits were never excessive, were mainly recycled for the benefit more of the consumer rather than the stockholder.

Freeman: . . . Popular concern . . . is heightened by a growing concentration and growing profits in the basic fuel industry, which suggests that competition may not be adequate to assure reasonable prices to the consumer.

Rebuttal: Arrant claptrap! We have effectively refuted the price and profit charges before, but here will explode the myth of growing concentration. The U.S. Bureau of the Census report on "Concentration Ratios" shows the following:

That the four largest refiners garnered 37% of the shipments in 1947 and 33% in 1970.

That the eight largest refiners accounted for 59% of the shipments in 1947 and 57% in 1970.

Evidently, concentration was decreasing.

Slippery Rhetoric on Oil

> *Freeman:* . . . On the average . . . energy represents 4 percent of the final cost of most products we buy and use. (Page 139)

Comment: Very enlightening. This calls for a close scrutiny of the ramifications and implications. The profits on that 4% are less than ten cents on the sales dollar. The production of the other 96% of purchased items depends on the availability of energy. It would be farsighted to stop nit-picking about energy profits so as to ensure adequate economic growth. It is absurd to disseminate misinformation about profits because, while they are an insignificant percentage of GNP, they provide the spark for the generator of the capitalist economy. Coal and petroleum profits of $7.4 billion comprised 6/10 of 1% of the GNP of $1,294.9 billion in 1973. The total of corporate profits was 5.6% of GNP. The worker should be aware of the adversary relationship his sham protectors are fostering for their own self-serving ends.

> *Freeman:* Until very recently, the price of energy has been one of the great success stories of America. (Page 13)

Comment: How magnanimous of Freeman to volunteer such an admission! He should recognize that it was the cost discipline of the incentive for profits that made that success possible.

> *Freeman:* Inter-fuel competition seems to have played a beneficial role for consumers during the 1960's . . . (Page 163)

Comment: The above two remarks contradict what he wrote on page 11 when he said, "Concerning prices, there is a serious doubt whether the fuel industry is sufficiently competitive to assure consumers of prices reflecting only a reasonable profit."

The whole book abounds in biases, contradictions and inconsistencies and belies the fulsome praise accorded the book. We will discontinue our probing as this chapter would take on the size of a book itself. We will just add a number of items we find objectionable as per the following:

>   ... windfall profits. ... (Page 145)
>   ... fatten the profit margin. ... (Page 146)

We are a bit perplexed by five serious omissions by Freeman:

1. Nowhere in the book does Freeman comment on or mention the obstructionist tactics by environmentalists that delayed construction of the Alaska pipeline.

2. Freeman neglects to mention the Paley Report of 1952.

3. He does not mention President Eisenhower's warnings about overdependence on foreign oil.

4. He neglects to give any attention to technological developments that will transform the automotive industry.

5. He ignores completely the potential of methanol— which is probably destined to become one of the prime fuels for motor vehicles in the 1980s.

Throughout the book, there is a pervasive anti-profit bias that is not justified by the facts. This is unfortunate, not only that it is unfair to the oil producers, but more important because it obfuscates the issues and delays the real solution that is so critically needed so that economic growth can be resumed and sustained.

Slippery Rhetoric on Oil

In the chapter on profits, we pointed out that the manner in which profit figures are reported gives readers an erroneous impression. The crux of the matter is that while the handling of profit data is true and factual, truth is not served because of the wrong impressions that eventuate.

An illustration of the type of profit reporting to which we object has been furnished by the *New York Times* in its Sunday edition of February 3, 1974 when it captioned a box of corporate reports with the following:

CORPORATE PROFITS SURGE

Consider a reader who is not conversant with the facts. What is his reaction to the word *surge,* which is defined as "to rise suddenly to an excessive or abnormal value"? Also, what impression does he get when he peruses the column on percent changes? It is certain that, unless he is given data in historical perspective and also figures on margins on sales, he will conclude that he and the rest of the public are being ripped off. Is this the impression the Newspaper Guild-oriented copy writer meant to convey? With Anthony Lewises and Tom Wickers in influential positions, this would not be surprising.

How well the sowers of distrust have succeeded is indicated by a recent poll of Opinion Research Corporation. In its survey adults were asked to give their best estimate of after-tax profits on each dollar of sales for several different kinds of business. The nature of the wildly erroneous results is incredible.

Given a sustained diet of falsely impressionistic reporting, the public estimated the average manufacturer's after-tax profit at 33 cents per dollar, more than six times the actual amount; the auto companies, at 39 cents, more than 20 times the actual amount; and the oil companies, at 61 cents, more than eight times the actual amount.

Perspectives on profits would show that profits and profit margins fluctuate upward and downward in phase with the business cycle, whereas wage rates are relentlessly upward. Nowhere do the detractors of profits and the profit system add a cautionary note to maintain objective perspectives. This but recalls the dictum of William James—"There is no lie worse than truth misunderstood by the listener." All in all, this is a basic fundamental of this book.

To get some meaningful perspective, we have compiled the tabulation below giving the earnings per share, the profit margin in cents per dollar of cents, and the percentage of profits paid out in dividends.

If one were to show only the first column, obviously a picture is conjured up of a grandiose rip-off. When the second column is considered at the same time, the portrayal changes dramatically, when cognizance is taken of the fact that the margins in 1973 increased from record lows.

However, to prove the profit perspective, note should be taken of the fact that the increases in per share earnings and margins in 1973 over 1972 included foreign exchange and inventory revaluations.

Again looking at the dramatic rises in per share earnings from 1973 to 1974, a false impression would be gleaned unless one also scrutinized the margin data and saw that they declined to record lows.

Such figures as are presented in the second column are seldom if ever reported. When they are, they are usually

Table XVII-3

	Earnings per Share	Profit Margin		% Dividends to Income
		EXXON		
1972	$ 6.83	7.5%	(L)	56%
1973	10.91	9.5		39
1974	14.05	7.5	(LL)	36
		TEXACO		
1972	3.27	10.2	(L)	51
1973	4.75	11.3		36
1974	5.84	6.8	(LL)	36
		MOBIL		
1972	5.64	6.3	(L)	47
1973	8.34	7.5		34
1974	10.28	5.5	(LL)	31
		STANDARD (California)		
1972	3.22	9.4	(L)	45
1973	4.97	10.9		31
1974	5.71	5.6	(LL)	34

L indicates 9-year low.
LL indicates 11-year low.
Source: Value Line Investment Survey.

inserted at the end of the article and subject to withdrawal in the composing room by the editor and compositor when space allotments are tight.

An important story is told in the third column, scarcely if ever constructed. This column tells us that less is paid out to stockholders, that more is retained in the business and spent for drilling, exploration and plant capacity.

If the public relations and publicity departments were negligent in these respects, they did their companies and our economy a flagrant disservice. Managements that encourage or condone these kinds of exercises in horrendous public relations must bear a major share of the blame for the erroneous fabrications and misinformation about so-called obscene, unconscionable and excessive profits.

The conclusive facts are that the lies, half-truths, and distortions about profits have damaged our economic and social fabric and that the slippery rhetoric on oil profits has provided a major contribution to that effect.

In the next chapter, we shall try to assess the blame for our energy mess and present a program that squares with reality.

XVIII

PERSPECTIVES ON ENERGY

Economic warfare was declared on the industrialized countries and the United States in particular in October of 1973, and confirmed in January of 1974, putting this country into an energy mess. Naturally, the question arises: Who is to blame?

Never looking far for a convenient scapegoat, the "new class" almost without exception will pick on the establishment, or a "ready-made" target that propaganda had already set up. Their most obvious target was the oil industry. Freeman in that respect was quoted by Jensen, but we will repeat it here for sake of emphasis.

Freeman: The energy crisis is not a giant conspiracy concocted in a smoked-filled hotel room by politicians and oil company executives (Page 6)

Here Freeman absolves the oil industry of the collusion theory but in the same paragraph he continues:

... The record of industry dominance of government policy amid public indifference is an open book. (Pages 6-7)

This elicits the following questions:
If the oil industry dominated government policy to the degree alleged by Freeman—why wasn't the industry able to arrange for higher natural gas prices?
—why wasn't the industry able to connive for permission to drill in offshore areas?
—why wasn't the industry able to get instant approval for laying the Alaska pipeline?
—why was the industry hamstrung in nuclear and coal activity?

Freeman continues, still in the same paragraph:

The crisis results from a failure of private, corporate energy policies originating in Houston and Dallas and New York and rubber-stamped over the years by the Congress and a succession of Presidents. (Page 7)

We object to two implications in the above charge. Note that he blames private, corporate energy policies. This is consistent with one of his main recommendations, that we must turn to a public agency to solve our problems. On the contrary, the facts are that the bureaucrats and politicians, as we explained before, are mainly responsible for the petroleum crunch. History is replete with instances of bureaucratic bungling followed by quixotic appeals to new bureaucratic panaceas to remedy the damages wrought by prior bureaucratic adventures.

We are not absolving industry of all blame. Oil company managers have made mistakes. However, we object to the double standard practiced by the "new class" that insists on perfect performance by capitalism, exaggerates its imperfections, but condones or glosses over egregiously poor performances of statists and bureaucrats. As we argued before, the free market redresses mistakes sooner and at less economic and social costs than the mistakes perpetrated by Gosplanners and empire-builders in public service (disservice).

Second, Freeman reiterates the trite theme of industry control of public policy.

In our opinion Congress must bear the major burden of the blame because it created the inept, counterproductive regulatory bureaucracies and because it listened to well-meaning but misguided and overzealous consumerists, environmental extremists and TV commentators.

Oil import quotas are a subject of much loose rhetoric and fuzzy thinking, and Freeman, with his addiction to contradictions, made his contribution in the following quotations from his book:

> In the late 1950's a major breach opened in the anti-competitive wall that the petroleum industry had erected with the support of federal tax breaks and production controls. Oil from the Middle East and Venezuela began to be imported. The limitation was 12.2 percent of domestic production, thus guaranteeing the domestic producers some 88 percent of the market protected from price competition. During the 1960's, consumers were de-

prived of billions of dollars each year in savings which the lower-priced imported oil could have afforded them.

The oil import quota system was justified in the name of national security, a vague and elastic phrase, but most students of the quota program outside the oil industry believe its major function was to protect the domestic industry against foreign competition. It is perhaps the most glaring example of federal intervention in the marketplace to prevent competition in the energy industries.

Debate over the oil import control program continued throughout its 13-year history, but the industry was politically stronger than its critics. The program finally outlived its usefulness, even for the industry. By early 1973 the price of oil in the world market had approached domestic prices. More importantly, supply was so short that domestic production was not threatened. Indeed it was clear that the U.S. would suffer severe shortages unless imports were permitted to flow in whatever quantities the marketplace demanded. The President's Energy Message of April 18, 1973, finally buried the import quota program.

In the last paragraph, Freeman says that "supply was so short." It is strange that it didn't occur to him that the shortage in supply would have been much worse because the oil industry would have developed less drilling and refining capacity in this country if no import quotes were in effect.

Also, the Mr. Freeman on page 769 was not the same Mr. Freeman on page 8 who wrote that "in 1972 the oil necessary to sustain our rapid rate of growth began to come from the Middle East. Within less than two years, this U.S. dependence produced the crisis challenging the independence of American foreign policy."

In other words, national security was and is of prime concern, and Freeman's remarks about national security on page 169 don't square up to the facts.

With the benefit of hindsight, we can now assert that the import quota system, perhaps through political and/or economic accident, actually increased our potential for the short and middle terms—serendipitously our reservoir for secondary and tertiary recovery has been increased. As *Fortune* has pointed out, a combination of decontrol and the unitization of our oil fields can increase our supplies within months.

At this juncture, our position is not as hopeless as pictured by some Cassandras. Pollyanish exuberance should also be avoided. We have resources, the technology and the managerial expertise that is necessary to extricate us from the energy mess and from economic and political blackmail. What is needed most is a moratorium in politicking that appeals to envy, prejudice and ignorance.

A price has to be paid for the quirks of nature that concentrated a superabundance of low-cost fuel under the sands of the Middle East. That price is higher energy prices—guaranteed for a relatively long time. To get insurance of energy supplies, we must pay a premium.

Private enterprise cannot operate in an atmosphere of uncertainty. You cannot expect the energy industry to invest billions in alternate energy resources that will cost 500 times or more what it costs the Arabs to extract oil at about 12 cents a barrel and risk the chance of ending up with some white elephants. It would not be unreasonable to expect the shahs and the sheiks to play the part of spoilers by suddenly dropping prices below the costs of alternate energy sources. Thus, we are confronted with a geopolitical reality of high prices, political pressure and price manipulation to undermine our efforts toward energy independence. Thus, reluctant as we may be, we are forced to resort to price manipulation.

After the guaranteed price is established through tariff control and we develop alternate resources, we should be aware that another problem is apt to arise. Ten or fifteen years from now, perhaps sooner, a glut of energy will emerge, with the result that the nations most dependent on imported oil, such as Japan, will benefit unfairly from cheap oil that was precipitated by our costly energy program in alternative supplies. In such a case, it would be economically prudent to allow for this in our tariff structure in competitive goods.

The higher energy prices would not only provide incentives and funds for alternate sources, but also provide the funds to solve the pollution problem, besides ensuring a sustained economic growth.

The guaranteed floor price need not become a permanent feature. Let us not underestimate our brainpower, technology and managerial talent. A good case can be made for the proposition that once our latent and potential technology bears fruit, energy could become as relatively cheap as it was before.

Our technology in the past has served us well in providing cheap energy resources. In fact, it has been a contributing factor in making our country too complacent about our situation. In unguarded moments, Freeman himself sang the praises of oil industry efficiency, as attested by these citations from his book:

> Until very recently, the price of energy has been one of the great success stories of America. For example, over the past 40

> years the price of electricity has halved, while prices in general have doubled. (Page 139)
> The energy industry in America developed swiftly because it was innovative and dynamic. (Page 23)

The industry was innovative and dynamic and became a great success story because it stressed technology by pouring billions into research and development.

What are needed to unleash energy know-how are an environment and funds conducive to and supportive of more research and development toward self-sufficiency in energy. A floor price for energy will enable us to tap a tremendous reservoir of potentials.

Higher prices and favorable tax treatments would accelerate the responses of industry and the innovators.

Potentials reside in hydrogen power, laser-fusion research and such energies as could be derived from solar, wind and geothermal powers, among others.

A salutary and serendipitous side effect of new technological breakthroughs would be more interfuel competition.

It should not be overlooked that technology will not be limited to the fuel supply conditions but will also apply to fuel consumption. In Europe, gasoline for years was selling near and in some cases over a $1.00 a gallon—equivalent to the U.S. gallon—and this is one reason that European cars are much smaller than their U.S. counterparts. Higher prices in this country are forcing people to stress economy and spur the automakers and the satellite parts suppliers to accelerate more economically operating power plants. And this is the area where the much-maligned space program comes down to earth to revolutionize the automotive industry with the development of computerized engines. These new engines will culminate from previous and ongoing technological wizardry in the computer, semiconductor and space programs.

We should get down on our knees, face Mecca to the East, bow and thank Allah. The Moslems have done their bit to arouse our technological giant. But wait, politicians and bureaucrats are vying for the title of "OPEC'S Best Friends," a subject of an editorial in *Barron's* of June 30, 1975, by Editor Robert M. Bleiberg. Some excerpts follow:

> Price ceilings have effectively discouraged exploration and development, to the point where both domestic production and U.S. reserves of crude have steadily dwindled. In turn, allocations—or "entitlements" as they ironically are known—strike us as grossly unjust; moreover, as Professor Milton Friedman has pointed out, to the mounting detriment of Project Independence (and whatever became of that?), they serve to subsidize imports of OPEC crude. And without a shred of Congressional sanction, FEA has just moved to extend its beneficent sway over not only petroleum but also the distribution of coal. Oil operators may exploit a relative few; the powers-that-be are ripping off the country.

* * *

> There is much at stake. Only the wilfully blind can fail to see the damage which government controls have inflicted on the domestic supply of energy. Thanks largely to price ceilings and allocations, relatively few new refineries are under construction in the continental United States. At last month's auction of offshore leases in the Gulf of Mexico, bids were disappointingly low. Domestic production of crude oil is running at only 8.3 million barrels per day, down 5% or more from last year's levels; oil men estimate that controls are costing the U.S. at least two million barrels daily. "I know that the FEA," so Milton Friedman wrote in *Newsweek* the other day, when he condemned the

agency and all its works, "is not in fact being run by secret agents of the Shah and Sheikhs. No need, when unwitting volunteers" are doing their work for them.

Price rollbacks as advocated by Democratic Congressmen and consumerists would scotch the momentum generated by the price rises. Demagogic politicians, doing only what is easy, convenient and popular, do not meet their responsibilities to their constituents and the country. More damage is inflicted when they unite with anti-business radicals and circularize the Big Lie against profits and the market system. President Ford is to be commended for showing political guts in taking a politically unpopular side of the issue when he recommended decontrol of "old oil."

What decontrol is to oil, deregulation is to natural gas. In this respect an adequate and perceptive analysis was presented in *Energy Regulation by the Federal Power Commission*, by Stephen G. Breyer and Paul W. MacAvoy, sponsored by the Brookings Institution, Washington, D.C., 1974. Major conclusions excerpted from the book follow:

> The authors investigate the three major areas of the FPC's work—natural gas pipeline prices, natural gas field prices, and electricity production. They conclude that the commission helped neither the consumer nor industry. They contend that regulation had little effect upon pipeline prices and that it did not significantly promote a better coordinated electric power industry. Although the commission kept gas field prices low, in doing so it may have created a shortage that hurt consumers more than low prices helped them. (Kermit Gordon, President, in his Foreword)
>
> ... The actual transactions prices on regulated sales apparently did not differ consistently from those on unregulated sales, if account is taken of variations in costs of transmission and in demands for natural gas.

Unhappily, these assessments lead to one inescapable conclusion. Namely, the value of Federal Power Commission price-setting activities has been either very low or zero. (Page 54)

The arguments against continued efforts to control the exact price of natural gas are strong. Regulation is not necessary to check the market power of producers. Moreover, there is no practical way to calculate and capture rents in competitive gas markets; setting the prices for producers individually is not feasible; setting area rates is administratively complex and of necessity produces a gas shortage. (Page 87)

The alternative is de-regulation. Our analysis strongly indicates that less, not more, regulation is required. The commission could obtain, through economic analysis, a rough idea of whether competitive conditions exist in each producing region. Unless the evidence strongly suggests that producers possess monopoly power, the commission should allow new gas prices to approach market-clearing levels. At the same time, by using prices in the competitive areas as benchmarks, the commission could set prices in those few producer regions where monopoly power existed. (Pages 87-88)

The quintessence of the contentions of Breyer and MacAvoy is that the heavy hand of regulation renders inoperative effective incentive or stimulus that makes private enterprise operate so efficaciously in the public interest. Even without the most effective of incentives, the performance of the private electric utilities merits deserved approbation. The average unit price for electricity paid by consumers fell by almost a half from 1926 to 1968, while consumer prices generally rose by almost 100 per cent according to figures cited by Freeman from the 1970 *National Power Survey*. So the much-maligned private monopoly acted like other capitalist enterprises—exploited technology and managerial expertise to lower costs for the benefit of the consumer. This proves another sad fact that truth, as Joseph Goebbels and *Pravda* could testify and most of the nineteenth and twentieth centuries stand witnesses, is rarely a match for the Big Lie.

However, the performance of the utilities could be improved if the regulators could constrain their ill-considered phobia about profits and allowed the utilities to capture some of the cost reductions as profits on a sliding-scale basis roughly as follows. The first year 80% of the cost reduction would go to profits and 20% to lower prices; the second year the ratio would change to 60 and 40; the third year, 40 and 60. At the end of five years, all cost-reduction benefits would accrue to the benefit of the consumer. This would remove the lid from the enormous reservoir residing in the know-how of the utility production engineers and the product design and production engineers of the equipment manufacturers. Thus, we apply the cost-control discipline of the profit incentive to the energy industry. The socially redeemable elements of the profit and market system have no bounds. All that is necessary is to recognize them for their utilization to make life pleasant and enjoyable for the greatest number.

The greatest impediments to the attainment of the benefits inherent in the free enterprise system are the propaganda and rhetoric of the "new class" and the counterfeit intellectualism of dogmatic Marxism. The succeeding and final chapter is devoted to an assessment of measures that are necessary as a counteroffensive to scotch the rhetoric before it obliterates our political and economic freedoms and before it sidetracks what appears to be inevitable—worker and middle class-capitalism.

XIX

CONCLUSIONS:
THE REAL ISSUES

Increasing the welfare of the lower income groups is the crux of our social and economic issues. This encompasses the issues of the creation of jobs and the removal of impediments thereto.

The problems of job creation and inflation are the reverse sides of the same coin. In order to solve problems, it is necessary to diagnose them properly. Perceptive contributions to the understanding of our problems have been made by Sommers, chief economist of the National Industrial Conference Board, previously cited, and E. J. Mishan, reader in economics at the London School of Economics and professor of economics at American University, Irving Kristol and Ben Wattenberg. It cannot be overstressed that inflation, with its underlying causes of demand-pull and cost-push developments, impedes job creation because of its negative impact on capital formation.

Reverting to Sommers, we find that "the failure of our political system to contain the growth of social demands within limits tolerable to the free market is the essential first cause of inflation in this society."

Quite right. In terms of delivery, it means that social demands have outstripped our productive capacity. The economic implications are threefold. In the first place, the excessive social demands, arising not from income generated by production, but from monetizing debts, create a demand-pull inflation where more money is chasing a limited amount of goods. Second, the portion involving transfer payments channels funds exclusively into consumption, thereby decreasing capital formation and the capacity to produce not only goods but also jobs. And finally, excessive social demands crowd the private sector out of the capital markets. Interest rates are increased on two counts: (1) competition for funds, and (2) the inflationary premium. This diverts funds from capital formation, increases its costs and makes home ownership more burdensome. High interest rates and inordinately high construction wages have combined to price even many middle income classes out of the housing market.

It is sad to observe that too many overlook the economic truism that larger public spending promotes the public sector of our economy and lower taxes expand the private

Conclusions: The Real Issues

sector. The former increases the ranks of non-producers; the latter, the producers. The former decreases the amount of goods produced; the latter increases goods production. The former decreases the economic base of a workers' capitalism; the latter serves to increase the base. With these precepts in mind, it should be obvious to union leaders and the rank and file that espousals of excessive and unnecessary government spending lead to absurdities and contradictions. It would be ludicrous and negligent on the part of labor not to promote an economically meaningful tax exemption for qualifying corporations. It would be the height of economic folly for labor not to strive to revive the work ethic where a day's work is rendered for a day's pay.

While we are on the subject of a workers' capitalism, we should devote some attention to what is being developed in Europe regarding workers' participation. Embodied in this concept is a requirement giving workers a say in company operations. A management board would be held responsible for directing the business; but its members would be appointed and dismissed, if necessary, by a supervisory board set up for outlining broad policies.

Shareholders would elect one-third of the board; the employees, one-third; and the remaining third would be chosen by the first two groups to represent the general interest. This is an offspring of the "codetermination policy" introduced into West Germany by the Allied military government after World War II. This shared responsibility explains to a great degree the productivity of German workers that has led to the competitive efficiency of German industry.

However, participation in this country should be viewed only as a transitory stage—a training period—because the groundwork has been laid for a workers' capitalism. Participation implies a concession to labor; but, in a workers' capitalism, labor will be in a position to exercise ownership and control as pension fund moneys keep on increasing to make it inevitable.

Getting back to Sommers' observation about social demands exceeding the capacity of free markets, we find that Kristol agrees and asks, "Who incited this explosion of expectations?" He blames the economists. We agree with Kristol but fault him for not including entitlements and inquiring on what the "explosions of expectations and entitlements" are based. The underlying reasons are misconceptions about profit margins, corporate pricing, labor costs, the limits of income distribution and the ensuing rhetoric concerning these factors.

In a special issue on "Inflation," *Skeptic* quoted Mishan in excerpts from an article first appearing in an English periodical, *Encounter* (1974). According to Mishan, "The monetary inflation cannot properly be understood without recognizing its connection with the universal *inflation of expectations*" (italics added).

We feel that Mishan makes a major contribution to an understanding of the problem when he asserts that "money wages were pretty rigid before World War II, as Keynes was then at pains to emphasize. In the present inter-union race to keep ahead of the cost of living, and *to keep ahead of each other*, wage levels cannot but escalate. A pattern of union militancy is emerging which threatens to be independent of demand conditions" (italics added).

Conclusions: The Real Issues

It is the recognition of intra-union and inter-union politics that has led us to advocate the wage policy outlined in Chapter Fourteen. At the moment, this appears to be the only way to decelerate what Mishan terms "the unabating struggle for (more) between the unions (white-collar no less than blue-collar)." This explains to a great degree the economic morass attending the construction industry, our educational structure and our municipalities, as exemplified by New York and Detroit among many others. It also should be recognized that union monopoly power has made a mockery of collective bargaining.

Wattenberg gets nearer the real crux of the matter when he states in *Real America* that "a good case can be made that a good part of our domestic malaise can be laid precisely at the feet of a media system that underreports progress." In our opinion, the media—a part of or a willing or naive captive of the "new class"—not only underreports progress, but also slants the news about profits and the free market system. Their activities bring to mind the astute dictum of William James: "There is no lie worse than truth misunderstood by the listener." In Kristol's opinion "the media—television especially—converted this nation into a vast echo chamber, in which fashionable opinions were first magnified and then 'confirmed' through interminable repetition. Gradually it came to be believed that, in the immortal words of a 19th Century utopian Socialist, nothing is impossible for a government that *wants* the good of its citizens" (italics in original).

With these items in mind, let us consider the events since 1965. The economy has been subjected to double-digit wage-rate increases in many years in the construction trades, wage-rate increases in other industries exceeding productivity gains, and bureaucratic throwing of taxpayers' money and monetized deficits at problems on an unprecedented scale. Profit margins were eroding, but the echo chambers reverberated with distortions about profits and corporate pricing. Thus, when the stagflation and slumpflation emerged, a handy scapegoat was available for the utopians and elitists to shift the blame from themselves to the establishment.

The success of the intelligentsist and "new class" propaganda is attested by the polls showing that corporations on average are believed to earn about 33 cents on the dollar rather than the actual 4 to 6 cents over the last 24 years. The population is further misled into believing that the rich individuals and "fat cat" corporations can be tapped for funds to finance government largess. There is no admission on their parts that social demands on productive capacity have exceeded their limits and aggravated the problem by denying funds to increase the productive capacity that furnishes goods and jobs. With profits at five cents on the dollar and dividends running at about 40% of after-tax earnings, we come up with figures showing that the stockholder gets two cents from the sales dollar and that only three cents of the sales dollars are channeled into new productive capacity.

The success of the anti-profit and anti-bourgeois rhetoric is further confirmed by Wattenberg in the following analysis:

> Consider the two attitudinal bedrocks discussed earlier in this volume. Americans say their own lives are fine and they say that America is in trouble. There is another way of putting that:

Conclusions: The Real Issues 379

What people know of firsthand, they think well of. What people know of secondhand, information gathered through the transmission belt of our system of communications, they think ill of!

Our major problems in this country involve unemployment, inflation, energy and crime. It has been stated that a change in attitude can change the life of a human being. Likewise, a change in attitude about profits and corporate entities could change for the better the country's social and economic fabric. An educational offensive must be launched to present the image of the corporation as it really is—the engine that recycles profits into a productive capacity that can meet reasonable social demands on a reasonable time basis, while simultaneously solving the pollution problem.

Instant cures to all ills are unavailable in any society. The political demagogue, who for ten years unleashed expectations and entitlements to an unfulfillable degree and helped engender slumpflation, serves no redeeming social function when he insists on instant and painless cures. In his rhetoric, pro-business proposals are deemed to be anti-populace.

It should be the function of a massive educational effort to squelch the rhetoric and show that what is pro-business is pro-country. It should be stressed that what is pro-business is not at the expense of the country but for the benefit of the country. Money recycled by corporations into new capacity and pollution control will do more for the underprivileged than the lame-brain panaceas of regulatory and service bureaucracies. It cannot be overemphasized too much that what is pro-business will be pro-workers' capitalism because it will enlarge the base and accelerate the workers' capitalism.

Pro-business is pro-worker when it is recognized and realized that contributions to pension and welfare funds exceed dividends and almost match undistributed profits. The profitability of corporations assures continuance of these allocations, besides routing funds into new capacity, new jobs and new pensions.

Working in an atmosphere antithetical to the adversary relationship, accountants, statisticians and economists representing labor and management should assemble in a summit conference to work on an agenda on corporate tax exemption, liberalized depreciation policies and inter-union disciplines. The labor unions among themselves should work out a rollback or a temporary freeze in areas in which wage rates, such as construction, trucking and printing, have outpaced other industrial groups. We have given reasons for wage guidelines. To placate labor and to induce labor to forgo featherbedding and strive for productivity gains, a good case can be made for dividend guidelines. Between these two areas, prices and profits would be exempt from guidelines because they would automatically work for lower prices and profit recycling. That has been the history of industrial capitalism, and all impediments to these operations should be removed.

The wage guidelines outlined in Chapter Fourteen are not to be construed as definitive and final, but only as a starting point or a rough guide for the suggested summit conference. In the event that the guidelines were adopted as outlined, it appears that the possibilities of double-digit inflation developing would be rather remote if we started from a non-inflationary base.

The main objective of the plan is to change the workers'

Conclusions: The Real Issues

attitude toward the work ethic and productivity. He will be assured that workers and consumers would derive the benefit from his increased productivity.

However, we are not starting in an ideal situation, and more drastic measures should be considered if double-digit or near double-digit inflation persists. The following anti-inflation plan is suggested for consideration:

1. Limit wage-rate increases to 6%—double the normal rate.
2. Freeze dividend increases.
3. No controls on profits and prices.
4. No accumulation of undistributed profits.
5. No corporate taxes within special guidelines.

It is obvious that, under the foregoing plan, profits would be absorbed by price decreases or diversion of profits into spending on new plant and research and development, or the funds could be allocated to price decreases and spending for new technology. In conjunction with the National Technical Center and the negative income tax, it should be easy to envision nothing but constructive developments.

One of our biggest problems is the pocket of poverty that exists in the lowest eighth segment of our population. The rise in female-headedness has been the main drag in impeding the progress of this group, besides being a major contribution toward the rise in crime. FAP, the Technical Center and vocational training should combine to provide major steps in solving this problem. Another major contribution to the decline in crime could be made by legalizing drugs. This would take the profit out of the drug traffic. Under legalization of drugs, the addict could get his fix by prescription, and a job would provide him a living as well as a "fix." He would not have to resort to robbery in order to get the large sums required to get drugs from the pusher. Most important of all, the incentive to drug pushing would be eliminated. Severe mandatory penalties for drug pushing should be instituted. Thus, we would have two deterrents against the rise in drug usage.

The educational process, a counteroffensive to the Marxist and pseudo-liberal rhetoric, should be initiated by business itself. Profits should be reported in a manner depicting their true social and economic function. Profit margins should be stressed at the outset in all profit reporting. As quarterly reports become available, profit margin data should be attached to all paychecks. The public relation and publicity departments should be alert to news slanting that distorts profit data and immediately insist on equal space and time for corrective reports.

It should be recognized that the Marxists and many of the "new class" will not give up their self-serving myths and cherished ideas. They have a vested interest in sowing confusion and discontent and in making the free economy unworkable.

Once the union leadership and the rank and file exhibit a properly sympathetic attitude toward profits, the educational complex could be persuaded to alter its tactics. The goal of a workers' capitalism should function to unite divergent groups that are erroneously at loggerheads because of misconceptions.

What of the future?

Conclusions: The Real Issues

Control of inflation is the object of immediate concern. It will determine to a great extent the viability of the budding start of a workers' capitalism. The most critical influence on future inflation will be pay increases.

An inauspicious start in this respect was given in the following report in the *Wall Street Journal* of July 1, 1975:

> *Construction Unions in Oregon take contrasting paths in bargaining*
>
> Five Portland locals and 250 contractors cheer inflation fighters with a rare five-year, multicraft accord paying a relatively modest 25% increase in wages over the first two years. The pact even empowers a board to okay limited crossing of craft jurisdiction lines to boost productivity. A union official says the package is designed to "stabilize the industry" because "the continuing spiral will destroy us."
>
> But in the same city, plumbers and pipefitters, much in demand for Alaska pipeline and utility plant work, pressure employers into a short, two-year pact paying 22% in wage boosts in the first year alone. "If it was exorbitant, we wouldn't have gotten it," a plumbers' leader says. A bitter employer complains, "We didn't have anything to fight with."
>
> One union business agent calls the plumbers' pact "ridiculous" and warns "there may come a point where you price yourself out of the market."

We find it hard to agree with the charitable attitude of the *Wall Street Journal* copy writer when he blithely refers to a "relatively modest 25% increase in wages over the first two years." It may be modest by construction workers' standards of recent years, but it is surely of great inflationary impact on the rest of the economy. The plumbers' increase of 22% in the first year alone is outrageous, but the Big Plumber in Washington, George Meany, bemoans the high unemployment in the construction industry and blames President Ford for unemployment and inflation. "The hypocrisy of the situation is stunning."

Current inflationary developments were portrayed vividly in the following editorial of the *Detroit News* on July 22, 1975:

> *High Cost of Labor Peace*
>
> The difficulty of keeping a cap on inflation was demonstrated again by the settlements reached with the railway clerks and the postal workers that kept the nation's rails and mails moving.
>
> The three-year agreement with the railway clerks calls for a 41 percent increase in wage and fringe benefits already approved for the seven train-operating unions, plus a cost-of-living adjustment on January 1, 1978, at the end of the new contract.
>
> In both cases, the settlements will mean higher costs to the public. In the case of the railway unions, the new pact also will mean a rate of wage increase for the next three years which will be much higher than the current rate of inflation.
>
> In other words, the rail contract has a built-in inflation of its own, in addition to the cost-of-living clause that is similar to such clauses in some other union contracts.
>
> As usual, the public will pay these new inflationary costs in the form of higher prices for rail service and higher rates for postal service.
>
> It is always convenient to blame the government for its failure to control inflation but when wage increases are granted far in excess of the rise in the cost of living, the unions which made the excessive demands ought to be held responsible for contributing to the resulting inflationary pressures.
>
> In other words, the public ought to understand the high cost it is paying for labor peace.

Meanwhile, Big George persists in wearing economic blinkers and flays handy scapegoats.

The two biggest causes of our problems of unemployment and inflation are long-continued astronomical govern-

Conclusions: The Real Issues

ment deficits and unjustified wage increases. But few politicians have the guts to say so because of fears that they may not get reelected.

It would be tragic if the engine of a workers' capitalism were stalled or wrecked by monkey wrenches thrown in by the little plumbers, the Big Plumber with assists from the demagogues.

The potentials of a workers' capitalism are extant.

Will labor screw itself and the rest of the population out of its socially redeemable benefits?

In 1976 labor and the rest of the nation are observing the Bicentennial of a great nation and democracy that can attain even greater heights by prudence and foresight on the part of labor. The year is also the Bicentennial of *The Wealth of Nations* by Adam Smith.

Labor's Spirit of 1976 can revive the American Spirit of 1776, and the Spirit of Adam Smith and bury the Marxist Spirit of 1848.

Will it?